P9-DIY-095

To S. [illegible] —
from [illegible] —

Cordially,
Aldea Todd
Dec. 9, 1964

JUSTICE ON TRIAL

BOOKS BY A. L. TODD

Justice on Trial
The Case of Louis D. Brandeis

Abandoned
The Story of the Greely Arctic Expedition

JUSTICE ON TRIAL

The Case of
Louis D. Brandeis
by
A. L. Todd

McGraw-Hill Book Company
New York · Toronto · London

Copyright © 1964 *by A. L. Todd.*
All Rights Reserved. Printed in the
United States of America. This book,
or parts thereof, may not be reproduced
in any form without permission
of the publishers.

Library of Congress Catalog Card Number 64-16300

First Edition

64916

*To the President who next appoints
a Louis D. Brandeis*

Preface

To most Americans, nearly a half-century after he became an Associate Justice of the Supreme Court of the United States, Louis D. Brandeis seems a distant figure. The world of that day is remote; the part the Supreme Court played in its life is clouded by the passage of time and the pressure of more recent events.

Many know of Brandeis' record as a distinguished jurist. They visualize an elderly man in a long, black robe, with a lean, craggy face and a shock of silver hair—as he is pictured on the walls of countless law offices and law-school classrooms.

Yet few of the millions who know something of the Justice, to whose name and memory Brandeis University each year brings fresh honor, are aware of the remarkable career of Mr. Brandeis of Boston, the "People's Attorney" whom President Woodrow Wilson called to Washington in 1916 to become Mr. Justice Brandeis. Few today can recall either the bitter struggle in the United States Senate over the confirmation of Brandeis as Associate Justice or the very close margin by which his nomination was confirmed.

Justice on Trial is an account of that struggle in 1916, when a determined President—by a highly controversial, courageous and symbolic act of appointment—helped the American people look and move forward.

Contents

PREFACE   *vii*

1 *"The Wonderful Year"*   1
2 *Vacancy on the Court*   16
3 *Mr. Brandeis of Boston*   40
4 *"A Little Knot of Men"*   69
5 *"An Unfit Appointment"*   96
6 *A Lawyer's Reputation*   128
7 *The Summing Up*   157
8 *Delay in Committee*   186
9 *Politics and Persuasion*   213
10 *Ten to Eight*   238

AUTHOR'S POSTSCRIPT   253
BIBLIOGRAPHY   263
INDEX   269

one

"The Wonderful Year"

All evening in the crisp December darkness the anticipatory rumble
mounting from the crowd in Times Square had grown in intensity.
Then, at the moment of midnight, as the brightly lighted signal ball
high on Times Tower slid down its shaft, the packed thousands in the
streets burst as if with one accord into that hysterical, raucous, self-
conscious public demonstration of bedlam that is seen and heard only
with the birth of the infant year.

Good-by, Nineteen-fifteen! Hello, Nineteen-sixteen!

By all estimates it was the most elaborate, most costly, gayest New
Year's Eve outpouring in the history of New York. Some 500,000
people had paid or pushed their way into the Manhattan theater district to demonstrate their joy at the symbolic transition to a new day
and new times.

The January 1 issue of *The Wall Street Journal,* spinning through
the presses while the horns blared in the streets outside, envisioned a
New Year pregnant with promise:

STATISTICAL RECORD FOR THE YEAR 1915
*Astonishing Story of the Rapid Rise of Prosperity
from a Spell of Great Depression*
WAR ABROAD THE GREAT UPLIFT OF BUSINESS THIS SIDE OF
THE ATLANTIC
Urgent Foreign Demand for Foodstuffs, Industrial Products,
Munitions Sets Everything Going
BETTER RAILROAD EARNINGS

The article below the headline proclaimed the record of 1915
"unquestionably the most pronounced and even dramatic recovery

in the world's economic history." As a striking example of the general trend, the *Journal* announced the triumph of America's premier industrial corporation, United States Steel, which ended the year with net earnings close to $130,000,000. So rapid had the pace of its business become—and so profitable—that the corporation had cleared $50,000,000 in the final quarter alone. Should its good fortune continue at that rate, all past records would be smashed in the New Year, the newspaper stated.

The officers of the steel firm had already determined how this bonanza would be shared with the people who had helped to make it all possible. Of the old year's profit, $75,000,000 would be paid out at once in dividends, amounting to earnings of 20.8 per cent for the holders of preferred stock and 10 per cent for those owning common. Nor were the workmen of U.S. Steel to be forgotten. The corporation promised an increase of 10 per cent in the wages of its ordinary laborers and graduated raises for other employees. Company spokesmen estimated the increase might add all of $15,000,000 to its yearly wage bill. This, in *The Wall Street Journal's* opinion, was a generous boost for the workers employed by U.S. Steel, who in the past few years had already enjoyed an annual wage averaging $905. Everyone was making money!

The happy fate that had overtaken the nation's biggest industrial company had likewise visited other sectors of the American economy. As the year-end totals were added and the prospects were projected into the year ahead, manufacturing, agriculture, transportation, trade, and banking concerns were, for the moment, wrapped in measureless content. The war in Europe was far enough across the Atlantic for safety; the security belt of ocean served also as a convenient avenue for commerce. The business of supplying belligerents had in seventeen months reversed the position of the United States from a buying to a supplying nation, from that of a borrower to that of a lender; America had a favorable balance of trade now of more than a billion dollars a year. And its rapidly swelling population had just crossed the hundred-million mark.

The war that brought prosperity nonetheless cast a dark shadow over America's conscience. As the bitter war in the trenches of France and Belgium continued through its first year and into its second winter the United States, though a nonbelligerent, was step by step being committed to the Allied cause. The memory of those Americans who had gone down with the *Lusitania* and other Allied ships, the sight of young college men leaving the campus to volunteer, the Sunday rotogravure ladies working for war relief causes—all brought an increasing sense of involvement. In contrast, the neutral tone of the correct, formal notes dispatched by President Wilson and Secretary of State Lansing in response to each new German outrage on the high seas seemed cold indeed.

Those few who openly stated that this wealthy, busy land and people must inevitably be drawn into the conflict, should it long continue, were still Cassandras. Yet almost every ship torpedoed by the Central Powers destroyed American lives or damaged American property, so that by the close of 1915 the nation wondered how long it could technically remain a neutral supplier of the Allied cause should the summer ahead bring no peace. It hoped with Woodrow Wilson that the country could stay out, yet it feared, as he did, that it would be dragged in.

Describing 1915 as "The Wonderful Year," a New Year's Day editorial in *The New York Times* marveled at the country's economic recovery from an early stagnation to the roaring boom with which the year ended. But the newspaper cautioned the country to turn its mind soberly to the suffering and destruction abroad on which American business was feeding fat. The dark side of the wonderful year, it declared, lay in the war's destruction of property and its death toll of some five million lives.

One did not have to cross the Atlantic Ocean or even leave New York, however, to find thousands for whom 1915 was more a year of bitterness than of wonder. Among them were men like the New York subway muckers—husky men, immigrants for the most part, who toiled beneath the streets to dig the tunnels for the booming city's expanding transit system. The common name of their occupation suggested the mixture of wet clay, runoff water, sewer-pipe leakage, and debris from the city streets in which they had to work. For following this calling six days in seven they were paid nine dollars a week.

The subway muckers' way of life was brought dramatically to public attention by an accident on the morning of September 22, 1915. The rush-hour traffic was rumbling over the heavy planking that formed the temporary surface of Seventh Avenue between 23rd and 25th streets above the subway diggings when suddenly timbers, planking, rocks, and earth along a hundred-foot stretch of the Avenue collapsed on the men below. A wooden trolley car jammed with passengers, mostly factory girls on their way to work, plunged into the gaping hole and smashed into a splintered mass. Fortunately, one work crew had just vacated the area and the next full shift had not arrived, so that no more than four of the muckers were crushed to death. Three of the trolley car passengers were killed. Close to 100 other people were injured.

A state legislative investigation after the accident noted that the muckers' total yearly wage, with no lost time or fines, came to only $468—exactly the amount New York City paid in pension to a widow with three children if her husband had died in the service of the municipality. But the dependents of the muckers killed beneath Seventh Avenue were not so lucky: their men, employees of a private contractor constructing the subway for a transit company, were not covered by the city compensation system. New men soon moved in to take their places, and the job went on as before.

At about the time of the Seventh Avenue accident, a report on the estimated cost of living for an unskilled laborer's family was drawn up by the Bureau of Standards of New York City, where public concern over such matters was as great as anywhere in the country. In establishing a schedule of wages for streetsweepers, the bureau report stated that "below $840 a year an unskilled laborer's family of five (husband, wife and three children under 14 years) cannot maintain a standard of living consistent with American ideas." Yet the muckers toiling beneath the streets of New York were being paid a little more than half this proposed minimal wage for the lowest form of labor. The budget on which economists based their report assumed the laborer would have to spend about 50 per cent of the total for food alone. Clothing and shelter allowances in the budget were miserly, and such items as medical care, insurance, recreation, and education were at the vanishing point.

If the employees of the U.S. Steel Corporation enjoyed considerably higher income than the subway diggers in New York, it was the result in part of their seven-day work week in the steel mills. Everywhere in the United States, in heavy industry and in service trades, the sixty-hour and even a seventy-hour week were common. So was the Saturday pay envelope that contained less than ten dollars. A big twelve-week strike of garment workers in Chicago ended at the turn of the year, the walkout having been precipitated by general dissatisfaction over piecework rates that brought the garment workers an average of less than ten cents an hour.

In 1915 Americans worked hard not only to supply the voracious needs of a great war in Europe but also because the father alone could not earn the family living. Many a family head became incapacitated through a work injury or was killed on the job without leaving his dependents either insurance or compensation. Women and children went to work in his place. The federal Bureau of the Census in 1915 enumerated the "population engaged in gainful occupations" starting at ten years of age; children that young formed a significant part of the national labor force.

Although by 1915 thirty states and the federal government had put into effect an eight-hour day for employees on public works, most of these workers were grown men organized in unions. Elsewhere the overwhelming majority of industrial workers, including women and children, were on the job nine and ten hours a day, six days a week. The half-holiday on Saturday, introduced by George Westinghouse in his plants back in the Eighties, was still a rarity granted by only a few benevolent employers. And while every factory worker was familiar with weeks of unpaid layoff when orders were slack, almost none had ever known a paid vacation.

By 1915 some of the states had enacted laws restricting the employment of women and children for excessive hours in certain industries, but these statutes were only scattered islands of protection in a great sea of employers' laissez faire. The federal Department of Labor, less than three years old, had virtually no power except to study and recommend. Regulation of the conditions of labor was the province of the individual states. Only six states prohibited night work for women in factories; only five states and the District of Columbia had an eight-hour law covering women workers. The U.S. Children's Bureau and social workers estimated that almost two million children under sixteen were employed in the United States, about one third of them girls. No one knew the true figure. One nation-wide firm of limited-price retail stores had invested some of its profits in a beautiful New York skyscraper, an architectural wonder that promoted the company name far and wide. It continued meanwhile to promote its stock to investors with the argument that its dividends had to be high because its employees were mainly young girls being paid very low wages.

Rapid industrialization since the Civil War had led job-seekers swarming into the cities and towns, so that by 1915 half the U.S. population was urban. The country was mining twice as much coal as it had in 1900 and was making three times as much crude steel. Recent immigrants had been pouring through the golden door of New York harbor less to become farmers than to man the mines, mills, and factories. For every happy craftsman or farmer living in the idyllic little clapboard home of a Currier & Ives print, ten others now dwelt in foul tenements, trapped in ill-paid work without real hope of improvement, and often without regular employment.

As the dispossessed grew in number, their frustration and resentment increased. They could see that the rich were growing richer from other men's toil, and they resented the widening gulf between life in the ornate mansion on the hill and bare existence in the company shack across the railroad tracks. To the immigrants and the first-generation Americans—Irish, Italians, Jews, Greeks, and Slavs of many ethnic subdivisions—this was not the American ideal of which they and their parents had heard and read.

From the 1870s onward, the stirrings among the discontented became more frequent and more vigorous. The small farmer, feeling helpless to protect the value of his crop against the gamblers at the grain markets, turned militant. He sought radical solutions to his problems with the bank and the railroad and joined in such movements as the Populists, the Grangers, and the Greenback Party. In the cities and towns, skilled workmen were organizing into unions and bargaining with employers for higher wages. A few of the workers and farmers had brought the socialist ideas of Karl Marx with them from Europe and talked of the class struggle.

Simultaneously, among a socially conscious fringe of the educated class there was a moral stirring in sympathy with the struggles of the impoverished. A new, pragmatic school of social work based more on a study of economics than the New Testament was emerging from the chrysalis of charity. In journalism a mixture of exhortation and factual reporting about the way most people were actually living—a school of reporting termed *muckraking* by the comfortable, whom it annoyed—was making readers aware that the days of the American frontier were over. Americans were told, harshly, that their smug, prim society of Victorian virtues covered a cesspool of exploitation, immorality, and human suffering.

By the turn of the twentieth century the country was divided roughly into two camps with antithetical outlooks. The owners of property, masters of finance, and employers of factory labor directed the conservative camp, and used the Republican Party as their primary political instrument. Their program was to resist the drive for change which the great, amorphous reform movement in the opposing camp demanded. In the years leading up to 1915, the urge toward social change concentrated more and more in the Democratic Party, which in turn attracted those politicians who sensed the power of this mass yearning for a better life. It was a movement based on certain commonly felt aspirations among a divergent mixture of people rather than an organization, and was variously termed reform, progressive, liberal, radical, or socialist, depending on one's viewpoint.

In the years just before the outbreak of the 1914 war in Europe, the reform movement through agitation and political campaigning won the enactment of new laws designed to better the conditions of labor and the farmer, to curb laissez faire in the market place, to promote the public welfare and protect the helpless individual from the combination with money or economic power. Wave by lapping wave, the rising tide of social legislation had by 1915 left the advocate of the free-for-all industrial society of the post-Civil War period gasping for air. The public now had a measure of control over certain areas of private enterprise by virtue of federal laws that provided, for example, for inspection of the meat-packing industry, government regulation of railroad rates, and control of trusts. The states had enacted laws to protect the rights of the worker against an exploiting employer and of the public against being bilked by merchants and manufacturers. And always, the industry or class coerced by law to spend more money or take more care under the imperative of the public good fought against reform laws with every means at its command.

The legislatures of the mining states, responding to the terrible toll of life taken in mine accidents, enacted inspection statutes that forced mine owners to observe certain minimal safety standards. By 1912 Congress had established the federal Bureau of Mines to assist in making this basic industry safer than would have been the case if the task had been left to the states. In one state after another, during the reform era that marked America's transition from the nineteenth to the twentieth centuries, factory owners felt more and more hedged in by vexing regulations governing safety guards on machines, ventilation, fire exits, lighting, and even provision of an adequate number of toilets and washrooms for the workforce.

Too, state laws were curbing the employer's right to hire anyone he wanted, for the reformers were pushing hard, industry by industry, to raise the minimum age at which boys and girls could be employed. They were attacking industrial homework, where jobs were taken to the workers' rooms for completion and then returned to the employer; they were concerning themselves with employees' health, with night work for women and children, and with the length of the workday. They were even taking aim at the most profitable operation of all— child labor per se. At the same time, the unions of skilled workmen were becoming more powerful and more vocal in their demand for more pay in return, as the employers saw it, for less work.

One way in which the owners of property who hired labor tried to halt this steady encroachment on their preserve was by defeating the reformist political demagogues when they ran for office. There were times as well when those elected could be fought off—or bought off. But when the combination of organized labor, the demagogues in politics, the reformers, social workers, and muckrakers finally did succeed in putting through a law that burdened business with costs, or hampered its freedom to compete, there still remained one last line of defense—the courts.

Judicial review of the acts of the legislature was a pillar of the American way of life. It could be traced back to Chief Justice John Marshall's assertion in 1803, in the case of *Marbury* v. *Madison,* that the Supreme Court of the United States could overthrow an act of Congress that did not square with the federal Constitution. The Supreme Court, or one of the lower federal courts, also had the power to void a state law that the judges found inconsistent with the U.S. Constitution. On the state and federal bench sat sound men, for the most part, who knew the law well. In the era of reform turmoil, few judges were of the reformer breed; they were conservative men from the owning stratum of society, who lived among private libraries and fine silver. Let one of these new social acts be shown contradictory to one line in the Constitution and the defenders of the status quo could count on good judges to discard it as null and void.

In a perilous sea of radical reform legislation, owners of property and their lawyers fortuitously found a lifeline in one clause of the

Fourteenth Amendment to the Constitution: ". . . nor shall any State deprive any person of life, liberty or property without due process of law. . . ." The Fourteenth Amendment had been adopted after the Civil War to assure the rights of the liberated slaves. But in a series of decisions from the Seventies on, the courts spelled out the doctrine that *any person* might also mean any corporate body, company, or association; and *property* might mean business or the profits of a business. The courts, by interpreting the Fourteenth Amendment this way, opened the door to a long line of attacks on state laws that governed wages, hours, safety provisions, and the like—because such laws increased the cost of doing business and thus ate into the employer's "property."

During the years when the propertied class made the greatest use of the Fourteenth Amendment due-process clause as a ground for voiding social legislation, judges differed in their application of it. Split decisions in appeals courts were frequent. Courts acknowledged that certain evils in an industrial society should be curbed by law in spite of the amendment. They therefore upheld some state laws benefiting women and child workers, and men employed in especially hazardous occupations. But during the same years every court ruling that invalidated a reform law discouraged the enactment of others. Consequently every employer of labor rejoiced in 1905 when the Supreme Court of the United States, in the case of *Lochner* v. *New York,* held that New York state had unconstitutionally deprived bakery owners of a property right when it enacted a law limiting the workday in bakeries to ten hours and the working week to sixty hours. There was no justification in a supposed protection of the public health or morals, the Court declared, that permitted such an invasion of the employer's property rights. Baking was neither that onerous nor that hazardous. For the next decade, the Lochner decision stood as a firm barrier to the enactment of further maximum-hours legislation by the states. The constitutional amendment designed to protect the rights of liberated Negro slaves had become an instrument for the exploitation of industrial wage slaves.

It was not surprising that from the turn of the century to 1915 America witnessed a growing dissatisfaction with the judicial system. Some reformers demanded laws to permit the recall of sitting judges. Others suggested methods of repassing legislation over the veto of the courts. It was proposed that the courts might be satisfactory as institutions but that they needed new men. And though vexation with the courts was directed at both the state and federal judicial system, it was on the Supreme Court of the United States that discussion centered, because this one mattered the most. After the suits and appeals in lower courts, a matter of constitutionality would come before the nine black-robed figures seated at the pinnacle of the American judicial system. In this era of rapid change, the Supreme Court of the United States was repeatedly called upon to decide what legislation was permissible under the Constitution of 1789 and what must fall from the evolving social contract in America.

In 1915 the Court had to decide a number of important and difficult cases involving property, personal freedom, and the Fourteenth Amendment. Just after New Year's Day it had announced its decision on a labor-boycott suit that had been in the courts at one level or another for twelve years. In the court record it was designated *Lawler* v. *Loewe,* but it was commonly known as the Danbury Hatters case. The issue had arisen from a suit for damages filed by Dietrich E. Loewe, a Connecticut hat manufacturer, against a group of striking workers who were urging union men all over the United States to boycott Loewe's products as the result of a wage dispute. The Supreme Court declared that the Danbury union men were acting as a trust that was illegal under the Sherman Act of 1890. It unanimously upheld a lower-court sentence that had levied fines and costs of more than a quarter-million dollars against the Danbury defendants for the damage they had done to their former employer.

The ruling struck not at a big organization with a rich treasury but at 186 individual workers, each of whom would lose his home if he owned one, and any other personal property that could be attached to pay his fine. This penalty might be severe, the Court noted, but every defendant was fully aware when he remained a member of the Danbury local of the United Hatters of North America that he was supporting an illegal union boycott—a conspiracy in restraint of trade. The antitrust law cut both ways, the Court held, against restraint of trade by labor unions as well as by trusts of businessmen.

The ink was scarcely dry on the Danbury Hatters ruling when the Supreme Court gave every employer in the country absolute freedom to fire a man for joining a union. In the sweeping decision of *Coppage* v. *Kansas,* the Court was divided, six justices to three. The majority, the spokesman for whom was Justice Mahlon Pitney, held that the Kansas legislature had acted unconstitutionally in 1903 when it outlawed what union men called the "yellow-dog contract." Under such a contract the employer insisted that a worker pledge not to belong to a union while in his employ.

In holding for the employer (a railroad) and declaring the Kansas law void, Pitney declared:

> To ask a man to agree, in advance, to refrain from affiliation with a union while retaining a certain position of employment, is not to ask him to give up any part of his constitutional freedom. He is free to decline the employment on those terms, just as the employer may decline to offer employment on any other; for "It takes two to make a bargain."

The Court majority, Pitney said, rested its view squarely on what it had declared in the case of *Adair* v. *U.S.* seven years before. Justice Harlan had said at that time:

> An employer has the same right to prescribe terms on which he will employ one to labor as an employee has to prescribe those on which he will sell his labor, and any legislation which disturbs this equality is an arbitrary and unjustifiable interference with liberty of contract.

The division of the country in social outlook in 1915 was in no other instance so clearly expressed as in *Coppage* v. *Kansas*. The dissenting opinions of Justices Holmes, Day, and Hughes seemed to be based on conditions in a world apart from that presupposed by Justice Pitney. To the three dissenters there was an obvious grotesque imbalance in the bargaining power of employers and workingmen. In accord with the entire body of liberal and reform opinion in the country, legal and lay, the minority could clearly appreciate the inequality between the wage-worker and the factory or railroad owner he solicits for a job. Legislation that to some degree makes him more nearly equal would not, to them, be law depriving anyone of liberty and property without due process.

Later in the spring the Court acted with more compassion toward women workers in California than it had toward union men in Kansas. This time it unanimously upheld a state law protecting women from

excessive hours of work. In 1908 the Supreme Court had set a precedent by upholding Oregon's ten-hour workday limit for women
employed in laundries. Now it upheld two California laws limiting
female labor to only eight hours in hotels and restaurants, despite the
claim of their employers that the Fourteenth Amendment forbade any
such denial of their rights by state law.

In April 1915 the Court agreed to hear argument, after its summer
recess, on a New York law banning industrial night work for women.
A ruling that this law was constitutional, employers feared, would
launch the reformers on a campaign against the employment of factory girls at night in other industrial states. Employers as a group
were therefore deeply concerned over the outcome. In a quite separate matter the Supreme Court in June found itself hopelessly dead-
locked over the government's antitrust suit against the International
Harvester Corporation. The Court therefore ordered the entire case
reargued in the fall. Should the government persevere and win, Harvester would face a forced breakup like that of Standard Oil and the
tobacco trust in 1911. As the year ended, the Court had still to rule
on an issue of special concern to every person of wealth in the country
—whether the United States personal income tax was constitutional
or not. The new federal tax had been challenged on the ground that
it was discriminatory against the rich, since it touched only personal
incomes above $3000 a year for single persons and $4000 for married
couples. On this matter the Court had heard oral argument and considered the briefs, and at the turn of the year the country was still
awaiting its decision.

In the most emotion-charged case of the year, the matter at stake
was the gravest that can come before a court—life itself. Again, the
Supreme Court Justices were divided. In February they heard oral
argument on the constitutionality of the trial of Leo M. Frank, sen-
tenced to death for murder by a court in Atlanta, Georgia. Frank, a
Jew and the college-educated manager of an Atlanta pencil factory,
had come south from New York a few years before. A young girl
named Mary Phagan who was employed in his plant was found dead
in the factory basement on a week-end night; Frank was accused of
having lured her there and killed her. His trial had been marked by an
ambitious prosecutor's shouting for Frank's blood, the blatant incite-

ment of anti-Semitism by the Georgia press, and by a lynch atmosphere in the courtroom and the streets outside. Long before it reached the Supreme Court of the United States, the Frank case was a national *cause célèbre*.

After two months of consideration, the Supreme Court rejected the condemned man's appeal. In 10,000 words of Justice Pitney's writing, the dry legal propositions were built one by one into the deadly syllogism that denied Frank's plea for a new trial. Justices Hughes and Holmes, dissenting, held that under the federal Constitution Frank deserved a fresh trial because the lynch atmosphere in and around the Atlanta courtroom had made it impossible for either judge or jury to give the accused more than a dumbshow of due process.

Shortly after the Supreme Court disposed of Leo Frank's last appeal for justice, the governor of Georgia commuted his death sentence to life imprisonment. But the prisoner's lease on life was short. One hot August day a body of armed men pushed their way into the state prison camp against virtually no resistance, drove the prisoner away in an automobile, and lynched him in revolting fashion. At the subsequent state inquiry, no one was formally accused of this crime, nor was any state officer found negligent in the performance of his duty. Official Atlanta in August was as blind to the crime of Frank's physical lynching as seven Justices of the Supreme Court in Washington had been in April to his juridical lynching.

As 1915, "The Wonderful Year," drew to a close, one of the Supreme Court Justices lay dying in the capital. Joseph Rucker Lamar, fifty-eight, had been a sick man since late spring. During the summer recess he had not returned to his home in Georgia but had tried to recover his strength by relaxing at the quiet watering resort of White Sulphur Springs, West Virginia. Here in midsummer he suffered a stroke which partially paralyzed his left arm and leg. His physician, finding heart enlargement and high blood pressure, prescribed a long rest. At the time of the opening of the October term, Justice Lamar was not on the bench. The Court carried on its work without him.

A round-faced, pleasant man, Lamar was well known in the capital by virtue of his distinguished office. A distant cousin, older by one generation, Lucius Quintus Cincinnatus Lamar of Mississippi, had sat on the Supreme Court bench before him. Born and reared in Augusta, Joseph Lamar had made a specialty of railroad corporate

law. The high point of his career was his work in saving the Georgia
Railroad Company from a heavy property tax hastily levied on it by
the state—an act which brought him to Washington in the fall of 1907
to argue the issues before the Supreme Court of the United States.
In his printed brief and oral argument Lamar convinced his future
colleagues that Georgia had imposed the tax on the railroad without
the due process guaranteed by the Fourteenth Amendment. The victory made him a hero to the railroad companies of Georgia.

On President William Howard Taft's occasional visits to Augusta
for the relaxation and golf he loved, he and Lamar met socially. During these meetings the President found Lamar was his kind of lawyer
—sound, conservative, thorough, not given to social theorizing or
experiment. Taft admired the traditions of the South and appointed
many Southerners to federal office. It therefore came as no great surprise when the Republican President reached into Democratic Georgia
in December 1910 to pick his Augusta friend for the Supreme Court.
True, only twice within memory had a President chosen a Supreme
Court Justice of the opposite political party, but the Court, after all,
was supposed to be made up of men above partisan politics. The
Senate confirmed the nomination in three days' time.

During his five years in Washington, Justice Lamar was known as
a quiet, noncontroversial judge, a good craftsman who knew his law,
even if he thrilled no one with the rhetoric of his opinions or the
novelty of their thought. Editors of the law journals did not find any
new ground broken in his decisions.

As the yellow leaves fell from the elms before the Lamar home on
New Hampshire Avenue, the Justice was bedridden. President Wilson
kept in touch with the ailing man and frequently sent a message or a
bouquet. Through the fall and into the winter, therefore, he knew
that the jurist would not return to the Supreme Court bench. In late
December Lamar appeared to rally, but shortly before New Year's
Day he suffered a relapse, and his breathing was impeded by a heavy
chest cold. On Sunday night, January 2, surrounded by his family,
Lamar quietly died.

When he heard that the end had come, Woodrow Wilson was preparing to leave The Homestead, the beautiful resort hotel in the
Appalachian Mountains near Hot Springs, Virginia, where he had
gone on a honeymoon following his marriage two weeks earlier to
Mrs. Edith Bolling Galt. Lamar's death now added to the President's

burdens one more critical matter requiring his decision. It was one that faced a President of the United States only two or three times during a term of office. He must name a man to fill the vacancy on the Supreme Court, the tribunal of last resort for all the forces engaged in the ceaseless struggle for social power in America.

two

Vacancy on the Court

The event that caused the President to break off his honeymoon ahead
of schedule and return to Washington was the crisis in American
policy precipitated by another outrage on the high seas. At one o'clock
in the afternoon of Thursday, December 30, the British passenger
liner *Persia,* bound from London to Bombay, was skirting the coast
of Crete. Suddenly her hull was torn open by a terrific explosion. Only
four lifeboats could be put out before the vessel went under with
heavy loss of life. The attacker, assumed to be a submarine, was not
seen.

Three days after the event, neither British nor American officials
seemed to know for certain just which power had been responsible
for the sinking, or whether any American lives had been lost. It was
feared but not confirmed that Robert N. McNeely, an American con-
sul, was one of the victims. Several other Americans were known to
have been aboard. There were rumors that the British vessel had not
only been armed with deck guns but that she was also carrying munitions and troops. If so, Americans should not have booked passage
on the *Persia.*

Given the circumstances, it was imperative that the President get
back to the capital to determine what action the United States should
take in asserting its rights as a neutral toward the guilty party—when
determined. The issue was too explosive to be left to a government
divided between Secretary of State Lansing in Washington and a
President honeymooning in the Virginia mountains, their only means
of rapid communication a telegraph wire.

Wilson would have left the mountain resort during the day on Monday, January 3, but since he found no train would be available until evening, he took his bride on an afternoon drive through the mountain country around The Homestead. By the time they returned to the hotel, the lobby was buzzing with curious guests and outsiders who sensed the excitement of watching close at hand a President facing a hard decision that might bring the country to the edge of war. The Wilsons smiled their way through the crowd, thanked the hotel manager for a pleasant stay, then went to their suite for a quiet dinner. They boarded their special train at 8:45 P.M. and by seven the next morning were in Washington.

Already the President's telegram of condolence had reached the widow of Justice Lamar:

> MY HEART-FELT SYMPATHY GOES OUT TO YOU IN YOUR TRAGIC LOSS, WHICH THE WHOLE COUNTRY HAS REASON TO MOURN. IT HAS LOST AN ABLE AND NOBLE SERVANT. I HAVE LOST IN HIM ONE OF MY MOST LOVED FRIENDS.

Though Wilson must have given at least fleeting thought during the past few months to the matter of Lamar's successor, he had confided neither the general lines of his thinking nor a specific name to anyone.

As the President brought himself quickly up to date on the *Persia* crisis and once again picked up the myriad executive threads of government from substitute hands, the Supreme Court was in recess. The three junior members—Justices Pitney, Van Devanter, and McReynolds—accompanied Lamar's body on the funeral train that afternoon and represented the Court at the service the next morning in the First Christian Church of Augusta. According to his wish, Joseph Lamar was buried in old Summerville Cemetery on the Sand Hills in a spot he himself had chosen years before. The Reverend Howard Cree, who had also buried the jurist's father, recited Tennyson's "Crossing the Bar" as the casket was lowered. Their duty to their departed brother done, the three Justices returned to Washington the same afternoon to resume the pressing business of the Court.

Top man on the Supreme Court, both in years of service and in his office of Chief Justice of the United States, was Edward Douglas White. At seventy he was still an imposing figure, but the former stern regularity of his features had somewhat softened of late. Fleshiness and lines of age about his cheeks and chin made his appear a baby face grown old and heavy. A symbol of the reuniting of the American people since the Civil War, White was a veteran of the Confederate Army, a Louisiana Roman Catholic who had been first a state senator and then a judge of the supreme court of Louisiana before entering the United States Senate in 1891. President Grover Cleveland had placed White on the Supreme Court in 1894. Now, nearly twenty-two years later, he was its dean in point of service by a margin of four years. He had been Chief Justice since 1910, when President Taft had broken precedent and promoted him from Associate Justice to replace Chief Justice Fuller.

White's senior by more than two years, and second to the Chief Justice in length of service on the Court, was Associate Justice Joseph McKenna. When he sat silent, lips compressed and white choker collar standing stiffly above the neck of his black robe, McKenna could look the forbidding judge. He had a trick of holding his pince-nez, as if waiting for an explanation from the truant schoolboy of an incompetent lawyer down below him, before he donned them to resume his reading of the appeal brief. Yet from another aspect McKenna's face, with its small pointed nose, was that of a disarming old pixie, completely encircled by a soft, silvery thatch of silken hair and a brush of trimmed cheek- and chinwhiskers below. Born in Philadelphia, McKenna had been taken by his parents to California in the wake of the Gold Rush, and there grew up with the Golden State. He served as state legislator, congressman, circuit judge, and as President McKinley's Attorney General for nearly a year before he was moved up to the Supreme Court at the turn of 1898.

Perhaps the most remarkable in appearance of all the Court members was Oliver Wendell Holmes, now approaching seventy-five. Bearer of the same name as his father, the Boston physician turned poet, Justice Holmes had long since dropped the Junior. Anyone coming into his presence, on the bench or elsewhere, was quickly made aware that in Holmes' case at least, the general rules of geriatrics did not apply. The tall man with the soldierly bearing who sat at the left of the Chief Justice was at once the oldest man on the Supreme Court and its most vigorously youthful member. Despite the snow-white hair and somewhat slow mode of speech, one could easily picture the youthful Holmes—the Civil War soldier who had returned, grievously wounded, to Boston and survived to teach brilliantly at the Harvard Law School. This was the scholar who had synthesized the experience of centuries of Anglo-Saxon jurisprudence into his book *The Common Law,* now a classic in its field. Twenty years on the supreme judicial court of Massachusetts and another thirteen years here had added to his luster without dulling his intellectual or physical polish. His wit crackled, his eyes sparkled. On the street his step was light and his Homburg was set at just the right tilt. People turned their heads to look when Justice Holmes walked by.

Whereas his upswept white mustache gave Holmes a debonair look, the drooping black mustache that cut across the hawklike face of Justice William Rufus Day made him appear grimly solemn. This, added to the exceptionally long and straight nose, the wide brow shining below and through strands of thinning hair, and, finally, the unusually long ears, completed the effect of a hanging judge from the pages of Mark Twain. Day was sixty-seven and looked it now, after thirteen years on the Supreme Court, to which President Theodore Roosevelt had named him a few months after appointing Holmes. Day had held many posts of honor and trust. Following fourteen years of private practice, he had been a state judge in Ohio before William McKinley appointed him Assistant Secretary of State. He had been later appointed Secretary of State, serving briefly in the McKinley cabinet that Joseph McKenna had just left, then had resigned to head the commission that negotiated the peace treaty with Spain at the close of the Spanish-American War. Day had left Washington in 1899 when the President named him to the U.S. Circuit Court in Cincinnati, returning to the capital early in 1903 when he joined the Supreme Court.

Seated immediately to the right of Holmes, as visitors to the Supreme Court viewed the bench, Charles Evans Hughes attracted instant attention. In recent months a crown of political question marks had clustered like a halo about the head of this imposing, handsome former governor of New York whom many Republicans considered the ideal candidate to unite their badly divided party in the coming Presidential election. Hughes' gracefully parted mustache and whiskers had shone like burnished bronze in his heyday as a federal antitrust prosecutor, and later as reform governor of the nation's most populous state. Now they had turned gray, a bit prematurely for a man in the prime of his intellectual vigor at fifty-three who was, despite his appearance, the youngest man on the Court. The impeccable neatness of Hughes and his bearing, close to majesty, reminded one of King

George V of England somewhat matured. When Hughes spoke, his listeners strained to catch a hint by which they might divine the intentions of this enigmatic Justice, now five years on the high bench, who had so far done nothing publicly either to promote or to halt the campaign to push him into the 1916 race for the Presidency.

Justice Willis Van Devanter, like Hughes an appointee of President Taft, had also been a member of the Court for five years. Smooth-shaven and long-faced, he had grown up in Indiana, then moved as a young man to Wyoming Territory to become one of its pioneer lawyers. His active practice led him to the chief justiceship of the Territory, then of the state. Sustained work as a Republican Party stalwart brought its reward as Van Devanter was named Assistant Attorney General of the United States by President McKinley, then federal circuit judge (by Theodore Roosevelt) until Taft elevated him to the Supreme Court.

The third of the Taft men remaining on the supreme bench after the death of Lamar was Mahlon Pitney of New Jersey. He had come up the same well-worn path—lawyer, Republican politician, lower court judge. Even more than Van Devanter, Pitney in his fifties was the kind of man whose face could easily be forgotten after being once seen. He was of that undistinguished-looking majority just pleasing enough and just plain enough to pass unnoticed in any gathering.

James Clark McReynolds, the one Supreme Court Justice appointed by President Wilson, was born in Kentucky and raised in Tennessee. A rugged-looking man with an intense air, McReynolds had the broad brow, piercing eyes, and eagle nose symbolic of the investigator. Under appointment by President Roosevelt he had served the government as special prosecutor in antitrust suits brought by a Republican administration against the tobacco trust, the anthracite coal–railroad combination, and others. Following a Taft-administration interim in private practice in New York City, McReynolds had been recalled to Washington early in 1913 by a Democratic President, Woodrow Wilson, whom he served as Attorney General until he was placed on the Supreme Court in the summer of 1914.

Taken together, the eight Justices represented the sort of distinguished and mature statesmen the American people expected on their Supreme Court. Their average age was sixty-three, and their records included membership in a President's cabinet by three, one former governor, a former United States Senator, and for the group as a whole many years' service on federal circuit courts and the higher state courts. All eight were Christians, all were native born, and all but Van Devanter bore surnames of ancestors from the British Isles.

Only two, Chief Justice White and Associate Justice McReynolds, were appointees of Democratic Presidents. The other six were considered Republicans, having been named to the bench by McKinley, Roosevelt, and Taft during the sixteen-year Republican tenure between the second Grover Cleveland administration and the accession of Wilson. If the Justices had divided sharply in the past on such issues as the right of laboring men to join unions, as in *Coppage* v. *Kansas,* or the power of the states to regulate men's working hours in bakeries, as in *Lochner* v. *New York,* the public and the legal fraternity knew that these judges were basically the same kind of American in blood and spirit, their family roots imbedded deep in the soil and traditions of the country.

For one American in particular, respect for the Supreme Court of the United States had increased through his mature years to the point of veneration. This man had been given the power to make the high tribunal over almost in his own image. William Howard Taft, nearly three years out of the White House and now Professor of Constitutional Law at Yale University in New Haven, was in constant demand outside the university as a speaker on public affairs. A huge man who managed to keep his weight below 300 pounds only by careful dieting, Taft was an engaging platform personality. There had been few former Presidents with enough vigor and interest to travel the lecture circuit after having served in the highest United States office. Nor were many public speakers so well informed and articulate on a variety of important questions. Taft thrived on public appearances, and on short notice could pull from his files an instructive and entertaining address on anything from life insurance and the tariff to international relations and the federal budget. When he told a joke, his listeners found something essentially comical in this big, jolly former President with his sweeping mustache shaking in amusement at their appreciation of his joke from the platform.

The place of the Supreme Court in the American system of government was a frequently recurring theme in the Taft lectures. Though he had served only one term as President, Taft had named five new Associate Justices to the Court and had appointed the present Chief

Justice. Although two of his appointees, first Justice Lurton and now Lamar, had passed from the stage, he still felt a strong proprietary interest in the tribunal.

Taft's feeling went beyond a close personal involvement with the Supreme Court members. He was a strong traditionalist, conservative on public questions, who regarded the Court as a learned senior council of the nation's wisest men. They formed, in his eyes, the kind of board of review required in a discordant society to settle with finality those constitutional conflicts that inevitably accompany personal freedom under law. Once the Court had ruled, Taft believed, there should be no going back, no further questions asked. American constitutional law was to him a framework of fixed principles, much like the laws of physics or structural engineering, in which the considered opinion of juridical authorities became fact. He had sought for his Court sound judges who *knew* the law. Such men could fit into the spaces between the laws already declared the solutions to those new legal problems that might arise, just as a competent librarian knows how to place new books within the established classification system of an old collection. Law to Taft was a matter of knowledge and reasoning intelligence, not sentiment, not experiment.

So strongly did Taft feel about the need to preserve the dignity of the Supreme Court that in 1911, when preparing to run for a second term as President, he had told an interviewer that he very much regretted the Court's being forced to consider the constitutionality of a federal income tax a second time. The Court had ruled in 1894 that such a tax was unconstitutional. It should not, Taft believed, be subjected to the possible humiliation of reversing itself. Solely in order to preserve the Court's prestige, Taft said, he preferred to submit the income tax to the state legislatures as an amendment to the Constitution. Should the Court now uphold the tax, something would be lost of its dignity. It would be a bad thing if the country were to think that the Supreme Court could easily change its mind.

For a long time William Howard Taft's veneration for the Supreme Court had been mingled with a craving for one of its seats. Never before had a public man so obviously displayed his desire for the place; nor had any such prize come so tantalizingly close, and so frequently, without the taking. Now fifty-eight, Taft had started his campaign to reach the Court when he was thirty-two and a member of the superior court of Ohio. On the occasion of President Benjamin Harrison's visit to Cincinnati in 1889, Governor Foraker of Ohio had suggested young Judge Taft as a candidate worth considering for the United States Supreme Court. The bright young judge had much to recommend him. He had distinguished himself as a scholar both at Yale and at the Cincinnati Law School; his family owned a major Cincinnati newspaper; and he was a Republican with sound views on property rights.

A few weeks later the President called Taft to Washington to become Solicitor General of the United States. This post in the Department of Justice was continually in the political spotlight. Not only did it offer the man who held it the chance to represent the federal government in argument before the Supreme Court, it also held promise of making one's name known quickly at the seat of power, with all that meant in terms of political reward. Taft took the job but he never felt really at home in it. He had become so imbued with the mystique of judicature that after only two years in the capital he welcomed the opportunity the President gave him to return to his home city on the Ohio River, to take a seat there on the United States Court of Appeals for the Sixth Judicial Circuit. He now saw himself as a judge for life.

"Perhaps," he wrote to his brother in one of his frequent ventures at self-analysis, "it is the comfort and dignity and power without worry I like."

Through eight years as a federal circuit judge, Taft was continually on the alert for any chance of stepping upward to the Court at the apex of the American legal pyramid. His name was suggested to President Grover Cleveland by the widow of Justice Howell Edmunds Jackson in 1895, and Taft himself, visiting Washington in 1896, reported to his wife that his being placed on the Supreme Court eventually was "the expectation" of "almost every person I met." Even most of the Supreme Court members "seem to regard it as very probable," he proudly wrote Nellie Taft. Disappointment smote him hard in 1898 when President McKinley, a fellow Ohioan much beholden to his brother Charles Taft for help in paying his debts, bypassed William Howard Taft and filled a Supreme Court vacancy with Joseph McKenna.

Early in 1900, when he was forty-two, Taft faced the big turning point in his life. With the Philippine Islands newly delivered from the yoke of Spain, President McKinley asked Taft to serve on the commission which was to establish civil government for the islands. Taft was not at all sure that it was wise to leave his comfortable bench in Cincinnati, from which he could keep an eye on Washington. When he voiced his concern over his future chances, McKinley assured him the Philippines task would be temporary. He could make the sacrifice only if he were made chairman of the Philippines Commission, Taft countered. The President agreed to the condition. Taft hesitated long, repeating his wish to sit on the Supreme Court. McKinley then gave this verbal promise:

"If you give up this judicial office at my request, you shall not suffer. If I last and the opportunity comes, I shall appoint you."

The task in the Philippines stretched far beyond the year that had been estimated. Two and a half years had elapsed; Theodore Roosevelt had replaced McKinley in the White House and Taft had become governor of the Philippines when Justice Horace Gray created a vacancy by resigning from the Court. Roosevelt consulted his close friend and advisor Senator Henry Cabot Lodge about a replacement, then appointed Oliver Wendell Holmes. A few months later, Justice Shiras told the President that he would step down from the bench at the end of the year. This time Roosevelt cabled Taft in the Philippines, offering him the position.

But now the would-be Supreme Court Justice found that he had been gripped, for the first time in his life, by responsibilities that fully challenged him. He wanted for reasons of personal pride to finish his work in the Philippines, a matter of perhaps another year he thought. He was haunted, moreover, by the suspicion that somehow the President's primary motive was to remove him from his governorship of the islands rather than to strengthen the Supreme Court by appointing him to it. After considerable correspondence and cabling over a period of months, Taft ended by declining Roosevelt's offer. He was, after all, only forty-five. He was thinking now that there were other places one might occupy quite happily before taking one of the black leather swivel chairs in the Supreme Court chamber. He had time.

The better part of a year passed. Late in 1903 Roosevelt called Taft home to replace Elihu Root as Secretary of War. A few months of authority in Roosevelt's cabinet, then taking part in his chief's winning campaign for the Presidency in 1904, gave Taft a taste of the political life that savored well on the whole. But life in Washington had another effect: It refined his taste for the Supreme Court to the point where he told Roosevelt that he coveted no mantle but that of the Chief Justiceship when it should fall from Fuller's shoulders.

In the early months of 1906 there was a great temptation for Taft to lower his requirements just a little, when Roosevelt offered him a subordinate place on the Supreme Court vacated by Associate Justice Brown. Should the Chief Justiceship later become vacant, Roosevelt pledged, Taft should certainly have it. But by this time Roosevelt had also made plans to direct a victory for the Republican Party in 1908 by selecting his own heir to office and making his right to the succession plainly apparent to his colleagues. He told Taft, and Secretary of State Root agreed with him, that the Secretary of War was the best man in sight to lead the party two years hence.

Again Taft hesitated, balancing the responsibilities and unpleasantnesses of political life against the serene dignity of the Supreme Court. Again, but only after long and tortured thought, he decided that it was too early for him to make the final career decision of his life. Accepting a lifetime appointment to the Court would mean bypassing the one office that would make his name immortal. He was only forty-nine and still had time. So Taft once more rejected Roosevelt's offer of a justiceship, this time to accept his tender of the Presidency.

In due course Taft succeeded Roosevelt in the White House, and the Colonel went off to Africa to hunt big game. During Taft's administration he filled a majority of the seats on the Supreme Court and replaced Chief Justice Fuller with White. Given the fact that Chief Justice White, Taft's appointee, was twelve years Taft's senior, the chances seemed fairly good that after his term as President, another Republican President might appoint Taft Chief Justice not far from his sixtieth birthday. To be the first man in American history to serve in the two most exalted posts within the gift of the Republic was a glowing prospect.

But the humiliation of his defeat when he ran for re-election in 1912 nearly cut Taft's heart from him. Roosevelt, the former chief with whom he shared an intimacy known by few men in high public office, the man who had groomed him for the Presidency and offered him everything, had come storming back into the political wars from his brief, self-imposed Elba. With withering scorn Roosevelt attacked Taft as a bungler who had mismanaged the job that had been handed him. Going to the crowds and arousing them against the man who had been his own choice as President, cutting the Grand Old Party down the middle with his Messianic Bull Moose campaign, Roosevelt in 1912 had drawn the majority of Republican votes to himself and his rump Progressive Party, leaving Taft a poor third in the race. The Colonel's egocentric drive for power had insured the handing over of the Presidency and control of both houses of Congress to Woodrow Wilson and the Democrats after sixteen years of Republican administration.

Yale, Taft's alma mater, embraced him again under her sheltering elms and derived a measure of glory in the return of her distinguished son. As Professor of Constitutional Law, Taft delivered four lectures a week, two in the law school and two in the humanities division, for which he was paid an annual salary of $5000. By Wednesday afternoon Professor Taft managed to get away from New Haven for his public-lecture schedule. He usually filled four engagements a week before his Sunday of rest, at an honorarium of $300 each, plus travel expenses. If the dignity of being a professor-lecturer did not quite measure up to that of Chief Justice of the United States at a salary of $13,000 a year, the earnings from Yale and the platform were considerably greater.

Not long after settling at New Haven, Taft found a genuine love for his new mode of life and employment, as he had previously become pleasantly habituated to governing the Philippines, to running the War Department, and to being President of the United States. Yet he still looked with wistful eye toward the chamber in Washington where, but for his sense of duty and a series of unfortunate turns of event, he might now be seated. The death of Justice Lamar, Taft's second appointee to die in less than three years, understandably aroused in Taft emotions not shared by any other man in the United States. Now, with the lean, ascetic-faced political science professor from Princeton in the White House, Taft's thoughts of what might have been were bitter indeed. They came flooding back, borne to him in the correspondence of his close friends and in the press.

In its eulogy of Lamar, *The New York Times* sounded a call that the President rise above party in filling the vacancy:

In considering the choice of a successor to Justice Lamar one name comes first of all to mind. President Wilson would give new strength and dignity to the court, he would recognize proved and distinguished judicial capacity by appointing ex-President Taft.

It mattered not, the editorial went on, that the present Court included only two Democrats—White and McReynolds. The Supreme Court should be made up of men of the highest caliber without regard to their political origins.

In the following days Taft's name was frequently proposed in the press. If the publisher did not speak for him directly through the editorial columns, the news pages persisted in reporting that Taft was the favored candidate of various leaders in politics and at the bar. On January 12 an editorial in the Washington *Herald* boldly put the issue of "Mr. Taft and the Supreme Court" where every government official could read it with his morning coffee:

> The whole country would commend the selection of Mr. Taft. . . .
> His profound legal knowledge, fortified by a broad experience in
> statecraft, would add greatly to the strength of the highest court
> in the land. As is well known, Mr. Taft, before he became Presi-
> dent, was ambitious to become a justice of the Supreme Court. . . .
> President Wilson would serve his country well by appointing him.

Hardly a January day went by without Professor Taft's receiving in his mail at New Haven evidence that his friends and admirers all over the country were at work in his behalf. Some letters included clippings of editorials promoting the Taft candidacy, some told of messages that Taft's correspondents had sent on his behalf to President Wilson and his advisors. Answering these communications with a warm glow of pride, the former President expressed his doubt that Wilson could see the situation with any objectivity. To his old Yale classmate Clarence Kelsey, a well-to-do New York corporation attorney and director, he wrote somewhat coyly:

> *My dear Kels:*
>   I have your letter of January 15th. Wilson never made a promise
> to put me on the Supreme Bench, and I don't know whether I
> could accept if he offered it to me now. I don't say that I would not,
> because of course I love the Bench and would like to be on that
> Bench, but it would seriously interfere with plans I have for the next

two years. Still, when one goes on to the Bench, he can not be a chooser as to time.

I agree with Judge Edwards that it is quite likely that while the Bar would like to have me on the Bench, the politicians would not care to. . . . I am wicked enough to enjoy the irritation that Wilson probably feels at getting those letters.

Myron T. Herrick, president of a Cleveland savings bank and an old colleague of Taft's in Ohio politics, received an acknowledgment in which the former President was somewhat more candid:

> *My dear Myron:*
> I have your note of January 10th. . . . I haven't the slightest idea that President Wilson will offer me an appointment to the Supreme Bench. . . . My own idea of Mr. Wilson's breadth of view is that he could not in any way be made to see a political advantage that he could derive from such an appointment; and while I may do him an injustice, I feel certain that he could not recognize a generous impulse if he met it on the street.

This was not the first time President Wilson had been importuned to appoint to office the man he had soundly defeated when they had gone to the people three years earlier. The ballots of the 1912 election had scarcely been counted when Wilson began receiving suggestions on ways in which Taft could be used to ornament his administration. It was as though there had been no great principle at stake in the election, as if Taft were regarded as the representative of a body of opinion in the country that somehow had a vested right to office. William S. Bennet, a former Republican congressman from New York, touched it all off. He wrote to Wilson that Justice Holmes, who was approaching seventy-two, would soon retire. Bennet's suggestion must have startled Wilson by its audacity:

> I imagine that irrespective of politics, a majority of the voters of the U.S. would be pleased if President Taft were to go upon the Supreme Court Bench. He could scarcely appoint himself to succeed Judge Holmes.
> My suggestion, which I hope you will not deem impertinent, even though you may not agree with it, is that it would be a splendid thing if you wrote to President Taft and said to him that if he would permit the vacancy to remain until after the 4th of March, it would be a pleasure to you to appoint him to the Bench.

There was never the slightest sign from Wilson as he awaited his moment to take over the Presidency that any deal with Taft was in the making. Yet soon rumors were spilled to the press that such was the case. Letters of applause and of protest bombarded the President-elect. One irate Democrat wrote the President from Denver early in December:

Sir:

I see by the paper this morning (though I am far from believing all I see in the papers) that you would be pleased to appoint Mr. Taft to a vacancy on the Supreme Bench. I do not believe you would do it under any circumstances, but I wish to enter my strong protest. It would seem to me like our Savior appointing a Judas to an apostleship after the betrayal.

The rumors were lulled somewhat by Holmes' failure to hand in the resignation predicted by ex-Congressman Bennet. But resistance to Taft flared up like a prairie fire every time during the next three years that rumors went out about his appointment. In 1914, a year after he took office, Wilson's mail was again filled with pro- and anti-Taft argument when it was merely rumored that a replacement on the Court was due. Again that summer, when Justice Lurton's seat fell vacant, the claques contending over Taft's qualifications were more active than ever. Now, with the death of Lamar, Taft's following was at it again.

A vacancy on the Supreme Court of the United States precipitates a deluge of advice upon the President as surely as thunderheads carry a storm. A place on the Court has long been regarded in the U.S. as juridical Valhalla. By 1916 only sixty-six men had achieved the distinction of sitting as members of that august body since John Jay presided over its first session in 1789. Everyone active in politics or the law who helped put his friend on the Court could feel a bit of its glory reflected on him. What finer tribute could one pay to a colleague on the bench or at the bar? And what more practical way to move everyone in a state political organization up one rung on the ladder than to fill a vacancy at the top? Sending one of its leading men to glory in Washington was a favorite move, and a smart one, in any political group.

The Washington *Times* on January 12 carried a front-page item indicating how well the path to the White House was worn by persons urging Supreme Court candidates on Wilson:

> Speaker Clark today saw the President regarding Judge W. W. Graves of Missouri, Senator James talked to him about Judge James M. Benton of Kentucky, and Representative Ralph Beagle of Texas recommended Presley K. Ewing, a Houston attorney.
>
> Various other persons called on the same errand. To all the President indicated he was keeping an open mind.

Names came to Wilson from every direction. Congressman George M. Young of North Dakota sent a wire promoting the candidacy of Judge Charles J. Fisk of the supreme court of North Dakota, signed by "the entire membership of the Grand Forks bar." Texans urged the President by wire and letter to "honor the Supreme Court and grand old Texas by appointing ex-Senator Horace Chilton, the choice of all Wilson Democrats, and peace of mind will be your reward." Governor Stuart of Virginia led a delegation up from Richmond to plead the merits of Congressman Andrew Jackson Montague, a former governor of the Old Dominion. Arkansas pushed forward Chief Justice Edgar Allen McCulloch of the state supreme court. Thomas Cowan McClellan of Alabama and William Reynolds Allen of North Carolina were other state supreme court judges whose names were presented.

Some partisans thought it wise to put forward their candidates in more subtle fashion and sent their endorsements to the President's son-in-law, Secretary of the Treasury William Gibbs McAdoo. If they hoped thereby to gain the President's attention by indirection, they promptly learned from McAdoo that their suggestions had been forwarded to Attorney General Gregory, in whose province it fell to recommend nominations to the federal bench. Self-confident B. F. Long, a member of the North Carolina superior court, did not hesitate to propose his own name to McAdoo. Governor Theodore G. Bilbo of Mississippi suggested Judge W. C. McLean of his state's supreme court. Various people in Atlanta sent in the names of Alexander Campbell King, a railroad attorney, and Judge John C. Hart.

Overwhelmingly, the candidates displayed for the President's selection were from the South. From the moment the press began to discuss the replacement for Lamar it had been practically assumed that the seat in question was a "Southern seat," as if the Court were somehow required to reflect an unchanging geographic balance. The venerable Chief Justice White and the relative newcomer Mc-Reynolds left a large sector of the country between Louisiana and Tennessee unrepresented, if indeed such a term can fairly be applied to service on the Court. In fact, it often was, fairly or otherwise.

Some of the correspondence concerning the vacancy commanded more than casual attention because it brought to Wilson a measure of genuine thought on standards to employ in choosing a new Justice. Jacob Dickinson, a railroad attorney based in Chicago and a former president of the American Bar Association, cautioned Wilson that he should think carefully before appointing a federal official who, like McReynolds, might be forced to disqualify himself from certain "great cases" to which the federal government was a party. The President assured Dickinson, a Republican, that his advice was "certainly first class."

Not everyone saw it this way. On January 17 Wilson received a confidential letter from Henry White, who had been Theodore Roosevelt's ambassador first to Italy and then to France. Shortly before Lamar's death, White wrote, he had talked with "one of the senior Justices of the court, an old friend of mine," and to him posed the question of "the most likely person" to succeed Lamar. The jurist had replied with a strong recommendation for John W. Davis of West Virginia. As White put it to Wilson:

> My friend at once said the President will have the greatest opportunity for strengthening the Bench which has befallen any President for a long time past in the person of his own Solicitor General, Mr. Davis. He added that Mr. Davis has produced a great impression—an unusual one upon the Court by the ability of his arguments and the depth of his legal knowledge and particularly by his breadth of view. I remember his also saying that besides his legal qualifications the Solicitor General would be not only politically but geographically in line for the place.
>
> I have since then mentioned this conversation to another Justice, also an old friend and he replied: "Mr. Davis is certainly a remarkable man and has impressed us all very deeply."

On the day of the Lamar funeral, Senator Robert L. Owen of Oklahoma had written Wilson:

I wish to strongly urge upon your attention the importance of putting upon the Supreme Bench, in place of the late Justice Lamar, a man who has demonstrated his complete sympathy with the Progressive view, and shown himself to regard the interests of human beings as superior to the interests of property holding.

I feel very strongly on this matter, and hope you will not lose sight of this vital distinction in making your nomination. We have not on the bench a single progressive man, in my point of view.

Wilson replied: "I warmly sympathize with the views expressed in your letter . . . and I hope with all my heart I can find just such a man."

More than he may have known at the time, Senator Owen had touched on the aspect of the nomination that most concerned the President—the social outlook of his nominee. The entire business of cementing political friendships with rewards and keeping party organizations in various cities and states happy by awarding each his patronage plums was alien to the scholarly occupant of the White House. Although he had rapidly developed political expertness at the policy level, and although he knew how to use men and to put issues vigorously from the platform, Wilson had little taste for the camaraderie of the professional politicians and almost no relish for the deal. Further, he had a keen sense of the way the minds of the mass of the American people were tending. It had been his ability to articulate a proffer of something better, of help through government for those in need, that won him first a governorship and then the Presidency. Millions of Americans, plagued by economic insecurity, interpreted his advocacy of "the New Freedom" as a hopeful sign of change in their lives.

Now, just short of completing three years in office, Wilson was laying the groundwork for his re-election campaign. Although his intimates felt certain that Wilson was planning to run again, the President had not publicly confirmed his intention to do so. Senator Owen had used a propitious phrase to characterize the kind of man Wilson believed he should appoint—"a man with the Progressive view."

The arithmetic of the 1912 election results, set against the characteristics of the campaign and the personalities involved, made it obvious to Wilson what he must do to win again. Wilson was a minority President. He had benefited from the split in the Republicans between Roosevelt with his so-called Progressive Party and Taft, candidate of the Republican regulars. Wilson had been elected with fewer than 6,300,000 votes of the 14,000,000 rolled up by all three candidates combined.

The signs were gathering that there would be no division in the year ahead between the Progressive Republicans and the regulars, so Wilson would have to lead his ticket against a united Republican Party. He could not hope to win away the conservative, traditional Republicans who had cast nearly 3,500,000 ballots for Taft in 1912. His best chance for victory lay in wooing and winning the nonpartisan liberal voters who had been attracted to the Roosevelt Bull Moose by the glitter of the Colonel's progressivism. No one really knew how many there were, as opposed to confirmed Republicans who had voted for Roosevelt because he was a more dynamic party leader than Taft. But Wilson knew that he could take a giant stride in the direction of winning the nonpartisan liberal vote by nominating to the Supreme Court a man who would symbolize his dedication to progressive principles.

It was clear to Wilson that the campaign promoting Taft for the Court stemmed from conservative roots. Paying honor to a former President, honoring the Court by putting an ex-President on it— these were really side issues. Taft was the symbol of conservative stand-patism, of which Wilson was convinced the country had had enough, not only in candidates for office but also on the Supreme Court. This had been shown long since by the vehemence of the opposition stirred up by the rumors of Wilson's supposed intention to put Taft on the Court. One letter the President received early in 1914 on this issue is typical:

> *Orchard Knoll Homestead Dairy, Klamath Co., Oregon*
>
> From a lonely cabin in the Far West I write to implore you not to do it. I have no grudge against Mr. Taft, but I believe him to be unfit for the place; that he is out of harmony with the spirit of American Liberty and the equality of the people. Born with a golden spoon in his mouth and never having had to fulfill the Divine command, "By the Sweat of thy face shalt thou eat bread," it is impossible for him to sympathize with the common man, and, unconsciously, his decisions would favor aristocracy and be against democracy. The trend of his thought is backward, not forward.

Organized labor had more specific reasons for urging Wilson not to put Taft on the Supreme Court. The whereases of a resolution adopted by the Central Labor Union of Indianapolis and sent to the President explained the union man's view:

> Whereas the said W. H. Taft has shown an opposition to labor organizations by speeches and otherwise that can readily be accepted as hatred, and
> Whereas there can be no justice rendered by a Court composed of men who permit their disappointments to become prejudices, as under such mental conditions no judge can be impartial. . . .

Plumbers Union 34 of St. Paul, Minnesota, was another group that let the President know its feelings:

> Whereas the said Mr. Taft, when he was a judge, inaugurated the abuse of the injunction power of the courts in its unwarranted application to labor disputes, and invoked and used against the working people of the country other forms of judicial tyranny; and
> Whereas, while he was President he upheld and defended this judicial tyranny with all the power required. . . .

But Taft's name engendered not only a class opposition; it did not sit well with loyal Democrats. When, two days after Lamar's funeral, a meeting of the Chattanooga Bar Association passed a resolution endorsing ex-President Taft to succeed him, Secretary of the Treasury McAdoo received a report of the meeting from two members who had waged a losing fight opposing the resolution. Thomas H. Cooke wrote:

> The non-partisan cry captured the crowd. . . . Mr. Wilson can surely find a competent democrat to succeed a democrat. Any way he certainly knows what is best to be done.

The President's son-in-law, thanking his Chattanooga informant, replied:

> I do not know that the President has as yet made up his mind as to whom he will name, but I can confidently predict that the country will be satisfied.

On January 11 the national committee of Theodore Roosevelt's Progressive Party held an executive session in Chicago, without its leader in attendance. At issue was the course for 1916—to reunite with the Grand Old Party or to go it alone. When the group opened its doors at the end, Roosevelt's right-hand man, George Perkins, announced to reporters: "We are hopeful that both parties will agree on somebody, and it need not necessarily be Mr. Roosevelt." Perkins went on to spell out the Colonel's views—that the paramount issue was national defense. It was further announced that the rump party would hold a national convention starting on June 7 in Chicago, same date and place as the Republican convention. All signs pointed to the collapse of the third party and reunion with the GOP. Implicit in the emphasis on national defense was a scrapping of the progressive domestic program for which T.R. had thundered during his Bull Moose campaign. The body of voters attracted in 1912 by Roosevelt's promise of liberal progressivism were now ready to be taken by the Democrats, provided Wilson's party could pick up the mantle of militant reform the Colonel had cast aside in favor of his old military uniform.

January 1916 was an especially busy month for Woodrow Wilson, as he laid out his strategy for the decisive months ahead. In his role as ceremonial chief of the American nation, his schedule had to make room for such duties as addressing the Pan-American Scientific Congress and later entertaining the 4000 delegates at the White House. The new Mrs. Wilson passed her ordeal of inspection gallantly as she presided with charm and grace over the season's social events. Intimates remarked that the President seemed to have taken a new lease on life since his December marriage, and that at fifty-nine he seemed fit, even eager, to join battle with whatever opponents, domestic or foreign, the new year might bring. On week ends he and Edith Bolling Wilson would escape for a few quiet hours down the tranquil Potomac aboard the Presidential yacht *Mayflower* or, if time did not permit a cruise, motor into the countryside.

Although the President possessed an unusual capacity to relax amid great stresses, his duties would not permit a day to pass without imposing on his consciousness that he was the leader of a political party, a government, and a nation. Wilson was obliged to divide his winter diplomatic dinner into a pair of dinners, so arranged as to avoid the unpleasantness of seating representatives of the Allies at the same table with their diplomatic foes from the Central Powers. Their sympathies in no way neutral, the President and his lady were forced to maintain a pose of disinterested courtesy on both evenings.

In a cloud of uncertainty over the cause of the sinking, the affair

of the *Persia* faded from view. In early January, Pancho Villa's marauding Mexican revolutionaries threatened the safety of Americans
living just across the border. How far, Wilson asked himself, should
he permit the U.S. Army to pursue them? Was this Mexican business
really a diversionary trick of the Germans? He could not take time
to settle one issue before another was pushed upon him. Which faction of Democrats should be awarded the prize plum, the postmastership of New York City? The Tammany crowd was pushing
Joseph Johnson on him. Should he appoint this hack to keep Tammany quiet, or name Robert F. Wagner, his own kind of liberal? And
he had to plan his speaking tour of the Midwest, scheduled for the
end of the month. Should he keep it strictly nonpolitical, devoted
to the theme of preparedness? How frank could he afford to be in
warning the country of the danger of war that lay ahead? In response
to the charges hurled every day by Colonel Roosevelt, Senator Henry
Cabot Lodge, and Elihu Root that he was displaying weakness
toward the Central Powers, should he in the coming series of speeches
reach for his holster just a little?

As each day passed, the vacancy on the Supreme Court seemed
to call more insistently for his decision. On January 17 the *Evening
Star,* a Washington partisan of Taft, pointed out that the Court was
not qualified that day to hear any matter involving the federal government, because the law required six Justices to hear a case. Chief
Justice White was at home with a cold, Day was recuperating from
the grippe, McReynolds was disqualified because he had recently
been Attorney General of the United States—and the seat formerly
held by Lamar was still vacant.

Meanwhile, action in a federal court in New Haven, Connecticut,
brought the Danbury Hatters to the end of their long, bitter trail.
The final order of foreclosure was granted against the homes of 141
union members surviving from the strike they had undertaken years
before against their employer, Loewe. Their houses would be sold
to pay the damages that the union men had incurred by defying the
Sherman antitrust law. The only thing that could save them from
being thrown into the street would be a generous subscription raised
by their fellow unionists in the American Federation of Labor. Samuel
Gompers, president of the labor federation, had previously washed
his hands of the Danbury Hatters because he did not believe in their
boycott tactics. But now that the law and the courts had decreed

eviction, those in sympathy with the defeated strikers looked to Gompers to extend his influence in their behalf.

On Monday, January 24, the Supreme Court ended a long period of suspense concerning the personal income tax by upholding it as valid. The case challenging the tax as unconstitutional, *Brushaber* v. *Union Pacific Railroad,* had been argued in October. Some form of federal income tax had seemed inevitable since 1913, when the states had ratified the Sixteenth Amendment, written specifically to authorize one. But the foes of the tax had hoped to outlaw the particular tax attached by Congress to the Underwood Tariff Act of 1913, claiming that its progressive rates amounted to an inequitable seizure of property without due process. In fact, the income tax touched fewer than 2 per cent of the families in the country in 1915, but because it struck the wealthy directly and in a way they considered discriminatory, it was doubly painful to them.

As soon as the Court ruled, Representative Cordell Hull, the Tennessee Democrat who had written the income tax law, declared that he would offer a broadened tax to the House. The Washington *Times* asserted that the Democrats planned to raise an additional hundred million dollars in the coming year by imposing a heavier income tax, "most of it wrung from the wealthier classes." There was a sense of economic class in the air when men discussed such issues as the income tax and the Danbury Hatters.

Late in January, Wilson quietly sought intelligence he required from Senator Robert Marion La Follette, the Progressive Republican from Wisconsin, spiritual leader of those Senators in both parties who considered themselves progressives with a small *p*. If, Wilson let it be known, he should nominate a certain man for the Supreme Court who was personally very close to the Senator, could La Follette assure him the support of the Republican Progressives in his bloc? The President might need their votes for confirmation by the Senate. La Follette's word came discreetly back to Wilson through Attorney General Thomas Gregory: Yes, the Progressive Republicans would stand by him.

With this assurance, the wheels of Wilson's Supreme Court nomination machinery turned rapidly. Attorney General Gregory sent word through an intermediary to the man of Wilson's choice. Would he accept? Almost immediately Gregory received a one-word reply by telegram: YES.

Knowing now that he was ready to set off an explosion that would blast the true progressives apart from the Republican stand-patters, Wilson must have derived ironic pleasure from the news from New York in the evening papers of Tuesday, January 25. In his role of right-hand man and political fund-raiser to Theodore Roosevelt, George Perkins announced that the Progressive Party stood ready to unite with the Republicans "to remove from the White House the man who has brought so much discredit and dishonor to our country." After firing this shot, Perkins then shifted into his principal role of corporation lawyer to attend the board meeting of U.S. Steel, which he served as general counsel. With him were Judge Gary, U.S. Steel board chairman, and its most powerful directors, J. P. Morgan and Henry C. Frick. The steel company's profits in the final quarter of 1915, Gary announced at the end of the meeting, came to a record-shattering $51,232,788, a million dollars above *The Wall Street Journal*'s estimate on New Year's Day. Business had never been better, or bigger.

The President held his nomination secret for two days more. On Thursday he rode in his special train to New York, where he addressed the Railway Business Association dinner at the Waldorf-Astoria Hotel, then went to the Biltmore to say a few words to the Motion Picture Board of Trade before going to his sleeping car for the night journey to Washington. On that evening, the Central Labor Union of Washington, D.C., held a dinner at the Elks' Home in celebration of the sixty-sixth birthday of President Samuel Gompers of the American Federation of Labor. The American labor movement, Gompers revealed to the diners who came to honor him, would be asked to give an hour's wages to pay off the fines of their union brothers, the Danbury Hatters, to save their homes. He pledged his word "to assist the men victimized by the vicious greed of the corporation, aided by the willing hand of the judiciary." The courts, Gompers' words implied, were part of the machinery of injustice in this case.

Shortly after the noontime opening of the Senate on the following day, during the humdrum of routine business, a clerk was recognized by the chair to read a message from the President. The few Senators present looked up at the dais.

"To the Senate of the United States," the clerk read aloud. "I nominate Louis D. Brandeis of Massachusetts to be Associate Justice

of the Supreme Court of the United States, vice Joseph Rucker
Lamar, deceased. Signed, Woodrow Wilson. The White House, 28
January 1916."

On the Senate floor there was a sudden, busy scurrying as several members conferred with their colleagues. Some quickly carried
the startling news downstairs to Senators still lingering over their
lunch.

In the press gallery above the Vice-President's chair on the dais,
reporters dashed for the telephones.

three

Mr. Brandeis of Boston

Forty years before the reading of Louis Dembitz Brandeis' name in the Senate caused an immediate flurry of excitement, he had already impressed his colleagues at the Harvard Law School as a young man who would command attention. Arriving in Cambridge fresh from two years at the Annen-Realschule in Dresden, Germany, Brandeis had entered the law school in the fall of 1875, shortly before his nineteenth birthday. He had not been through the undergraduate course that was the common preparation of his classmates, most of whom were several years his senior. But he soon showed that he was the brightest student among them.

Brandeis' parents were well-educated, German-speaking Jews of Bohemian origin who had emigrated from the Austrian Empire shortly after a wave of reaction had crushed the democratic revolutions of 1848 in Central Europe. Inspired by the American ideal eloquently expressed by De Tocqueville, the Brandeises started out afresh in the New World as free spirits, bound neither by religious dogma nor by the nationalistic loyalties of the continent they had left behind. They settled in Louisville, Kentucky, where young Louis was born in November 1856. In the wake of the 1873 financial panic and a failure in the family grain-brokerage business, the Brandeises temporarily went back to Europe. When they returned to Louisville in 1875, Louis had made up his mind to study law. His vocational motive stemmed from a deep admiration for his uncle, Lewis Dembitz, a man of sagacity and culture whose life of the mind in the law appealed to young Louis as far more stimulating than his own father's business of buying and selling. It was in honor of Uncle Lewis that Louis changed his middle name from David to Dembitz.

Louis was completely bilingual in German and English, without a trace of accent other than the soft border-states inflection of certain vowels acquired from his Louisville upbringing. In class at Harvard his lucid oral explanation of the complexities of case and textbook made students and professors alike recognize they were in the presence of a person of uncommon mental talents. Brandeis showed that he was well grounded in the classical authors, languages, mathematics, and history. But it was the speed and accuracy with which he absorbed new knowledge, and his ability to relate it to the pattern of facts already acquired, that marked him as the distinguished student. Brandeis was not yet twenty-one when he graduated in 1877, the leading scholar in his class, with what President Charles W. Eliot termed the most distinguished academic record the school had known —yet his characteristic thoroughness impelled him to stay on for a third year of study at Harvard because he wanted a deeper grounding in the law than the university required for the degree.

This intellectual center of New England in the time of its brightest flowering offered stimulating diversions as well as academic opportunities—lectures, concerts, new friends, and discussions with thinking people. Young Louis Brandeis looked on it as the Athens of the New World. Those years at Harvard, Brandeis told an interviewer years later, "were among the happiest of my life. I worked! For me the world's center was Cambridge."

Small wonder, therefore, that Brandeis felt unfulfilled in St. Louis, where he went in 1878 to put in his first year of legal practice and found himself boringly bogged down in petty cases involving petty issues. The following spring he happily accepted the proposal of Samuel D. Warren, his law-school classmate, that he return east. Sam Warren had been second in the class scholastically, immediately behind Brandeis. Since Boston, where his family ran a successful paper business, was Warren's home, he offered good social and business contacts. The two of them, Warren wrote Brandeis, could pool their abilities and self-confidence and start their own Boston law practice. In the summer of 1879 the firm of Warren and Brandeis opened its one-room office on the third floor of 60 Devonshire Street in downtown Boston. In this and the successor firm, which Brandeis founded some years later when Warren left the law to direct the family business, Brandeis was to practice law for thirty-seven years.

The firm succeeded from the first. Although in the early years

Brandeis and Warren had to work hard, they took time to enjoy themselves. Louis found his world expanding on all sides, and adapted himself readily to the society into which Sam Warren introduced him —club life, riding, tennis and gymnasium work to keep in trim, and social evenings with cultivated people such as Oliver Wendell Holmes, who had employed Sam in his law office while Brandeis had been in St. Louis. Brandeis felt accepted socially and intellectually. He was a happy, well-adjusted young man about Boston, feeling no self-consciousness for being Jewish or born of immigrant parents. To his Massachusetts acquaintances he was a Harvard man, Sam Warren's friend and partner.

As he practiced, Brandeis continued to study deeply into the history of the law and its social foundation. Always he sought the whys that lay behind the whats. Between 1879 and 1881 he devoted some of his time each week to serving as law clerk to Chief Justice Horace Gray of the supreme judicial court of Massachusetts. The older man was profoundly impressed with his ability. As early as 1880, before he left Boston to become a Justice of the Supreme Court of the United States, Gray wrote of his young assistant, then twenty-four: "I consider Brandeis the most ingenious and most original lawyer I ever met."

Louis in these years gave considerable thought to his beloved law school across the Charles River, where he had grown from a schoolboy into a full-fledged member of the profession. When Professor James Bradley Thayer asked his aid in raising funds for a new building and for broadening the curriculum, Brandeis proved a helpful and resourceful alumnus. In 1881, a few months after the penetrating Lowell Institute lectures delivered by Oliver Wendell Holmes were published in book form as *The Common Law,* Thayer sought a way to endow a teaching chair for the distinguished author. Brandeis promptly convinced a classmate who had just come into a fortune to give the money that brought Holmes, though briefly, to the law-school faculty. On the heels of his having taught the law-school course in evidence while Thayer was absent for a term, Brandeis, at twenty-five, was offered a Harvard professorship. He enjoyed teaching but preferred practice even more, so he declined. His work for the law school in the Eighties took other forms: in one instance taking the initiative with a small group of other men to organize the Harvard Law School Association. In 1887 he became one of the founders of the *Harvard Law Review*. A trustee of the publication for nearly thirty years, Brandeis contributed occasional articles to it, and to other law journals.

His most significant article in this period appeared in the *Harvard Law Review* in 1890. Entitled "The Right to Privacy," Brandeis wrote it with Samuel Warren. Sam had transmitted to Brandeis his indignation against a sensational weekly paper that had spread out in its columns details of Warren's personal and social life. The material Warren resented catered solely to the prurient interest of the readers; it had no genuine public value. What, Warren and Brandeis asked, could good citizens do to prevent the personal injury done them by such distasteful invasion of privacy? Reasoning closely from the history of personal-injury law, the authors argued that those offended against might sue for damages under the common law of torts; or they might seek court injunction to forestall injury in public print. If carefully drawn, statutes might furnish an even stronger defense against the yellow press, the article proposed. Discussion among members of the bar following this *Harvard Law Review* article led to litigation in many parts of the country that curbed, if it did not completely halt, the sort of invasion of privacy of which Warren had been the victim.

Like every alert and socially conscious attorney, Brandeis became involved in public issues as a natural by-product of his work, and felt his appetite for public cases steadily increasing. There was stimulation for him in a cause he thought to be for the common social good. Yet he was no blind zealot who appropriated the truth to himself, denying any to his opponent. Brandeis frequently sought a way in which the conflicting interests of his client and adversary at law could be constructively resolved. He looked for a harmony larger than either side had conceived when they called in their lawyers. Trial by combat, he thought, was a hangover from medieval times.

When he represented the Protective Liquor Dealers' Association before the state legislature, Brandeis found himself opposed to the Citizens' Law and Order League, a temperance group of puritanical standards. Brandeis believed that liquor-control laws were needed, but he could see why the Massachusetts liquor laws, being unrealistically severe, had been regularly disobeyed both by dealers and the consuming public.

"Liquor is desired by a large majority of the voters of the Commonwealth, and consequently people will sell it," Brandeis told the legislators. "You enact laws which the habits of the community will not permit liquor dealers to obey, and as a consequence you invite into the business the professional lawbreakers or those who are ready to become such."

Everyone in the state was aware of corruption in the liquor industry. Brandeis argued: "You can remove liquor dealers from politics by a very simple device—make the liquor laws reasonable."

The young attorney learned about poverty and human suffering when he visited the Boston poorhouses and the state reform schools, in which his interest was aroused by socially minded friends. He met Henry Demarest Lloyd, who had written a vigorous exposé of the Standard Oil trust for the *Atlantic Monthly,* and discussed with him the social results of concentrated economic power. As his legal practice with manufacturers and businessmen increased, he found that in order to furnish sound legal advice he must know the bases on which businessmen made decisions. He therefore had to learn the arts of business management, from simple cost accounting to the intricacies of high corporate finance. He made it a point to learn more about the client's business than the client knew himself.

In one instance, Brandeis was called upon by a shoe manufacturer named William H. McElwain to help settle a strike in his plant at Manchester, New Hampshire. McElwain had recently introduced a piecework system of payment, which precipitated a walkout by the union members. Upon looking into the situation, Brandeis found that the employer's piecework payment was fair enough while the men were employed, but in this seasonal industry the workers' families were left stranded for weeks on end each year when the plant shut down. Earning more money on piecework in a shorter period did not help when there was no work.

Bringing owner and union leaders together, Brandeis managed to get both to tackle the problem of regularizing the work schedule so that the factory could stay open the full year. From this experience onward, Brandeis preached the doctrine of year-round employment— and placed the responsibility for carrying it out squarely on management, where it belonged. The way to deal with "labor trouble," Brandeis often counseled his employer clients, was to understand labor's grievances. Capital, he said, should recognize the right of employees to join into unions and should deal fairly with their spokesmen. Yet labor could be wrong too, Brandeis held. He could not share the class-struggle outlook of the Socialists. To the extent that there was a struggle between capital and labor, Brandeis deplored it as a sign of men's failure to regulate their affairs rationally. Most industrial conflicts, he maintained, could be avoided by cooperation.

Brandeis was still in his early thirties when the president of the Massachusetts Institute of Technology invited him to teach a course in business law. Brandeis had long been interested in education of a practical nature, so he looked forward to directing the course at M.I.T. when, in the summer of 1892, the violence at the Carnegie-Illinois steel plant at Homestead, Pennsylvania, forced a revision in his thought. Looking back on his change of outlook years later, he told an interviewer:

> I think it was the affair at Homestead which first set me to thinking seriously about the labor problem. It took the shock of that battle, where organized capital hired a private army to shoot at organized labor for resisting an arbitrary cut in wages, to turn my mind definitely toward a searching study of the relations of labor to industry. . . .
>
> One morning the newspaper carried the story of the pitched battle between the Pinkertons on the barge and barricaded steel workers on the bank. I saw at once that the common law, built up under simpler conditions of living, gave an inadequate basis for the adjustment of the complex relations of the modern factory system. I threw away my notes and approached my theme from new angles.

The public service which was destined to occupy a major part of Brandeis' time and attention in his mature years was presaged early in 1893 when he opposed the attempt of the West End Railway to extend its tracks across Boston Common, a historic park. He testified against the proposed desecration with masterful effect. A friend who listened to Brandeis' testimony complimented him in a letter:

> Never before this morning had it been my good fortune to hear so logical, clear and convincing an argument on the very important question of street franchises as that made by you at the State House. I wish that your remarks could be printed and sent to every taxpayer in the city.

Brandeis himself much later called his maiden venture into the drawn-out struggle over control of the Boston transit system "my first important public work."

The 1893 Boston Common affair was followed by the city transit contest that raged intermittently from 1897, when electrically powered public transit was competing with horse-drawn vehicles for space in the crowded Boston streets, to 1911, when automobiles and trucks were pushing the horse out of the city permanently. The basic issue in the long war was whether the city should retain effective control over public transit operated by private companies. At stake were the duration of leases granted by the city to various transit lines, conditions under which company mergers were effected, fares to be charged, and ownership of rights of way. The issues were too complex for the average person to grasp, since they involved legal and fiscal matters beyond his scope. At least so it seemed on the surface.

Brandeis became intensely concerned with educating the public concerning the difference between a fair franchise and a giveaway. He explained how the company directors planned to milk the riding public of millions of dollars extracted in the form of pennies tinkling into a thousand cash boxes far into the indefinite future. By helping the public understand this grab for unreasonable profits by a public utility, Brandeis helped save Boston's public transit system. Through it all he was for years the central figure, combining the roles of attorney, strategist, organizer, propagandist, and spokesman for the public interest. He wrote articles, delivered testimony, helped organize such citizens' committees as the Public Franchise League, and stimulated others to action.

At one stage in the fight against granting a long-term lease at lucrative terms to the Boston Elevated Railway Company, he told a legislative committee:

> We are here to see the control rests with the community, that the Elevated Railway Company, or any company that serves us as transporters of passengers, is the servant and not the master of the public; and this company will be the master of the public if you do not reserve this power of control.

Later, when the fight he helped to lead had been victorious, Brandeis told a convention discussing municipal ownership:

> Boston will own all the subways which are the connecting links in both the elevated and surface systems through the heart of the city. Without these subways no practical elevated system is possible and no surface system could be successfully operated. So long as Boston

retains this ownership and the right to revoke surface locations, the city will control the transportation system and will have power to compel the corporations to pay adequate compensation for the use of the streets.

By frustrating the men with capital, many of them from the oldest Boston families, who had been counting in advance their dividends from a captive Boston transit system, Brandeis incurred their undying enmity. These men termed him Socialist, muckraker, and every other epithet then applied to one who stirred up the people. They were annoyed at other prominent figures, like Edward Filene of the department-store family, who sided with him; but Brandeis was their particular vexation because he was the most annoyingly articulate of their opponents.

During the transit fight Brandeis established a rule to which he adhered for the rest of his days as a practicing attorney: he would never charge a fee when working in a public cause. Others might give enormously of their wealth to charities; Brandeis chose to give of himself. His time and talents, as the hundreds who appreciated his assistance were aware, proved more precious than gold.

In 1891 Louis Brandeis married his second cousin Alice Goldmark, a charming and talented young woman who shared his ideal of a life of community service. When they first set up housekeeping in Boston the newlyweds agreed that they should limit their personal income each year to an amount that would furnish them a reasonably comfortable standard of living. Beyond that, Louis had Alice's full support in devoting his time and energy to the public causes that interested him most. It worked out that as a highly successful lawyer at the head of a well-organized and growing firm, Louis earned several times more than the $10,000 a year he and Alice had set as the ceiling on their personal needs. Brandeis invested the surplus in securities that would liberate him from the necessity of earning in later years. And at the end of each year Brandeis regularly paid into the law firm's profit pool as much money as he thought he might have earned in the time he put into his public work. His partners, he believed, should not be required to lose their share of the firm's earnings because he pursued his own enthusiasms.

To Louis Brandeis' intimates, this self-imposed limit on dollar income was part of the man, whom they knew to be almost a zealot for modest living. But there were politicians, businessmen, and other lawyers who never could understand his point of view. Somewhere, they believed, Brandeis must have an angle that led him into the public struggles by which he became famous. They thought he must have a hidden and special axe to grind.

Brandeis' talent for composing public conflicts was never better illustrated than in the reorganization of the Boston gas system. In 1904 there were eight overlapping and inefficient companies supplying Boston and Brookline with gas for heating and light. They were mismanaged, their agents were corrupting political officials to keep the authorized gas rates high, and the public was paying the bill of waste. The firms decided to consolidate. The terms under which they proposed to merge, however, involved a gross overvaluation of their assets at $24,000,000; Brandeis and his colleagues thought the figure should have been a little more than $15,000,000. The valuation point was important, because the consolidated company would use the valuation as a base on which to establish the rates to be charged the public for service. Gas in Boston already cost household users $1 per 1000 cubic feet; it would doubtless go higher if the company's reshuffling of figures were allowed.

When Brandeis got into the gas-company consolidation struggle as unpaid counsel for the Public Franchise League of Boston, he was caught in a crossfire. On the one side were the conservative utilities men who could not conceive of running their business in any but the same old corrupt, wasteful way—extracting high rates from consumers, watering stock, and paying off public officials as a regular business expense. On the other side, Brandeis found himself ranged against irreconcilables in the reform camp, to whom every utility company was an evil to be endured only until the achievement of municipal ownership as a cure-all. Brandeis sought a path between the two, one that would allow a fair profit to private enterprise, with gas produced cheaply and efficiently.

Fortunately, the consolidated company was headed by a man new to the industry, James L. Richards, who had been selected by the investment house of Kidder, Peabody and Company to operate its gas properties. Brandeis persuaded Richards to accept an entirely new scheme: capitalization of the merged company at a little more than $15,000,000, dividends to be set at a high rate—7 per cent—and the basic charge for gas to be lowered to ninety cents per thousand cubic feet. The crowning ingenuity of the Boston gas formula was a sliding scale, adopted from one in effect in London, under which the company could raise dividends 1 per cent for every five cents reduction it could effect in the price of gas. Thus the holders of company stock could earn more on their investment, provided management would cut its costs of operation and pass a fair share of the savings along to the public.

The Brandeis-Richards sliding scale plan was put into effect, and within a few weeks the price of gas in Boston was cut from ninety to eighty-five cents. A year later it was down to eighty. Writing shortly afterward in the *Review of Reviews* on Boston's solution of its gas problem, Brandeis stated that while the public saved an estimated $800,000 a year and stockholders earned higher dividends, the most notable achievement was that "the officers and employees of the gas company now devote themselves strictly to the business of making and distributing gas instead of in lobbying and political intrigue."

It was characteristic of Brandeis that he could change his mind. He was a generally self-assured person because he based his conclusions on a thorough examination into facts. But when a position previously taken seemed not to square with new facts, he was willing to alter his earlier view. Brandeis changed his mind with respect to woman suffrage, which he at first thought would be poor public policy but later advocated when he observed the admirable leadership women were assuming in social-reform movements after the turn of the twentieth century. Another change in view, which later caused him considerable trouble, was his disaffection from the United Shoe Machinery Company, of which he had once been a stockholder, a director, and legal counsel.

Formed in the late Nineties from a merger of smaller makers of shoe-manufacturing machinery, United dominated its field by requiring that its customers, shoe manufacturers, use its line of machines exclusively in all their operations. The company offered the same terms to all customers, regardless of size. It held its monopoly position by insisting that shoe manufacturers sign leases with a so-called tying clause enforcing the exclusive policy. Brandeis generally opposed monopoly and favored competition in business, and the tying clause made him uneasy. But he thought that on balance the United system of equal terms for all customers helped stimulate competition in the manufacture of shoes, which he deemed of far greater public interest than competition in shoemaking machinery. In 1906, when the United

Shoe Machinery Company's tying-clause system was under attack in
the Massachusetts legislature, Brandeis testified against a bill to outlaw it. The many shoe manufacturers Brandeis' law firm had represented as counsel for a number of years raised no concerted complaint
against the United. Some of them had certain grievances which the
United president, Sidney Winslow, promised to smooth out if the bill
were defeated, which it was.

As time passed, however, a number of things occurred that caused
Brandeis to see the United position quite differently. First, Winslow
took no steps to confer with the shoe manufacturers, whose complaints began to increase. Next, the United Shoe Machinery Company
inserted a thirty-day cancellation clause in its leases, which gave it
the right to pull its machines quickly out of the plant of any shoe
manufacturer who stepped out of line. This was a threat to use economic power that made the lessee company the servant and United
its dominating master. Brandeis heartily disapproved this kind of
economic coercion. Then came the development of a competing line
of shoe machinery by a man named Thomas G. Plant. United saw
the newcomer as a threat. Suddenly all doors to credit were slammed
shut in Plant's face, because the United Shoe Machinery Company
had swung its weight at the source of ready money. In a tense midnight session that resembled a scene in an 1890 melodrama, Plant
was forced to sign his properties over completely to the shoe-machinery monopoly and go out of business.

The fact that one company could kill a competitor by influencing
banks to choke off his credit struck Brandeis as a monstrous denial
of freedom. Finally, with recent Supreme Court decisions in the American Tobacco and Standard Oil cases having clarified the meaning of
the Sherman Antitrust Act, Brandeis concluded that United's tying
clause was illegal.

Well after he had severed his connection with the United Shoe
Machinery Company and after having for some time remained strictly
neutral in its struggles against a group of Midwestern shoe manufacturers who were trying to break out of its grip, Brandeis finally consented to assist the Midwesterners. Simultaneously, a number of
congressional committees and government agencies called on him in
1911 to testify as an expert witness on the monopoly problem. Among
his examples Brandeis cited the United Shoe Machinery Company
experience. Company officials in Boston hurled charges of inconsist-

ency and betrayal at him, hinting darkly that he had shifted sides to line his own pocket. Actually, Brandeis charged the Western Alliance of Shoe Manufacturers a modest fee, turning half over to his partners and returning his portion to the client. The days he spent delivering testimony in this case, in preparation and traveling to Washington, he considered part of his public work. After a long battle in the courts, the shoe-machinery monopoly was finally broken.

Other legal work originating in Boston led to matters of broad public policy of national import. In 1905 Brandeis was approached by a group of Boston men who held life insurance policies issued by the Equitable Life Assurance Society of New York. They had become gravely concerned over the struggle for corporate control that had broken out in the top command of the insurance company and sought Brandeis as counsel to represent their interests. Since he had already heard rumors of the directors' looting of the company and their doctoring of company books, Brandeis became very much interested. He insisted that he be retained by the policyholders' group without a fee, on condition that he be given his freedom to conduct an inquiry into the entire insurance business, well beyond the immediate interests of those who had approached him. After much discussion, he was retained on his own terms.

At this time the life insurance industry in America was rotten-ripe for investigation, exposure, and reform. Few people knew its true state, and those on the inside who had seen the books were not inclined to share their knowledge. Brandeis spent day after day and evenings at home poring over insurance industry reports and figures, studying the situation from every angle. He kept in close touch that same year with the investigation of the New York life insurance scandals held in Albany by the legislative committee headed by State Senator William W. Armstrong. Charles Evans Hughes, then a forty-three-year-old attorney from New York City, was put in charge of the Armstrong investigation to bring out the facts. Brandeis was acquainted with Hughes, for whose law firm in New York the Boston law office of Brandeis, Dunbar and Nutter acted as New England representative.

On October 6, 1905, Brandeis delivered a vigorous address before the Commercial Club of Boston, in which he spoke the blunt truth about the unhealthy condition of the life insurance industry. Basically, he declared, it was too tightly controlled by a very few men. Of ninety life insurance companies in the United States holding more than $2,500,000,000 in assets and with an annual income of more than $600,000,000, close to half the assets were held by three giant Wall Street firms—Mutual Life of New York, Equitable, and New York Life. Most of their assets were in the form of liquid capital, which enabled their directors to shift quickly from one investment outside the insurance industry to another, and so realize financial killings for themselves while risking policyholders' money. Their economic power, wielded in concert with a handful of big bankers such as J. P. Morgan, was far greater than was healthy for any small group of financiers to have. The United States Supreme Court had ruled that controlling the industry was not within the federal government's domain, and state laws regulating the insurance industry were ridiculously weak. No other multimillion-dollar industry was so lawless, Brandeis declared.

To underline his belief that a reform of state insurance laws was overdue, Brandeis exposed the simple arithmetic of the so-called industrial sector of the insurance business. Industrial insurance was the type of policy sold in low-income neighborhoods by collection agents working down the street door to door, and up tenement-house stairs. These men sold new policies as they collected on those already in force. Industrial insurance policies were generally written for sums ranging between $100 and $1000, and were paid for in weekly installments of nickels and dimes. At best they paid for the insured man's funeral and a little more. So wasteful was the system that forty cents of every dollar collected was eaten up by agent's fees, directors' salaries, and other administrative costs of the company. About three quarters of the policies in effect in America were industrial policies, sold by high-pressure methods to people who often were forced by poverty to let them lapse without recovering a cent. Brandeis pointed out that only one policy in twelve was carried to maturity. The other eleven, allowed to lapse through neglect or paid off at a discount before maturity because an impoverished family needed cash, represented a never-ending bonanza to the companies. In fact, the Armstrong investigation in New York brought the admission from industry spokesmen that industrial insurance provided the companies all their profits, whereas ordinary life insurance was operated at a break-even point.

Brandeis proposed a solution, which he touched on in his Commercial Club address, and extended in an article for *Collier's* magazine:

Let the savings banks offer life insurance. Using their existing staff and place of business, banks could reduce overhead costs to a minimum.

Backed by a committee of prominent Massachusetts citizens aroused to the need for safe, low-cost insurance for low-income workers, Brandeis toured the state for months, speaking wherever a group of interested citizens would furnish him a platform. He wrote articles and letters to newspaper editors—as he had done during the transit fight and the struggle for cheaper gas in Boston. Steadily during 1906 and 1907 the movement in favor of a Massachusetts experiment in savings-bank life insurance grew. In 1907 the legislature passed Brandeis' bill authorizing the savings banks to issue life insurance under state regulation.

The natural conservatism of bank officials was overcome only slowly, but when the system got under way, bank management proved so efficient that the insured received dividends ranging from 8 per cent on one-year policies to 20 per cent on policies of five years' duration. In order to meet the competition, the standard companies selling industrial life insurance promptly reduced their premiums an average of 20 per cent shortly after the Massachusetts plan went into effect, and changed a number of their rules in major respects in favor of the small policyholders. Brandeis estimated in 1914 that the reduced premiums alone had already saved American policyholders at least $20,000,000 a year. As to the spur his plan offered to a general reform in the entire American life insurance industry, Brandeis in later years said he considered savings-bank life insurance in Massachusetts "my greatest achievement." By this time, too, Charles Evans Hughes had become so distinguished a public figure through his work in the Armstrong committee investigation that he had been elected governor of New York.

By the time he was fifty, Louis D. Brandeis was known to literally thousands of people with whom he had come into contact, but he retained a reticence in his personal mode of life that seemed out of keeping with his public stature. From the turn of the century onward he was rich as professional men go, yet the outward signs of wealth were completely absent. His dress had none of the custom-tailoring display and flashing of gold and silk that many men at the bar affected. Sam Warren and Brandeis had been among the first law firms in Boston to install a telephone, because it was an instrument that pro-

moted efficiency, yet Brandeis was repelled by showy gadgetry for
which he could not see a useful purpose. Whereas others of his income
class fed their appetite for status by riding in a chauffeur-driven
limousine, Brandeis clung to his faithful horse and buggy with the
tenacity of a Mennonite.

For recreation the Brandeis family found that books, music, and
the stimulation of thoughtful company at the dinner table supplied
most of their needs. Conspicuous consumption and display repelled
Brandeis as vulgar; the furnishings of his home were so plain as to
be almost drab. Brandeis retained his membership in the Dedham
Polo Club in order to go riding; in bright weather he could be seen
in the late afternoon paddling a canoe on the Charles River; and even
when the pressure of legal work was on him, he took regular walks
between home and office. These were mentally relaxing forms of
exercise which he could engage in as he wished, with time for con-
templation while enjoying them. It would have been impossible to
imagine Brandeis at Braves Field amid a raucous crowd watching
tobacco-chewing professionals play baseball; Harvard College could
have played football games until Doomsday without Brandeis ever
setting foot in the University stadium.

This distaste for social, extroverted sporting made for an aloof
quality about the man which some of his colleagues at the bar and in
business resented. When he did mix with them socially at luncheon or
a professional meeting, Brandeis took sherry or ale when they drank
whisky and soda. Anyone so indiscreet as to tell a dirty story in his
presence was made to feel mortified by the cold face and deaf ear
he turned. Some may have considered him prissy on this score, but
those who knew the man well saw him as different in his tastes from
the run-of-the-town lawyer and quite consistent in maintaining his
own standards. Indeed, it was in his private reserve, as opposed to his
dynamic public personality, that Brandeis caused a certain amount of
dislike on the part of those who could have warmed to him had he
bent in their direction even slightly.

Just as the big boys who cut up in every schoolroom resent the
little fellow whose brightness in class shows them up as dolts, so
Brandeis' personality only stung his opponents the more after he had
beaten them in court. And he was a consistent winner at the bar.
In the eyes of those he defeated he was not a good winner or a
gracious one, because he let his opponents know he thought himself

a kind of modern St. George defending the right against the dragons of evil. Many of them did not enjoy being beaten and preached at by a Jewish upstart who had not even been born in Boston. They might have thought him all right if he had joined them in backslapping camaraderie after hours, but he had neither time nor taste for such fraternizing. He joined or helped found civic reform committees by the dozen but eschewed lodges, smokers, and men's clubs. Poker and golf were simply not in his world.

Brandeis was intensely disciplined in his working routine, yet in his effort to extract the most value from his time he did not court ulcers with a frantic intensity of work. He rose early and whenever possible spent a morning hour reading aloud with his daughters, Susan and Elizabeth. Every August the Brandeises sought a quiet retreat at the beach. Musing some years later on his belief in pacing the demands on his energy, Brandeis recalled: "I soon learned that I could do twelve months' work in eleven months, but not in twelve." A vacation, he believed, was an essential for a hard worker.

He read the daily newspapers rapidly, got through his office correspondence with dispatch, and scheduled appointments with precision. It was widely known in Boston that Brandeis' office furnishings were so uncomfortably bare that they induced the visiting client to leave promptly after stating his business rather than to lounge. It was a busy, efficiently organized place. Junior men in the firm, which in 1897 was changed from Warren and Brandeis to Brandeis, Dunbar and Nutter, were paid a salary plus a share in the firm's annual profits, which Brandeis calculated at the year's end. As the years passed and Brandeis' reputation as an attorney grew, a position in his office became an honor much sought after by young men starting out in law, because there they knew they could learn from one of the very best. When he was a member of the Massachusetts Supreme Judicial Court, Oliver Wendell Holmes sent his nephew to Brandeis for his first job.

"My special field of knowledge is figures," Brandeis once said, characterizing his specialty of business law and public questions revolving about corporation finance. He stayed away from criminal practice. It was not that he lacked the actor's quality that perennially attracts performers to criminal-trial work. Brandeis' acting was of a different genre. He was not in the least self-effacing when dealing with a matter on which his feelings were intense, but he never sought the platform solely for the spotlight and the applause. When he did take the public stage he played a cerebral drama rather than the shouting, puffing melodrama of the jury-swayer. He sought to elucidate and to educate, as in the fight to save public transport for Boston and in his design to bring life insurance within the reach of working people. Behind each hour of public performance lay many hours of study. When Brandeis wrote a brief or a magazine article, he redrafted his words five or six times so that his meaning would stand out clearly, in contrast to the prolix jumble of technicalities other lawyers often employed, to the reader's confusion. When he delivered oral testimony before legislative committees, his listeners saw a clear picture take form because Brandeis had thought the matter through so as to draw the essential lines with bold, sure strokes.

Fifty-nine when Wilson nominated him to the Supreme Court, Brandeis in physical appearance was a lean man slightly above average height, whose vigorous pace and gestures marked him as one who had in no wise slowed down. There was just a touch of gray around the edges of his hair, which was generally cut short and somewhat tousled. The prominent dark eyes of his student days had receded into sockets shadowed by dark eyebrows, and the lines of his narrow, clean-shaven face had since his mid-forties given him somewhat the look of Abraham Lincoln. There was a quick keenness about him, however, that was quite different from the brooding quality of the Emancipator President, and only at certain camera angles or moments when Brandeis' face was in repose was the resemblance noticed. His speaking voice was soft when low volume was called for and his consonants were clear without the harsh exaggeration of the declaimer. Yet when it was appropriate, Brandeis could make himself heard in a large hall without sacrificing the flowing modulation of volume and pitch that brings clarity to spoken sentences. Eyes might not automatically be turned in his direction in a crowd, as they would to the huge Taft, the regal Charles Evans Hughes, or Oliver Wendell Holmes with his magnificent stature and sweeping white mustache. But it was said by many of Brandeis' admirers that once he began to develop a thought from the platform or at the bar, he could hold men's attention riveted to him until he was through.

Perhaps the most remarkable feat Louis D. Brandeis performed in all his years of legal practice took place in 1908, when he won a victory for all the working women in America before the Supreme Court of the United States. In winning it he also added *Brandeis brief* to the terminology of students of American law.

In the fall of 1907 the owner of the Grand Laundry in Portland, Oregon, Curt Muller, decided to appeal a ruling against him by the Oregon supreme court. Some months previously Muller had been convicted by a lower court of having forced a Mrs. Elmer Gotcher, one of his employees, to work longer than the ten hours a day permitted by the Oregon law governing women workers in factories and laundries. He was fined $10 for the offense. The Portland laundry incident might have had little importance, except that since the 1905 ruling by the United States Supreme Court in the case of *Lochner* v. *New York,* which struck down a ten-hour limit for men working in bakeries, employers had been encouraged to challenge every law restricting hours of work. The Portland laundry owners, employers of women, wanted a clear test.

At this time there was one organization of socially minded women particularly interested in promoting reform legislation that benefited working women and children. This was the National Consumers League, directed by Mrs. Florence Kelley, whose staff assistant was Josephine Goldmark, sister-in-law of Louis D. Brandeis. When it became known that Muller planned to appeal to the United States Supreme Court, Mrs. Kelley and her colleagues sought a prominent lawyer to assist the attorney general of Oregon in presenting the case for the state ten-hour law, because if the Oregon law were to be struck down, similar laws in nineteen other states would probably fall like tenpins.

Mrs. Kelley first called on the eminent and elderly Joseph H. Choate, former American Ambassador to the Court of St. James, who had distinguished himself in the civic-reform movement in New York. Choate, who had tilted gladly against the notorious Tweed ring, could see no evil in long hours for working women. There was no reason, he told Mrs. Kelley, why "a big, husky Irishwoman should not work more than ten hours in a laundry if her employers wanted her to." So much for the lawyer of great and imposing presence.

Mrs. Kelley and Josephine Goldmark hurried to Boston to consult Brandeis and found him at once sympathetic. The case of *Muller* v. *Oregon* was one to his taste—the test of a constitutional issue involving the welfare of underdogs in an industrial society in which relations between capital and labor were becoming steadily more critical.

From his study of the Lochner decision of 1905 and others involving the clash between Fourteenth Amendment liberty of the property-owner and state legislation designed to protect the weak, Brandeis recognized the kernel of his task: to convince the Supreme Court that the Oregon legislature had acted *reasonably* in passing its ten-hour statute. The Court had made clear that it would tolerate protective laws that curbed the employer in the free enjoyment of his property only if such laws were reasonably calculated to promote the social good. The words *reasonable* and *reasonably* ran like a thread through one Court decision after another.

Brandeis immediately put Josephine Goldmark to work pulling together evidence to prove the reasonableness of a law designed to curb the physical and social evils to women attendant upon excessive hours of toil. This evidence was to be from physicians, health inspectors, social workers, and industrial experts rather than from legalists. Medical libraries were combed for documentation; when this was assembled and edited, Brandeis submitted 101 pages of citations from experts in a dozen countries, all bearing on the physical requirements of women for a decent amount to rest if they were both to work and to fulfill their function as mothers. Some of his testimony dated back fifty years, and much of it revealed greater official concern with working women's health in the Old World than in America. Brandeis' brief showed that every reliable nonjuridical authority in Western Europe and North America knew that excessively long hours of work are harder on women than on men, and further, that because women bear children the physical well-being of humanity requires that their working hours be limited. One citation after another proved that long hours of work led to breakdowns in women's health and morals—to illness, to alcoholism, and to prostitution.

When he rose in the Supreme Court on January 15, 1908, to present this novel brief, in which his purely legal argument was limited to two pages, with a one-paragraph legal conclusion, Brandeis had just heard the attorney for Muller wave the sacred "life, liberty and property" of the Fourteenth Amendment in the faces of the Court members. Brandeis' brief had no constitutional argument from precedent, but only from rational human reaction to social necessity—101 pages of it. Step by step Brandeis unfolded his argument to prove the Oregon statute constitutional because it was a reasonable exercise of state power by the legislature for the good of the human beings it represented. The Justices listened with careful attention. There was an anxious wait of nearly six weeks during which the fate of the Oregon law and those like it hung in abeyance: then Justice Brewer announced that the Court had upheld the statute unanimously. In his ruling he noted "the course of legislation as well as expressions of opinion from other than judicial sources" and took the unusual step of mentioning "the brief filed by Mr. Louis D. Brandeis" as containing "a very copious collection of all these matters."

The historic Muller ruling of 1908 opened a door into which Brandeis stepped on many occasions during the succeeding eight years. Twelve times he either prepared briefs or argued orally in state or federal appeals courts on behalf of laws protecting laboring women and children. Not once was he defeated, and not once did he pocket a fee. Early in 1915, when the Supreme Court upheld two California laws limiting female labor in restaurants and laundries to eight hours daily, the victories were his. He had just filed his brief to test a new legal concept before the Supreme Court—a state minimum-wage statute for women workers—when his nomination to the Court by President Wilson caused him to withdraw.

Brandeis' argument, based on the experience of mankind, in the Muller case became the model for many other attorneys whose problem was to convince the courts that legislatures had acted reasonably rather than with caprice. The *Brandeis brief* of the Muller case had passed into lawyer's terminology to stay.

In roughly the same years during which Brandeis was piloting these working women's laws past the constitutional shoals into safe waters, he was also leading a New England struggle against absentee banker control of the region's transportation system. The 1905–1914 controversy pitted him against the New York, New Haven & Hartford Railroad officials who were aggressively trying to monopolize not only the rail systems but also the many interurban trolley lines connecting New England's scattered towns, as well as the steamship companies that handled most of the coastwise traffic north of New York. In the press and before state and federal commissions, the clash appeared a personal fight between Brandeis and President Charles S. Mellen of the New Haven. It was actually a contest between the economic beliefs of Brandeis, spokesmen for competition, and those of J. Pierpont Morgan, Sr., the immensely powerful New York financier and personification of monopoly, who controlled Mellen and the railroads he assigned Mellen to direct.

The New Haven struggle started in 1905 when word leaked out that directors of Morgan's railroad had been buying up enough stock of the Boston & Maine Railroad to effect control. At the same time, the New Haven had been acquiring majority interest in one trolley company after another and in the principal steamship lines of importance to New England's export of finished factory products. The New Haven Railroad was a Connecticut corporation and therefore paid no attention to the Massachusetts law designed to curb mergers of transportation companies. Its stocks were considered gilt-edged; they had paid 2 per cent dividends every quarter-year since the early 1870s —a lucrative 8 per cent a year. When it was ready to absorb the Boston & Maine, the company flooded New England—especially Massachusetts—with propaganda to the effect that a new era for the region was dawning with its taking over the B&M and bringing to all New Englanders the benefits of its splendid management.

Having become opposed in principle to monopoly because he believed it deadened business initiative, Brandeis called on New Englanders to resist. Studying the financial records of Mellen's company as thoroughly as he could from the scanty records the New Haven had been required to publish, Brandeis concluded that the company had been grievously mismanaged. Its owners, he said, were draining it of funds that should have been put into safety precautions and capital improvements, because the Morgan-Mellen group was more concerned with a profitable investment than with public service. The New Haven, Brandeis argued, was already in serious financial trouble and would soon be forced to admit its true condition. Mr. Morgan, with his immense resources of liquid capital, might juggle its financing for a while, but the day of reckoning was not far off because the New Haven had been disastrously weakened. "Time and arithmetic will do the rest," Brandeis predicted.

In response, the railroad and its apologists launched a personal campaign of defamation against Brandeis that treated him first as a fool, then as an insidious menace. As the struggle went on, paid propagandists for the Morgan interests were disclosed in legislatures, in newspaper offices, and even on the Harvard Law School faculty (in the person of Professor Bruce Wyman, who resigned after he

admitted taking an annual retainer of $10,000 to give scholarly lec-
tures on transportation problems). Hostile cartoonists pictured Brandeis as "King Louis," seated on the throne of New England, wearing
ermine and a crown, puffed with his own ego, his face caricatured
just enough to give a subtly anti-Semitic impression. Brandeis was
"ruining" the railroad by waging psychological warfare against it,
some of the New Haven's defenders claimed. Brandeis was accused
of secretly acting both for Jewish bankers in New York to "wreck"
the New Haven and for that rapacious railroad tycoon Edward H.
Harriman, who allegedly was scheming to add the New Haven to his
Illinois Central empire. The personal vilification to which Brandeis
was subjected was almost unprecedented. In response, he attacked
not individuals but institutions, not businessmen personally but their
ways of doing business. As for issuing replies to personal attacks, he
explained to a friend at the height of the New Haven struggle:

> I determined many years ago not to make any denials of any
> kind or any explanation of any of the vile charges which the interests
> whom I am fighting put out. I did this partly because a denial would
> dignify the attack, and partly because if I once began to make
> denials or explanations, it would easily be in their power to occupy
> me in this way eight hours a day, and divert my attention from the
> more important business of attacking their methods.

The struggle was a long and complicated one in which Brandeis,
leading the businessmen and public officials whom he rallied against
the New Haven–B&M merger, lost the early rounds. In the late months
of the Roosevelt administration a federal antitrust prosecution against
the New Haven was launched, but during the Taft regime it was
dropped by Attorney General Wickersham. In 1913, with Wilson in
power and James McReynolds heading the Department of Justice,
the suit was revived. The same year the New Haven Railroad announced it would cut its annual dividend to 6 per cent; later it determined to suspend all dividends until further notice. The Boston &
Maine also withheld dividends in 1913, the first such default since
before the Civil War. Then Mellen resigned from the presidency of
both railroads in his disagreement with the New York financiers who
were his superiors. Brandeis' 1907 prediction of the downfall of
Mellen and the New Haven had finally come true. In 1914 the Interstate Commerce Commission forced the New Haven directors to give

up their control of the Boston & Maine, which put an end to the Morgan plan for a New England transportation monopoly.

The decline of the New Haven held several lessons for America, Brandeis wrote in a magazine article in 1913. First, business requires competition if it is to remain efficient; monopoly uncontrolled leads to inefficiency. Second, there is a limit to the size of an enterprise that any one man or group of men can manage well. Third, there operates "the law of arithmetic by which two and two will always make four, despite reports of presidents and financial advisers who insist on stretching it into five."

Because of his prominence in the New Haven Railroad struggle, Brandeis in his middle years emerged as a figure of national importance. Magazine editors sought articles from his pen on the issues with which he was associated; his speeches to meetings of businessmen and to university audiences were reprinted. He was regarded as one of the key idea-men of the progressive movement. Nor did any other public figure of his time range more widely in his interest or probe more deeply: life insurance, antitrust law, public utilities regulation, labor relations, court procedure, civil liberties, and woman suffrage all presented problems he felt called upon to analyze and help solve. Congressional committees, the Interstate Commerce Commission, the Federal Trade Commission, and other official bodies solicited his testimony. Shippers retained him to draw up their case against increased freight charges which the railroads sought to impose. Businessmen sought him as counsel.

As often as possible, Brandeis used the opportunities offered in this employment to sound his principal themes: that monopoly in industry was a cancerous evil which should be met squarely by a stronger antitrust law than the Sherman Act of 1890; that giant accumulations of capital, which he termed "the Money Trust," were killing competition by rigging prices while at the same time they were squeezing labor's wages below the American standard of decency; that interlocking directorates should be broken up because no one man could intelligently or faithfully administer the affairs of more than one large company. Always Brandeis stressed that the criterion should be service to the public at a fair profit—not the jungle law of dog eat dog. He spoke often of "social justice," but he did so not as a sentimentalist or preacher, nor as a Socialist advocating public ownership, but as a pragmatist who wanted to preserve capitalism by removing the causes that made men bitterly hate its heartless excesses.

Brandeis took a special interest in railroads, which by their nature had to accumulate millions of dollars in reserves for capital improvements. By the level of their efficiency railroads affected the price of almost every article sold in the American market. Yet most of them, Brandeis said, clung to traditional practices without regard for efficiency. At one hearing of the Interstate Commerce Commission in Washington, Brandeis caused a sensation by boldly asserting that if all the railroads in America adopted scientific management methods they could save one million dollars a day. "Ridiculous!" snorted most railroad executives. "Moonshine!" is what the bankers retorted when Brandeis pointed to the baneful influence of bankers in industries in which their money spoke with the voice of power.

Brandeis named Money Trust names, but he did not engage in personal abuse. Through his speeches and articles ran the leitmotif of United States Steel Corporation, which he repeatedly cited as the archetype of industrial giant. In U.S. Steel mills, men without a union worked a twelve-hour day, seven days a week, and were worn out before their time. Brandeis pointed out that Judge Elbert H. Gary, in running the Steel Corporation, exercised the power of a Caesar, but that J. Pierpont Morgan was an even more powerful figure since he controlled the finances not only of U.S. Steel but also of railroads, on which steel products were shipped, and of the other companies that bought steel-mill products.

Senator Robert M. La Follette, the fiery Progressive Republican from Wisconsin, leaned heavily on material supplied by Brandeis to document his case when he spoke in the Senate and on the campaign platform of the evils of monopoly. He and other politicians inveighed against Morgan personally, employing such descriptions as "thick-necked financial bully, drunk with power." Brandeis continued to write and speak of Mr. Monopoly Himself as "Mr. Morgan." Others could refer to Morgan or Gary or their principal attorney, George W. Perkins, as liars—Brandeis stated that their claims "do not correspond to the facts."

In a series of articles on "The Money Trust" which he wrote in 1913 for *Harper's Weekly,* Brandeis exposed the demimonde of corporate finance in its relation to bank capital to the light of his readers' reason, without name-calling. He had faith that the facts spoke for themselves. Judge Kenesaw Mountain Landis wrote Brandeis apropos the series:

> I feel personally grateful to you for the work you are doing. The strength of your "Money Trust" articles lies in the fact that the blacksmith, the shoemaker, the farmer, and even the federal judge can understand the matter as they do the A.B.C.'s. . . . The great mass of folks in this country know that you are fighting for them.

Robert Marion La Follette alone matched Brandeis in stature and talent as a leader in the progressive movement of the time, and the two men worked closely together after their first meeting in 1910. On occasion Brandeis would send the Wisconsin Senator a draft bill on the antitrust problem. Or he would suggest an approach to the regulation of interstate commerce, or furnish material for a speech on banking legislation. In fact, from 1910 onward La Follette's colleagues in the Senate felt certain that whenever the Senator from Wisconsin took action on any important issue that was within Brandeis' field of competence, the Boston attorney had a hand in it. And had La Follette himself not been such a strong man of deep conviction and fiery zeal, it would have been natural enough for his enemies to have sneered at him as "Brandeis' mouthpiece" or "Brandeis' representative in the Senate."

As the cleavage in American society between the haves and the have-nots became even more bitter, Brandeis and La Follette were twin targets of the reactionaries' hatred. Both represented to men of privilege and property the same kind of menace. Both were dedicated, as their opponents saw them, to breaking down the traditional American way of life under which the freedom to accumulate was sacred in the eyes of those who worshiped property. La Follette, rabble-rouser in the Senate, and Brandeis, demagogue on the outside, were troublemakers. If such men as they should have their way, the man who had acquired wealth by hard work and brains could no longer hope to live comfortably on his investments and pass them, augmented by careful handling, to the next generation. The 12 per cent and 10 per cent return on capital was fast disappearing; investments bringing a safe 8 per cent were becoming hard to find. If a man like Brandeis, with his wild ideas of a shorter day for workmen and higher pay to go with it, his advocacy of the income tax, his schemes to break business into ruinously competitive units, his tight-control plans for public utilities—if such a man should come to a position of real power, then America would never be the same again.

Republicans who could see Brandeis only as a partisan Democrat had a distorted view of him. For years the Boston lawyer had remained a critical independent in his politics, voting the Democratic ticket most of the time, but never hesitating to fight a Democratic city hall in Boston, or a governor, when he thought they were wrong. He had, for example, prodded Democratic Mayor John F. ("Honey Fitz") Fitzgerald about the need for improvement of the city's auditing procedures, to permit taxpayers to keep a better watch over the way his aldermen were spending public money. He had also clashed with Fitzgerald on the legality of the New Haven's absorption of the Boston & Maine, and the consequences of the merger to Boston, when Fitzgerald had seen nothing wrong with it.

At one point in Brandeis' career the Socialists, attracted by his progressive views, had approached him with an offer of a candidacy for office. He was not interested. Reform elements among the Democratic and Republican parties had done the same, asking him to consider running at various times for state or municipal office. To all such offers he had remained cool; he found himself happiest, and most free of political entanglements, as a free-lance reformer. After 1910, when he became a close friend and advisor to Senator La Follette, Brandeis joined the National Progressive Republican League both to develop progressive issues and to promote the candidacy of the Wisconsin Senator for President. But when La Follette's supporters within the GOP dwindled away toward Teddy Roosevelt, Brandeis could not follow them to the Bull Moose. Although he knew Roosevelt moderately well and heartily approved some of the reforms undertaken during his administration, he believed that Rooosevelt was blind to the dangers of economic concentration. Roosevelt, he knew, was deceiving himself when he thought that government in the hands of righteous officials could control the excesses of Standard Oil, U.S. Steel, and the Morgan banking interests. Better than seeking to regulate such monsters, thought Brandeis, it should be government policy to prevent their growth to unmanageable size and power. He came out boldly in 1912 for the election of Wilson and called on all his fellow Progressives to do the same.

In the summer of 1912, Governor Woodrow Wilson of New Jersey, the Democratic nominee for the Presidency, was casting about for a way to seize the initiative from Roosevelt, who posed as the trust-buster, leader of a Gideon's army of little Americans against the malefactors of great wealth. Wilson's attention was called to newspaper articles of support from Brandeis' pen; in August he received a note from Brandeis, whom he had never met, congratulating the Democratic candidate on his stand for a gradual reduction of tariffs. Wilson responded cordially, expressing the hope that Brandeis would confer with him on the economic side of his campaign, and by the end of the month, at Wilson's request, Brandeis came to Sea Girt, New Jersey, for a three-hour discussion with Wilson on the trust problem and allied campaign issues.

During the next ten weeks, Brandeis worked mightily on three fronts in Wilson's behalf. He wrote a series of strong antitrust articles for *Collier's,* striking hard at the Janus-faced economic program of Roosevelt, encumbered by the presence of his political right-hand man, George Perkins of the U.S. Steel board. The articles were so strong that the *Collier's* editor, Norman Hapgood, felt compelled to tone them down. Meanwhile, Brandeis kept up a running correspondence with Wilson, feeding him one memorandum after another suggesting ways to put the economic issues of the campaign into his speeches. The man in the street had to understand them if Wilson, who lacked the dynamic personality of Roosevelt, were to win him over. Indeed, the human touch with which the former college professor managed to reach the masses in the speeches outlined his program of what he termed a "New Freedom" for the underdog could be traced back in many instances to the Boston lawyer. Finally, Brandeis took the stump himself. He went on an exhausting speaking tour of the northeastern states and into the Midwest, urging all Progressives to vote for Wilson as the candidate best representing their principles.

After Wilson's victorious sweep of forty of the forty-eight states, Brandeis' national prominence in the triumph led to talk of his being appointed to Wilson's cabinet. Speculation associated Brandeis with three posts, a testimony to the breadth of his abilities: Attorney General, Secretary of Commerce, and Secretary of Labor, the last a new cabinet post authorized by legislation enacted during the dying days of the Taft regime. As the March 4 inauguration approached, word filtered out to the press that President-elect Wilson was planning to entrust the Attorney Generalship to Brandeis. But on March 2

Wilson let it be known that James C. McReynolds, not Brandeis, would be his Attorney General.

Although he had spent weeks considering the appointment of Brandeis and had sought the advice of many men in whom he had confidence, Wilson was finally persuaded that the appointment of Brandeis would cause too much difficulty. Some believed he was swayed most by vigorous protests coming from business. Others assigned major weight to the Massachusetts regular Democratic organization, who took a dim view of "their" big job in the new administration going to an independent who had never been "one of the boys," in the sense that professional politicians use the term. Whatever happened behind the scenes, Brandeis was not particularly unhappy. He remained free to continue his public work unfettered by political obligations, and he used his liberty to advise the Wilson administration on a number of reform measures, such as the establishment of the Federal Trade Commission and passage of the Clayton Antitrust Act.

In 1914 two books of Brandeis' articles and speeches were published. *Other People's Money—and How the Bankers Use It* posed the problem of the domination of industrial credit by a handful of institutions tightly controlled by a few men. It made provocative suggestions by which independent business and the public, acting through new laws, might break the power of "the Money Trust." The second book, *Business—a Profession,* discussed the public issues Brandeis had grappled with in Boston and elsewhere, such as gas, transit, insurance, railroad and labor relations, and pleaded for a public-service approach to business.

"In the field of modern business," Brandeis had told the graduating class at Brown University in 1912, "so rich in opportunity for the exercise of man's finest and most varied mental faculties and moral qualities, mere money-making cannot be regarded as the legitimate end. . . . Real success in business is to be found in achievements comparable rather with those of the artist or the scientist, the inventor or the statesman. And the joys sought in the profession of business must be like their joys, and not the mere vulgar satisfaction which is experienced in the acquisition of money, in the exercise of power, or in the frivolous power of mere winning."

In the final chapter of *Business—a Profession,* a wider audience could weigh Brandeis' views on ethics in the legal profession than the small group that had heard him speak on this subject before the Harvard Ethical Society in 1905 at Phillips Brooks House. In offering the law as an avenue for men of conscience to express themselves in public service, Brandeis deplored the tendency of the most capable lawyers to gravitate toward the defense of property:

> The next generation must witness a continuing and ever-increasing contest between those who have and those who have not. The industrial world is in a state of ferment. The ferment is in the main peaceful and, to a considerable extent, silent; but there is felt today very widely the inconsistency in this condition of political democracy and industrial absolutism. . . .
>
> The labor movement must necessarily progress. The people's thought will take shape in action; and it lies with us, with you to whom in part the future belongs, to say whether it is to be expressed wisely and temperately, or wildly and intemperately; whether it is to be expressed on lines of evolution or on lines of revolution. Nothing can better fit you for taking part in the solution of these problems than the study and preeminently the practice of law.

four

"A Little Knot of Men"

The three-column headline on the front page of the arch-Republican New York *Sun* was no exaggeration. From the moment the name of Louis D. Brandeis was heard on the Senate floor and in the press gallery, it was clear that Woodrow Wilson had chosen to fight it out with his political enemies on an issue of basic social principle.

The United Press dispatch printed in the Saturday papers expressed in explosive terms the sudden, devastating surprise of the afternoon:

> President Wilson sent a bomb to the United States Senate yesterday. . . . The bomb exploded. With the reading of the nomination Senators started for the cloakrooms. To them it was the biggest sensation of the session.

The Associated Press emphasized the amazement of the lawmakers in which, the AP declared, "all official Washington joined, because Mr. Brandeis had not been mentioned among the long list of eligibles which President Wilson considered." The President had not consulted a single Senator about the nomination of Brandeis; on this point the press was unanimous. Had the newspapers known the identity of the one Senator who had been sounded out indirectly, they would have understood why nothing had been said about the consultation.

Brandeis had arrived in Washington from Boston on the day that the sound of his name threw the Senate into a state of excitement.

He was attending to some unfinished business connected with anti-trust work at the Justice Department, and that evening was invited to a dinner party at the home of Secretary of the Treasury William Gibbs McAdoo, an old friend. News reporters tracked him down late in the afternoon at the Gordon Hotel on 16th Street, a few blocks from the White House. Would he make a statement on his nomination to the Supreme Court?

"I have nothing to say," Brandeis told the newspapermen quietly, "nothing at all." In guarding his silence at the outset, he set a pattern of "no comment" to which he adhered through the months of struggle that followed.

The President joined Brandeis that evening at the table of his son-in-law before taking a night train to Pittsburgh to open his speaking tour of the Midwest. Several members of the Supreme Court had been invited as well. Wilson and McAdoo had timed the occasion nicely to provide a number of Wilson's ranking colleagues a chance to meet quietly, if only for a few hours, with the man whose nomination was on its way to dividing the nation into two contending camps.

SELECTION DECLARED TO BE BASED ON POLITICAL MOTIVES declared the January 29 headline in the New York *Sun,* following its revelation of "shock" in the great deliberative body. The other *Sun* headline foretold a struggle to come:

HE'S FIRST JEW EVER PICKED FOR BENCH
Long and Bitter Fight Expected in Senate over Confirmation
PRESIDENT NEEDS THREE VOTES TO WIN
Judiciary Committee Said to be against the Boston Lawyer

The article below the headlines found Brandeis wanting:

It is clearly apparent that if he were obliged to go before the Senate purely on his merits he would be defeated. There is, however, danger that the racial issue will become involved in the struggle, and in that event it would be difficult to predict how members of the Senate would vote. Already there are evidences that this phase of the situation is influencing those who will be called upon to pass upon Mr. Brandeis' qualifications.

As with numerous other press comments on the Brandeis nomination, the *Sun* article returned repeatedly to the fact that the nominee was the first Jew nominated to the United States Supreme Court, by its very emphasis indicating that this was a matter of gravest importance. It held that the nominee's being Jewish gave him a great advantage, on the ground that Senators did not want to be quoted as opposing his confirmation for fear of being labeled as anti-Semitic. Usually, the *Sun* went on, there had been little or no comment on the political effect of a Supreme Court nomination; but in the case of Louis D. Brandeis the politics of the nomination were being discussed on all sides:

> Some Democrats pointed out that as he is the first Jew to be nominated to the United States Supreme Court the circumstances would have a decided effect upon the attitude of the hundreds of thousands of Jewish voters in the United States toward President Wilson. This vote in New York is very large and without that state President Wilson would fail of reelection.

As if the attitude of the *Sun* were not abundantly clear from its news columns, an editorial headed *"Brandeis!"* deplored his nomination to what it termed "the stronghold of sane conservatism, the safeguard of our institutions, the ultimate interpreter of our fundamental law."

The press foresaw a hard fight in the Senate against Wilson's nominee, to be led by Republicans and aided by dissident Democrats. If the two Senators from Massachusetts, both Republicans, should invoke "Senatorial courtesy" and ask members to reject the nominee as personally objectionable to them, there was general agreement that confirmation could be blocked. But Senators Henry Cabot Lodge and John W. Weeks were saying nothing for the moment. Should they maintain their silence, the consensus held that the President would get the votes to win, because the party division in the Senate was decidedly in the President's favor—fifty-six Democrats to forty Republicans. It was considered highly likely that Senator La Follette of Wisconsin and several of his following among the Progressive Republicans would support the nomination, enough to make up for any defections from the President's party.

With all the amazed shock and surprise, however, members of the Senate were strangely reluctant to commit themselves on the way they would vote. Many, it appeared, were quite willing to indicate off the record to newsmen that they were unhappy over Wilson's nomination, yet virtually none would permit himself to be so quoted.

According to the Washington *Post,* Senator James J. Wadsworth, Republican of New York, was the only Senator who stated openly that he opposed confirming Brandeis for the Court, yet even he declined to say why.

On the other hand, some of those who were instinctively favorable to the nomination were quite open about it. Especially emphatic was "Pitchfork Ben" Tillman, a flamboyant small farmer's man in South Carolina politics, but in the U.S. Senate a partisan, regular Democrat. Tillman had earned his soubriquet years before on the stump when he threatened to "jab a pitchfork into the fat ribs of Grover Cleveland." Wall Street and big business had more recently become Tillman's favorite target. Asked his view of Wilson's appointment of Brandeis, the South Carolinian declared:

"Too proud to fight, is he? I guess this shows he isn't afraid to offend the predatory interests, which always have had too much influence in the appointment of Supreme Court justices. It looks to me as if the people who said the President is playing to big business will have to keep their silence now. . . . Senatorial courtesy! If Senatorial courtesy means that as big an appointment as a Supreme Court justice can be prevented by one Senator for personal reasons, why to hell with senatorial courtesy!"

Within twenty-four hours it became clear that the nomination would face detailed scrutiny within the Senate Judiciary Committee, and that for this purpose a subcommittee would be named to take testimony on Brandeis' fitness for office. At once speculation centered both on the make-up of the subcommittee and on the prospects for the nomination when it should come before the full commitee of eighteen members. In the absence because of illness of Senator Culberson of Texas, chairman of the Judiciary Committee, Senator Overman of North Carolina prepared over the week end to select the subcommittee. Yet Overman somewhat casually told a United Press reporter the day after the bomb went off that Brandeis would certainly be rejected if he were to face a vote of the full committee right away. But, Overman added suggestively, hearings might change some members' minds.

Preliminary canvasses of committee members bore out both parts of Overman's statement. They showed a leaning against the nominee by the majority, but it was difficult to tell a Senator's confidential statement from a partisan newsman's educated guess. The *Evening Star* of Washington, within hours of the nomination, quoted a "prominent Democratic member of the Senate Judiciary Committee" as saying: "There will be the biggest kind of a fight in the Senate over this nomination."

Newspaper editors responded to Brandeis' name as if by a reflex conditioned through years of familiarity with the man and his ideas. The Boston *Post* applauded the nomination, as did the liberal New York *World,* which the late Joseph Pulitzer had built into a crusading power. Also applauding were those few newspapers that had hitched their wagons in 1912 to the Progressive movement of Teddy Roosevelt. If their editorial policy was anti-Wall Street, if they actively sought the readership and the pennies of the little man in Main Street, they generally reacted with favor to the Brandeis nomination.

On the other hand, opposition was voiced most emphatically by the organs of business and of Republicanism. *The Wall Street Journal* exploded in its denunciation. Wilson, the *Journal* complained, had sent Brandeis' name to the Senate only a few hours after he had reassured the businessmen and railroad leaders assembled in banquet that he stood with them in furthering the business interests of the country. Said *The Wall Street Journal:*

> In all the anti-corporation agitation of the past years one name stands out conspicuous above all others. Where others were radical he was rabid; where others were extreme he was super-extreme; where others would trim he would lay the ax to the root of the tree. As "attorney for the people" before commerce commission and legislative committee and in cheap magazines the railroads have been held up as public enemies. Twenty-four hours after leaving the Railway Business Association the President appointed this man without previous judicial training to the bench of the United States Supreme Court, the highest office in the gift of the Executive.

The Detroit *Free Press* was bitter in its opposition:

> Of all the Americans who have passed before the public view in the last ten years Louis D. Brandeis is in temperament and in training perhaps the least fit for the calm, cold, dispassionate work of the Supreme Court of the United States. . . . It is the solemn duty of the Senate to reject this nomination. . . .

The nomination clearly caused great discomfort to *The New York Times,* which four weeks earlier had urged the appointment of Taft to the Supreme Court vacancy. Adolph S. Ochs, publisher of *The Times,* must have felt with every other Jew in America a certain gratification at the nomination of a Jew to the Court on which none had ever sat before. Yet as an organ of thoughtful conservatism in the money center of the country, *The Times* under Ochs had become a balance wheel in the national political system. It could not hail the nomination of Brandeis—neither could it denounce him in the strident tones employed by the *Sun, Wall Street Journal,* and Detroit *Free Press.* The first *Times* editorial on Brandeis turned out to be a lengthy essay discussing the many angles from which the nominee could be and would be attacked. But it skipped neatly away from committing the paper to a firm expression of opinion. Two days later, however, the sober second thoughts of *The Times* held that it was highly improper for Wilson and Attorney General Gregory to "pack" the Supreme Court with a sure vote on the government side of pending antitrust suits against U.S. Steel, International Harvester Company, and other corporations:

> Justices of the Supreme Court are appointed for their learning, their uprightness, and their independence, not because of their preconceived and known opinions. To nominate and confirm with intent to "pack" the Court for the Government would be as flagrant a breach of trust as to put on the bench an avowed partisan and active advocate of the defendant corporations.

In Brandeis' own city, the Irish Democrats applauded Wilson. Almost by instinct their political leaders could sense a winning combination of ethnic minority symbols that could, under the leadership of President Wilson, overwhelm the *Mayflower* descendants in the fall election. Who could resist a ticket headed by the President who had put Brandeis on the Supreme Court, with an Irishman nominated for the Senate against Henry Cabot Lodge? Mayor James Michael Curley called the appointment of Brandeis "a splendid compliment to a most able man." Ex-Mayor John F. Fitzgerald, the singing Irish smoothie known to his East Boston following as "Honey Fitz," had outgrown his primitive anti-Semitic feelings and termed the nomination "a very timely one. Mr. Brandeis believes that the law was made for man—not that man was made to be the slave of law." Former Governor David Ignatius Walsh, who had worked with Brandeis on reform legislation, was ecstatic:

> The nomination is admirable in every way. Mr. Brandeis is a real progressive, with a profound knowledge of law, and is certain to prove one of the greatest jurists that has ever sat on the Supreme Bench.

William Howard Taft happened to be in Boston on Thursday, the day before Wilson sent Brandeis' name to the Senate. The former President spoke at the annual banquet of the Knights of Columbus in suburban Waltham, then caught an overnight train to New York. Reporters missed him at the McAlpin Hotel in the afternoon when the news broke, but they caught him that evening in Trenton, where he was lecturing at a business college.

"I have no comment to make," was all the disappointed Taft would say that Friday evening.

He had a very special reason for viewing as a slap in the face the nomination of Brandeis to the place for which he longed. He could see that now the old story of the Ballinger affair would come out in the papers again. Six years before, in 1910, Brandeis had been responsible for smearing his administration in a way that had caused Taft acute embarrassment and had degraded his Secretary of the Interior, Richard A. Ballinger. Brandeis' work had set the stage for the election disaster in 1912.

It had started with an accusation leveled against Secretary Ballinger in 1909 by Louis P. Glavis, a young man of twenty-five who was chief of General Land Office field agents within Ballinger's department. Glavis charged that the Secretary of the Interior, his superior, was abandoning the national policy of conservation by letting the Guggenheim interests take over certain coal-bearing public lands in Alaska. Glavis prepared a detailed document explaining his charges. Taft examined them in the summer of 1909 at his vacation home in Beverly, Massachusetts, then called on Secretary Ballinger to furnish him a detailed reply. The Secretary did so, at great length.

Taft received the Ballinger documents, consulted with George Wickersham, his Attorney General, and within six days made public a letter that Taft said he had sent to Ballinger, exonerating him completely. Ballinger, the President said, should discharge Glavis as a faithless public servant. Secretary Ballinger then told news reporters that the matter was closed. But he spoke too soon, for in November Glavis' document was published in *Collier's Weekly,* whose editor, Norman Hapgood, believed it sounded a warning against the danger that Taft meant to abandon Theodore Roosevelt's policy of conserving America's natural resources.

The Glavis article in *Collier's* caused a national sensation. The Taft administration countered by arranging to have a joint committee of Congress set up, ostensibly to investigate the charges but really calculated to vindicate Secretary Ballinger. After the planned whitewash, Attorney General Wickersham would pursue *Collier's* with a costly suit for damages. Although the majority of the congressional committee was stacked with Republicans prejudiced in favor of Ballinger, some Democrats who leaned the other way were included. At the urging of editor Hapgood, Brandeis was brought in from Boston to take charge of the case for Glavis and for *Collier's.*

In the course of the long hearings in the spring of 1910, Brandeis completely turned the tables on the committee majority and its chief witnesses, Secretary Ballinger and his close associates. By persistent questioning, and by reconstructing the schedule of activity of the men involved, he brought out the fact that President Taft, busy with golf, social affairs, and ceremonial appearances during his vacation at Beverly, had not really had time to examine the matter. Brandeis proved that in fact Taft's "findings" had been prepared long in advance in Ballinger's own office, with the aid of Attorney General Wickersham. Then the trusting Taft had simply added his signature. The accused Secretary of the Interior and his confidential assistants had prepared his own Presidential whitewash!

When the press had finished telling the entire story of the Ballinger investigation, the Secretary looked to the public like a thorough scoundrel. Taft appeared at best an incompetent Chief Executive who could not even identify a dishonest public official in his own cabinet and who, when he was shown the facts, had blithely brushed them aside. Brandeis emerged seeming both a giant-killer and a defender of the public interest. The investigating committee voted the expected vindication of Ballinger by a bare party-line majority, but the minority raised a howl in a contradictory report. Ballinger soon resigned and disappeared into the political shadows.

This affair was not the only one, of course, but Taft looked back on it as one of the most important spurs that had brought Theodore Roosevelt charging back into the Presidential race of 1912. This led to the split in the Republican party and Taft's consequent defeat. Had it not been for Brandeis and his exploitation of the Ballinger–Glavis–*Collier's Weekly* affair, there easily might have been no third-party movement and Taft might have stayed in the White House.

Back in New Haven after guarding his silence about the Brandeis nomination over the week end, Taft in his Monday mail read a letter from Washington, sent by his close friend and confidant, Gus J. Karger. Veteran Washington correspondent of the Cincinnati *Times-Star,* the paper owned by Taft's half-brother Charles. Karger had been Taft's most faithful correspondent after he left the White House. The two men exchanged letters almost weekly, the newsman keeping Taft apprised of political developments as they unfolded before his eyes and within reach of his ears—the former President sharing with Karger his views of national politics from his detached vantage point at Yale and his deep fund of experience in office. It was the faithful Karger who performed perhaps the greater service in that he offered Taft the sympathetic companionship of an intellectual equal while maintaining a respectful deference for Taft's position.

"Well, how do you like it? If Mr. Wilson has a sense of humor left, it must be working overtime today," Karger's Saturday letter began.

> When Brandeis' nomination came in yesterday, the Senate simply gasped. Today some of the Senators are coming up for air and trying to take stock. There wasn't any more excitement at the Capitol when Congress passed the Spanish War Resolution. At first it seemed as though Brandeis would be doomed to terrible humiliation; today the situation has changed. Many Senators who might base their opposition to him on sound and logical grounds, if he were a Presbyterian, are reluctant to take a stand, lest their opposition be misconstrued. If the fight is carried to a finish—and I suppose it will—Mr. Brandeis will probably be confirmed and have the opportunity to make the Supreme Court bench the forum for his stump speeches. . . .

Letting all restraint go, the wounded Taft that afternoon poured out his heart to Gus Karger:

Dear Gus:
  Our worthy President has developed more qualities of Machiavelli than even I, with a full appreciation of the admirable roundness of his character, had suspected. When I think of the devilish

ingenuity manifested in the selection of Brandeis, I can not but
admire his finesse. Of course, joking aside, it is one of the deepest
wounds I have had as an American and a lover of the Constitution
and a believer in progressive conservatism, that such a man as
Brandeis could be put in the Court, as I believe he is likely to be.

He is a muckraker, an emotionalist for his own purposes, a
socialist, prompted by jealousy, a hypocrite, a man who has certain
high ideals in his imagination, but who is utterly unscrupulous in
method in reaching them, a man of infinite cunning, of great tenacity
of purpose, and, in my judgment, of much power for evil. He is only
one of nine on the Court, but one on the Court is often an important
consideration; and even if the rest of the Court is against him, he
has the opportunity to attack their judgments and weaken their
force by insidious demagoguery, and an appeal to the restless element
that can do infinite harm. I sincerely hope that he can be defeated in
the Senate, but I don't think so.

If his own secret disappointment, producing "one of the deepest
wounds" of his career, were not sufficient cause for Taft's emotional
outpouring, if even his own estimate of the black character of the
nominee had been insufficient, he was maddened by the deft stroke
Wilson had executed in drawing to himself the veneration of American
Jewry. What stung Taft most was the fact that Brandeis had never
been a faithful son of Israel. He had hardly ever stepped inside a
synagogue. Only in the past two years of war had he become identified
with Zionism, through the movement for relief of masses of Jewish
refugees made homeless in the war-torn Turkish, Austrian, and Rus-
sian empires. Surely Gus Karger, a conservative, thoroughly Ameri-
canized, Midwestern German Jew, would understand. Taft's denunciation of Brandeis went on:

> Your description of the outburst against him when nominated,
> together with the dark brown taste in the mouth of protesting Sen-
> ators the next morning, is an indication of the satanic skill in his
> selection. The intelligent Jews of this country are as much opposed
> to Brandeis' nomination as I am, but there are politics in the
> Jewish community, which with their clannishness embarrass lead-
> ing and liberal and clear-sighted Jews. I venture to think that the
> leading Jews of New York, Boston, Chicago, St. Louis, Cincinnati
> and other cities, who are not bound up in emotional uplifting, and
> who do not now tend to socialism, are as much troubled over his
> appointment and as indignant as any of us can be, but Brandeis'

foresight as to himself has strangled their expression lest they arouse bitter criticism against themselves, by their own people.

I talked with Isaac Ullman of New Haven some little time ago about Brandeis. Isaac is on all the great Jewish committees, and he says there is a great feeling of antagonism toward Brandeis among the leading Jews, because his present superlative and extreme Judaism is a plant of very late growth. He says that he was no Jew until he was rejected by Wilson as Attorney General, because the leading Jews of the country told Wilson that Brandeis was not a representative Jew.

Since that time, Brandeis has adopted Zionism, favors the new Jerusalem, and has metaphorically been recircumcised. He has gone all over the country making speeches, arousing the Jewish spirit, even wearing a hat in the Synagogue. . . . If it were necessary, I am sure he would have grown a beard to convince them that he was a Jew of Jews.

It was not just the hypocrisy of the man that stung Taft; there was also the obvious political effectiveness of Wilson's nomination. Yet as an ex-officeholder freed from the pains of further party responsibility, Taft gleefully noted the way Wilson's stiletto was tormenting the two Republican Senators from Massachusetts:

The humor of the situation I can, even in the sorrow of the appointment, not permit to escape. When I consider the heartfelt indignation of Lodge and Weeks at having to alienate the Jews of Massachusetts, with their candidates before them, I derive some wicked amusement. Weeks is the candidate of the Shoe Machinery Company, and of all organizations in the country, Brandeis is anathema to them. Lodge's friends in Boston . . . regard Brandeis as the most exalted type of dishonest trickster. Wilson has projected a fight, which with master art he will give the color of a contest, on one side of which will be ranged the opposition of corporate wealth and racial prejudice, and on the other side the down-trodden, the oppressed, the uplifters, the labor unions, and all the elements which are supposed to have votes in the election. This will lead to the confirmation because of the white-livered Senators that we have. The Senate has been LaFollettized and Gomperized so that it has ceased to be the conservative body it was.

Yet Taft was borne up by his faith that righteousness must eventually triumph over the chicanery of the President. His letter to Karger rolled on:

As so often happens in such a well devised Machiavellian scheme, the ultimate result is not going to be to Wilson's advantage, if we nominate any man whose conservatism appeals to the business men. His willingness to put a socialist on the Bench, and a muckraker, will drive from him the element that he might call upon because he has saved us from war, and that is strong among the business men. This appointment will be remembered long after the excitement of the confirmation has passed away, and it will return to plague him, as it ought to. It is too ingenious and too unscrupulous. Machiavelli's philosophy and policy were lacking in the same way.

Then back to his deep wound, laughing it off with a Yiddish phrase for Gus Karger's benefit that ill concealed its tragic Pagliacci quality:

> When you consider Brandeis' appointment, and think that men were pressing me for the place, *es ist zum lachen.* You know me well enough to know that my judgment on this subject is not in the slightest degree colored by the fact that men had suggested me for the place. I never for one moment credited the possibility of Wilson's considering my name. The thoughts of the Judges of the Supreme Court, if they could be interpreted, would form interesting language.
>
> I am coming down to Washington as you know, and I shall be glad to continue this subject when I see you. . . .
>
> > *Affectionately yours.* . . .

As he contemplated further the discomfiture that the Brandeis nomination was causing others who had wounded him in the not too distant past, Taft must have felt at least a moderate glow of pleasure. To his brother Henry W. Taft, a Wall Street lawyer, he developed this titillating aspect of the situation:

> I can formulate some of Lodge's sulphuric sarcasm and bitter indignation at Wilson's putting him in the situation he finds himself in. He has no breadth to look at it from other than a personal standpoint. . . .
>
> The humor of the situation over Brandeis grows as I think of it. Speyer, Schiff, Kahn, Louis Marshall all have to praise the appointment and all hate Wilson for making it. As I think the appointment over, of course I am deeply concerned to have such an insidious devil in the Court, but it is interesting to study the Machiavellian traits of our President. With Roosevelt shouting at him and

calling him names, and reeking with the gore of Germans that he would like to kill, he must smile to think how much Perkins, Roosevelt's political father in Good, enjoys the prospect of Brandeis sitting in the Harvester case on a rehearing.

I hope White will not end his judicial career with an apoplectic fit caused by the nomination.

Taft's humor had returned to him sufficiently by the end of the day to permit him to write jokingly to George W. Wickersham, Attorney General during his White House days, now practicing law in partnership with Henry Taft in Wall Street: "I have no doubt that you are telegraphing the Senate to assist in the confirmation of Brandeis."

Two days later Wickersham sent news that may have quickened hope in his old chief that at least a struggle would emerge from the pool of discontent in the Senate.

> I was in Washington yesterday and Sunday [Wickersham wrote], and talked with a good many people about it. I find a very stiff opposition is being organized. Some of the Senators told me that it would be impossible for the nomination to be confirmed, or even to be voted upon.

By February 3 Karger was informing Taft that "the Brandeis furor seems to have subsided." There was little opinion to the effect that the confirmation would be prevented, the newsman wrote, even though there were definite indications of "undue delay to emphasize senatorial displeasure. But senatorial displeasure is not courageous enough to come out in the open, when the coming-out might be provocative of charges of anti-Semitism and of undue friendship with the interest of Wall Street."

Three days later, hower, Taft was informing Karger that there was cause for hope:

> There is a movement on foot to carry on a real campaign against Brandeis. . . . It is quite probable that he will be confirmed, but I am not at all disposed to discourage the effort to bring out evidence against him even though it shall fail of its chief purpose.

Wickersham had not been idle in Wall Street, that bustling world within a world where bankers, lawyers, and corporation directors had almost to a man bristled in their electric reaction to the Brandeis nomination as if they had been shocked by the same high-voltage charge. Accustomed to swift decision and action, the financial-district men almost immediately set up a letter-writing campaign urging Senators to reject the Brandeis nomination. In addition, the lawyers among them set in motion a statement of protest of special prestige, in which Wickersham earnestly solicited the cooperation of former President William Howard Taft. It was this to which Taft referred cryptically when communicating with Karger.

Wilson's nomination of Brandeis had been a painful wound to Taft's self-esteem. But to Senator Henry Cabot Lodge, the President had savagely attacked the two things he held most dear: his concept of the enduring American values and his right to his Senatorship from Massachusetts. Lodge was now, at sixty-six, an elder in public life, with nearly twenty-four years of Senate service. He was a reserved man, proud and aloof, aware that he had read more books, and written more, and spoke a finer English than most other men in America. The sweeping gray whiskers, the erect bearing, the cane and the swinging pace as Lodge walked confidently down Massachusetts Avenue combined to give him that look of distinction expected of the patrician born to wisdom and leadership.

Senator Lodge had lately become somewhat tired, having suffered illness and loneliness following the death of his wife after forty-four years together. A passionate believer in maintaining the maritime and naval strength of his country, an instinct inherited from generations of Boston merchant-shipowners, Lodge suffered with the news of every ship from old England sunk by German U-boats. He had reached the stage of gloomy pessimism over Woodrow Wilson, whom he considered a spineless neutralist in the struggle between good and evil, and he was greatly discouraged by the grip with which Wilson held the powers of federal government. For three years Lodge had been frustrated as a minority Senator without a committee chairmanship, and he had been disappointed by the political eclipse of his old friend and comrade-in-arms, Theodore Roosevelt.

But there was another element underlying Lodge's pessimism. For a long time now something had been coming over his beloved country that made Henry Cabot Lodge infinitely sad. He had known a time when his New England marked the entire United States with its Anglo-Saxon stamp. His kind of people not long before had run the country and set the pattern for its growth. But since the 1880s, to Lodge's great regret, America had become a refuse ground for the unwanted human overflow from Europe. Lodge had for years deplored the policy of unrestricted immigration that brought all kinds of people —Slavs, Greeks, Italians, Jews, and others—pouring by millions into the land his ancestors had seeded and pioneered. The trickle of immigration from the British Isles, the shanty Irish excepted, was tolerable to Henry Cabot Lodge; but the flood that was pouring in from eastern and southern Europe was something quite different.

"More precious even than the forms of government," Lodge had declared on the floor of the Senate as early as 1896,

> are the mental and moral qualities which make what we call our race. While those stand unimpaired all is safe. When those decline all is imperiled. They are exposed to but a single danger, and that is by changing the quality of our race and citizenship through the wholesale infusion of races whose traditions and inheritances, whose thoughts and whose beliefs are wholly alien to ours and with whom we have never assimilated or even been associated in the past.

It was not merely that the immigrants were here, sullying the purity of America (which Lodge conceived as an English society in the New World) with their barbaric massacre of the English tongue and their odd-looking foreign-language newspapers. More than two thirds of the Massachusetts people now were immigrants or the children of immigrants. They were penetrating everywhere—into the schools, the better neighborhoods, and into public office. Even worse, since the ratification of the Seventeenth Amendment to the Constitution in 1913, these new arrivals could vote directly for members of the United States Senate. In November 1916, after having held his seat since 1892, Lodge would be required to face this new electorate and solicit its votes. No longer would he be chosen by the state legislature that had selected him four times previously. The Senator had opposed the amendment when it was pending before Congress, because at base he did not trust the electorate at large to select the right man.

Lodge had observed a disturbing sign of the change that had come over the people of Massachusetts in Boston's official Independence Day celebration held in Faneuil Hall. Back in 1879, when Brandeis and Sam Warren were on the point of opening their law office, a much younger Henry Cabot Lodge had delivered the Fourth of July oration there. But in 1915, at the invitation of Mayor James Michael Curley, Louis D. Brandeis had given the Independence Day address, taking "True Americanism" as his theme. According to all the newspapers Lodge had read, the hall was packed and an overflow crowd was gathered around the doors. The orator was cheered with such enthusiasm on his arrival that he had difficulty getting started. But once begun, he held his audience in close attention to the end. It was clear as daylight that this man Brandeis felt the pulse of the crowd, and should he ever run for office, he had the mark of a winner.

And what did Brandeis say that this crowd approved with such vocal acclaim? His oft-repeated theme of what he termed "social justice"—shorter hours and higher wages for the workingmen, the right of women to vote, an open door to immigration from all parts of Europe, trade unionism, and soak-the-rich taxes. Whereas Lodge spoke in 1879 for a return to the old-fashioned American heritage of self-reliant independence, and still believed in it, Brandeis had the audacity to say from the platform in Faneuil Hall:

> The citizen in a successful democracy must not only have education; he must be free. Men are not free if dependent industrially upon the arbitrary will of another. Industrial liberty on the part of the worker cannot, therefore, exist if there be overweening industrial power. Some curb must be placed upon capitalistic combination. Nor will this curb be effective unless the workers cooperate, as in trade unions. Control and cooperation are both essential to industrial liberty.

To Lodge it was a sign of sickening deterioration in public life that the city government of Boston had fallen into the hands of people like Curley, who would give Faneuil Hall to Brandeis to use as his forum for rabble-rousing on the Fourth of July. Of even more immediate concern, Brandeis had a following, and a large one, as his success at the Independence Day meeting made clear. The Irish Democrats understood how to do business with him. Lodge recognized that Brandeis could become extremely dangerous in the politics of Massachusetts if he should ever decide to run for public office.

Lodge was by nature a bitter, partisan opponent of Woodrow Wilson, but the nomination of Brandeis made him pause. The difficulties of the coming election campaign would be great enough, since he would oppose a ticket headed by the incumbent President. Now that President was whip-sawing him by nominating a perfectly impossible Massachusetts man to one of the highest offices within his gift. Should he openly oppose the confirmation of Brandeis? His position of influence as senior Senator from the nominee's state could probably bring about Brandeis' defeat if he were to invoke the rule of Senatorial courtesy. There wasn't a moment's doubt that Brandeis was personally objectionable to him, of course. But in view of the election ahead and the changed character of the electorate, would it be wise to make an issue of his stern displeasure? If Brandeis should be rejected through his efforts—what then?

Lodge was ill at home when the nomination reached the Senate on Friday afternoon, but he returned to Capitol Hill on Saturday and was seen by reporters in consultation with several members of the Judiciary Committee. He had nothing to say for publication.

Taft was not the only one to appreciate the acute discomfort the Brandeis nomination caused the Senator from Massachusetts. Arthur D. Hill, a State Street Boston lawyer and close friend who handled Lodge's personal legal affairs and investments, wired the Senator at once urging him not to oppose the nomination and so risk defeat in the election later in the year. Lodge responded promptly, marking his letter, as he did many, "personal and *confidential*."

> The principal reason which you give for supporting Brandeis seems to me to constitute the most serious objection to his nomination. For the first time in our history a man has been nominated to the Supreme Court with a view to attracting to the President a group of voters on racial grounds. Converting the United States into a Government by foreign groups is to me the most fatal thing that can happen to our Government . . .
>
> A man ought to be appointed without any reference to his race or religion, and solely on his fitness. If it were not that Brandeis is a Jew, and a German Jew, he would never have been appointed and he would not have a baker's dozen of votes in the Senate. This seems to me in the highest degree un-American and wrong.

As for the nominee's fitness for the place, Lodge was certain that Brandeis fell short, although he acknowledged to Hill that he could not at the moment document his case.

As to his professional character, although I am a member of the bar I have never practiced and I am conscious that I speak as a layman, I have had before me the proofs of Brandeis' action in several cases which seems to my uninstructed mind in the highest degree unprofessional, if there is any standard of unprofessional honor.

By the Monday after the Friday nomination, Lodge had already determined that he was not to be caught in no man's land leading a charge against the nominee and his allies. Those who turned their faces expectantly toward him, as senior Senator from Massachusetts, might look in vain for him to lead them out of the trenches for an assault against Brandeis. Those people did not have to wage a campaign for re-election all over a polyglot state in which an alarming number of semieducated voters, many just barely literate, looked on Louis D. Brandeis as their savior. Let the organization of lawyers take the lead in exposing the man's unsuitability for a seat on the Court. The Senate, largely made up of legally trained men, would listen to their peers at the bar. Lodge put this idea to Hill:

If the Bar Associations have nothing to say against his appointment I do not believe they will find that Senators are anxious to plunge into a very disagreeable contest, as this is sure to be. Of course no one questions Brandeis' ability. Everyone recognizes that the question is solely one of character.

The same day that Lodge was explaining his public posture and private views on the Brandeis nomination to Hill, the Boston attorney was writing to the Senator in an attempt to explain at length his reasons for immediately telegraphing Lodge, as a friend, not to join the fight against the nominee. Hill put the political argument first:

I have had rather exceptional opportunities for learning Brandeis' enormous influence with the thoughtful radicals of the country. There are very few men who have the same following that he has in that great body of opinion, made up partly of Republicans and partly of Democrats, to which the term "Progressives" has been loosely applied. If the Republican Party is to win next year it has to get the votes of these men, or many of them. . . .

His strength with the sober, righteous middle class, who read the ten-cent magazines and inhabit places like Somerville, is enormous, and the Jews, especially since his taking up Zionism, take great pride in him and his leadership.

Of course, Hill continued, he knew that all this talk of political expediency would have no weight with Lodge if the Senator thought Brandeis unfit for the Associate Justiceship. But, Hill declared, he honestly did not believe the nominee was unfit, in spite of the fact that a large number of influential people neither liked nor trusted him. True, the man suffered from "a lack of personal magnetism" that alienated certain of his colleagues:

> I have never heard any reliable evidence of any conduct on his part which would make him unfit for a judicial position.
>
> His unpopularity at the Bar, which undoubtedly exists, is the result, I think, of two things: first, that he has been always an active radical, constantly attacking all sorts of established institutions, and thereby inevitably inciting considerable enmity; and second, a certain hard and unsympathetic quality which is largely racial.
>
> He has no power of feeling or understanding the position of an opponent, and none of that spirit of playing the game with courtesy and good-nature which is part of the standard of the Anglo-Saxon. He fights to win, and fights up to the limit of his rights with a stern and even cruel exultation in the defeat of his adversary. It is not for nothing that in the Old Testament there isn't a word from beginning to end of admiration for a gallant enemy.

Hill concluded by insisting that Brandeis, though not a man he would seek as a close friend, had a clean record so far as his legal ethics were concerned:

> He is, I am convinced, a sincere idealist in his relations with the public, has done much good service to the community from disinterested motives, and would strengthen the Court, not only by his great legal ability, but by unusual knowledge of the ecnomic and social facts in the community. . . .
>
> If you get an opportunity I suggest your talking Brandeis over with Judge Holmes. He knows much about him and has, I think, more power of seeing men from a detached point of view than most of the people with whom one comes into contact.

Lodge's reply to Hill was indignant:

> Your argument is wholly political. I fear I cannot be governed by the political argument in the case of an appointment to the Supreme Court. . . .
>
> I am not so much in love with a seat in the Senate that I should

be willing to sacrifice my own self-interest by voting for or against a man because I thought the vote might benefit me politically. I can live without the office, but I should find it extremely difficult to live contentedly, in the few years that remain to me, without my own self-respect.

I did not know that Mr. Brandeis, who has been in and out of all political parties and of late has been a staunch Democrat, had such a hold on the Progressives. I know one Progressive who is pretty thoroughly against him, and that is Theodore Roosevelt.

Hill was not one to give up easily, nor did he accept the quick and vague generalization. Hill had recently been filling in at the Harvard Law School as teacher of the course in evidence since the sudden death of Dean Ezra Thayer. He asked Lodge—just as he required of his students—to prove statements by evidence:

I am greatly interested in what you say as to the "proofs" you have seen of his having been guilty of action "in the highest degree unprofessional." No such definite instance has ever been brought to my attention.

Responding to Hill in another of his letters stamped "personal and *confidential*," Senator Lodge tried to straighten out three tangled issues: the fact that Brandeis was a Jew, his fitness for a place on the Court, and election-year politics:

Your argument was chiefly on political grounds, which I do not think ought to enter into the question at all. I should not think of opposing Mr. Brandeis on account of his race, or his politics—which have been extremely varied—nor should I feel justified in voting against him because he held views on general matters with which I do not agree.

The only things that would weigh with me in deciding my action, and the only things that ought to weigh, I think, in deciding the action of the Senate on an appointment to the Supreme Court, would be those relating to ability, character and fitness. The ability of Mr. Brandeis nobody questions. His character and fitness are certainly in serious doubt.

Very grave charges have been made in regard to not one case but many where he appears, from all I know of the cases, to have behaved in what seems to me a most unprofessional manner and as no man of high integrity would behave. These charges are being brought before the Judiciary Committee, who will consider them and report to the Senate. My action will be based on these charges and facts as presented by the Committee.

Thus, in response to Hill's request for proofs, Lodge fell back on "charges."

In the days immediately following, Lodge did his best in one letter after another to promote an anti-Brandeis campaign by the bar associations. Henry Lee Higginson, eighty-one-year-old dean of the prominent banking and brokerage firm of Lee, Higginson & Company, spluttered his indignation over the Brandeis nomination in almost daily notes to Lodge. As he had done with Hill and other correspondents, the Senator shunted Higginson to the organizations of lawyers. "The apparent indifference of the Bar is undoubtedly making a good deal of an impression here," Lodge wrote.

Six days after the nomination Higginson had good news to report to his Senator. Emissaries of the United States Steel Corporation had visited Boston in order to organize resistance. One of the visitors was Raynal C. Bolling, General Solicitor for U.S. Steel in New York, who had for years been acting in a personal capacity for Chairman Elbert H. Gary of the U.S. Steel board. The other was James Hay Reed, one of the founding fathers of the corporation and a U.S. Steel director, with headquarters in Pittsburgh. Higginson notified Lodge that these two men

. . . members of the bar employed by the Steel Corporation have been here seeing members of the Bar, with a view to getting a protest from a little knot of men about Brandeis' appointment.

Mr. Louis A. Coolidge, Treasurer of the United Shoe Machinery Corporation, has been in New York and may go again. He is pretty lively in his talk, and perhaps has not much judgment, but he must have the "goods." . . .

Mr. Bolling thinks that all the Republicans are opposed to the nomination and that a good many Democrats would like to oppose it if they had the necessary information. . . . These lawyers from New York seem to think that I should join in any little protest about Brandeis, but I have thought to the contrary and shall be guided in the matter by Lawrence Lowell. (I am to see Lawrence Lowell this afternoon.) If you have any feeling about that pray advise me.

Higginson was certainly emotionally upset, and this, combined with his advanced age, rendered his grasp of detail less precise than it once

had been. But he was certain that he shared with his old friend Cabot
Lodge a scale of values based on Massachusetts family lineage, property, and Harvard University. Higginson measured the U.S. Steel men
by the scale they both respected:

> Bolling I have known for many years, and he is a very high-class
> fellow. He must have graduated somewhere about 1904 or 1905.
> He married Anna Phillips and of course is well known to Andrew
> Peters. He comes from Arkansas and was known in college as a
> very superior man. He graduated at Harvard and then was in the
> Harvard Law School. Reed is employed by the Steel Corporation in
> Washington, so Bolling said. They are men of the best kind. . . .
> I think we can get a remonstrance from certain lawyers here
> about Brandeis. . . . Any instructions which you can give me in
> any way I shall be much obliged to you for.

Draw up your brief and argue was the gist of the "instructions"
Lodge sent back to Higginson on Saturday, February 5:

> As to Brandeis, there are a number of cases in which his conduct
> has been in the highest degree unprofessional and which ought to
> debar any man from a seat on the Court. If those cases can be pre-
> pared for presentation to the Committee and through them to the
> Senate, I doubt if the Senate will confirm him, but his record must
> be shown. Somebody must come here and present it. The Bar As-
> sociation is apparently afraid to say anything. If they did speak it
> would have a very great effect.

Another of Lodge's friends went even farther than Arthur Hill in
counseling Lodge to support Brandeis for the bench. Charles H. Jones,
a shoe manufacturer, pleaded with Lodge to see the danger to his position in the Senate represented not only by the nominee's following in
Massachusetts, but by Louis D. Brandeis himself. If the Senate should
fail to confirm, Jones told Lodge, there would be considerable bitterness among the rank and file of the voters:

> They consider him, in a sense, the champion of their rights. . . .
> It is now being urged that if he fails of confirmation that he run for
> the Senate at the next election. His political friends claim that he is
> absolutely solid with the labor vote, both Union men and those
> who are not affiliated with the Union. This they claim will get him
> a lot of support outside of the regular Democratic party, and with

the Jewish vote, they claim that he would be an invincible candidate.

He would not consider such a self-serving political course, Lodge retorted to Jones, no matter what the friends of Brandeis might do at the coming election. Jones replied forcefully:

> Instead of considering him in any degree unfit, it is my firm belief that his qualifications for this position are pre-eminent, and that no man in the United States is as well qualified to serve the country effectively as Judge of the Supreme Court as Mr. Louis D. Brandeis.
>
> This opinion is not a haphazard judgment, but has been formed after an acquaintance of over twenty years, during the last twelve of which I have been intimately associated with him.

Jones went on to detail one legal struggle after another in which Brandeis had been prominently involved, and over which there were now rumors of improper behavior on his part. Jones assured his friend the Senator that

> . . . in none of these did anything occur which, when fully investigated, would leave the slightest stain on the personal or professional character of Mr. Brandeis. . . .

Then, returning to the argument of political expediency, to which he did not yet understand Henry Cabot Lodge's granite resistance:

> It occurred to me that it would be good management on the part of Massachusetts Republican Senators to assist in the confirmation of a Massachusetts Democrat, rather than wait for a Southern Democrat to be selected for this position, knowing as I did that the Massachusetts man was far better qualified for the most useful and important service to the country than the other man would be, and feeling, as I did, the possibility that his confirmation would prevent a political contest in Massachusetts that seemed to me wholly undesirable from every point of view.

Others who wrote to Lodge asking him to resist the nomination found it difficult to explain why they opposed Brandeis. Professor Barrett Wendell of the English Department at Harvard, for example:

> It is perhaps needless to urge that you use all your influence to prevent the confirmation of Louis Brandeis as a Justice of the Supreme Court. I have known him for at least thirty years. Through-

out that period, there can be no question in my mind he has steadily fallen in the esteem of such people as either personally or professionally command my confidence. Just why this is so I have never quite been able to satisfy myself.

A further prod from the pinnacle of Massachusetts intellectual life, the office of President A. Lawrence Lowell of Harvard, reached Lodge on February 1. And again, the call to do something about Brandeis proceeded from a conviction frankly based more on feeling and belief than on proof. "Are we," Lowell asked Lodge rhetorically,

> to put on our Supreme Bench a man whose reputation for integrity is not unimpeachable? It is difficult—perhaps impossible—to get direct evidence of any act by Brandeis that is, strictly speaking, dishonest; and yet a man who is believed by all the better part of the bar to be unscrupulous ought not to be a member of the highest court of the nation. Is there anything that can be done to make his confirmation less probable?

Not content to leave his duty half done, Lowell on the same day addressed himself to John W. Weeks, Republican, the junior Senator from Massachusetts. Lowell's approach to Weeks was a bit different from that he took to Lodge:

> I venture to write you about Brandeis. Perhaps you know his reputation as well as I do. An event occurred many years ago, within my knowledge, which convinced me that he was unscrupulous, and that feeling is now shared by all the better part of the bar. Surely a man who is not felt in his own profession to be above suspicion ought not to be a member of that body that stands at the head of the profession, and, after all, controls its moral standards.

Ten years younger than Lodge, John Wingate Weeks was twenty years his junior in Senate seniority. Weeks' formal education had been at the Naval Academy, after which virtually his entire adult career was investment banking. This background set him somewhat apart from the heritage of Harvard College and literary scholarship that stamped both Lodge and Lowell as intellectual superiors in that sector of the world of which Boston was the hub. Physically a big man, heavy-set and serious-looking, Weeks wore a thick mustache of a blackness accentuated by the shiny baldness of his ovate head. Indeed, the frontal outline of his face was like a capital O, the generously rounded jowls below almost matching the curve of the bare dome above. He had prospered greatly in the years since he and a well-financed young friend named Hornblower had formed the brokerage firm of Hornblower & Weeks, which by 1916 had offices in a number of major cities.

Weeks was a conservative who considered sound investments the water of life. He favored a high protective tariff and deplored the federal income tax. He was a safe Senator, chosen for the post by a Republican legislature dominated by Lodge; his political speeches were routine and his actions undistinguished. Yet somehow he had been promoted as a possible candidate for the Republican Presidential nomination. Now the Brandeis matter was causing him the same embarrassment that discomfited Lodge, for though the name Brandeis was anathema to a man of his brokerage-house mind, he knew that he must take the voters' regard for Brandeis into account. If only Lowell could give him the ammunition with which to justify his opposition to Brandeis! He asked the Harvard president for it:

> If the case to which you refer is in such shape that it can be used as evidence in such an investigation, I hope you will bring it to my attention. There is a disposition to approve the appointment for reasons which I need not repeat; but if any one of the half dozen things which have already been brought to the attention of the Senate relating to his professional conduct is true there ought not to be any question about the action which the Senate should take.

A. Lawrence Lowell had been a lawyer by training and vocation before he turned to teaching and later to university administration, and was sufficiently sophisticated in the use of evidence to know the difference between indication and proof. His purpose with Weeks, however, was not to prove a case, but only to stir the Senator to action. Lodge had been unresponsive to Hill's request for proof of Brandeis' moral unfitness; Lowell, on the other hand, frankly confessed to Weeks that he had none to offer:

> The case to which I referred was a personal matter, not of a professional nature, and although it convinced me that Brandeis was unscrupulous, perhaps as it affected me I am prejudiced. It might not have the same effect on others. Probably I had better not have referred to it; nor should I raise any objection on that ground, if it were not that his general reputation, as you know, in the better part of the Suffolk bar, is not what that of a judge should be.

This would seem to me, without proving a specific instance, a
sufficient reason for not confirming him. When a man has for many
years a reputation of this kind, without being able to shake it off,
even if a particular offense cannot be proved, one may feel confident that there is something wrong.

Lowell thus proposed to Weeks the argument that was to be repeated throughout the long struggle over the nomination of Louis D.
Brandeis: If some people, particularly attorneys, mistrust the man,
that fact alone should be enough to bar him from the Supreme Court.

On the Monday following the nomination, the Senate Judiciary
Committee was called together by Senator Overman of North Carolina, ranking majority member in the absence of the ill Senator Culberson of Texas. As freely predicted in the newspapers the preceding two
days, the Committee put the controversial nomination into the hands
of a subcommittee of five, to investigate the facts concerning the
nominee and the charges against him which had already found their
way not only into the press but also into the Senators' offices. The
subcommittee, under the chairmanship of Senator Chilton of West
Virginia, was to report its findings and recommendations to the full
Judiciary Committee, which in turn would consider the matter and
report to the Senate. How long the entire process would take was
anyone's guess, but it was clear to Senators from the outset that a
movement of protest against Brandeis was forming. If it should gain
sufficient momentum it might seriously delay or even completely block
confirmation of President Wilson's replacement for Justice Lamar.

As early as February 1, the day after the subcommittee was chosen,
Senators' incoming mail bore evidence of an organized pressure campaign to win their votes against confirmation of Brandeis. At 80
Maiden Lane in the New York financial district, for example, members of the law firm of Carleton & Moffat were in such haste to write
to a number of Senators that they used the same form message in
carbon copies, typing in only the individual Senator's name in the
address line:

Dear Sir:
   We protest against the nomination of Mr. Louis D. Brandeis to
be a Justice of the Supreme Court, and urge you to vote against its
confirmation.

From 49 Wall Street, a few buildings away, the attorneys of Seibert, Paddock and Cochran sent precisely the same message, varying it only by putting *I* in place of *we* when one individual signed the form letter. In fact, so many copies of this brief remonstrance written in exactly the same form turned up in Senators' mail together that the recipients were quick to note their common origin point on or close to Wall Street. And though such a naïvely conceived letter-writing campaign bespoke a clique rather than a movement, it was clearly a well-placed and well-financed group of men.

Within the next few days they were destined to join hands with the former President in New Haven, who had already hinted to Gus Karger that there was "a movement on foot to carry on a real campaign against Brandeis." George Wickersham, Taft's Attorney General and now Wall Street law partner of his old chief's brother, was to act as liaison between them. Their efforts were to be blended with those of a group in Boston which Henry Higginson had described to Lodge as "a little knot of men" best placed to disclose the past record of Mr. Wilson's nominee. They were to make common cause with the U.S. Steel Corporation attorneys, Raynal C. Bolling from the New York headquarters and James H. Reed from Pittsburgh, both of whom had already gone to Boston to incite a protest movement. Louis A. Coolidge, treasurer of the United Shoe Machinery Company, was already with them and had quickly journeyed to Washington to see what could be done. Finally, there was a seething dissatisfaction within the Senate over a nomination which many Republicans instinctively detested and on which administration Democrats felt slighted because they had not been consulted.

Louis D. Brandeis was a man about whom it seemed that no one in public life could be indifferent.

five

"An Unfit Appointment"

The first subcommittee hearing on the President's nomination was called to order on Wednesday, February ninth. The ornate Judiciary Committee room at the northwest corner of the ground floor of the Capitol did not have enough seats for all who wanted to attend, so standees packed against the windows and walls. A visitor searching the room for the much-talked-about nominee might look in vain, for Brandeis had not been summoned.

In attendance were the five subcommittee members named by the acting chairman of the Senate Judiciary Committee to hold hearings on the nomination, a few committee staff members, several witnesses, and a considerably larger than usual cluster of news reporters. The spectators were that breed of roving onlookers congressional committee hearings in Washington perennially attract—some seething partisans, some amateur students of the arts of legislative procedure, others merely curious, drawn to Capitol Hill in hope of seeing a good show.

Seated as chairman at the head of the committee table was Senator William Edwin Chilton of West Virginia. Chilton was an energetic and intensely partisan Democratic Party leader in his state and publisher of the Charleston *Gazette*. He had long been active politically but had persistently failed of election until 1911, when the state legislature had chosen him for the U.S. Senate. Now approaching fifty-eight, he was facing a campaign this year for re-election to his second term. Despite his relatively short time in the Senate, Chilton ranked third in seniority of ten Democrats on the Judiciary Committee.

Seated with Chilton was Senator Duncan Fletcher of Florida, a legislator more interested in the price of farm products than in passing on the merits of federal judges. The third Democrat was Thomas J. Walsh of Montana, at fifty-six the youngest member of the group and a Senator for less than three years. On the Republican side of the sub-committee table sat the venerable Clarence Clark of Wyoming, who had been twenty-one years in the Senate, and Albert Baird Cummins of Iowa, a Senator for eight years.

Of the five, Cummins was in national reputation far and away the biggest man in the room. He was an avowed candidate for the Presidency, and had started counting his delegates to the coming Republican National Convention. An articulate, distinguished-looking former governor of Iowa, Cummins was a political straddler. His right foot was firmly planted in the Republican organization of his state, which he dominated; his left foot marched with the Progressives (he announced in 1912 that his vote was cast for Theodore Roosevelt). Cummins was the kind of middle-ground man in the intraparty struggles who by that fact thought he had a good chance to attract the nomination. He had made his reputation first as a railroad attorney, but he had quickly switched loyalties to the farmers, manufacturers, and shippers of farm products who had longstanding grievances against the railroads because of their high freight charges. Cummins at one point took the case of an independent manufacturer of barbed wire who was accused by Eastern steel interests of patent infringement; in winning, Cummins broke the trust-administered price of barbed wire to about half its former rate and became thereby a hero to the farmers of the Plains country. As governor, Cummins led a reform administration. He struck a blow against railroad corruption of state officials by outlawing the much-abused free pass, by which the carriers had won friends in the right places. From his political background, as well as his work in the Senate, Cummins could be grouped with the progressives whose leader was Senator La Follette of Wisconsin, close friend and co-worker of Brandeis.

The first witness was Clifford Thorne of Des Moines, chairman of the state Board of Railroad Commissioners in Iowa, a man of great political ambition and, like Cummins, a Republican who broke away from the party in 1912 because he could not vote for Taft. Although for twelve days the country had known that the opposition to Brandeis was strongest among defenders of the legal and economic status quo, Thorne surprisingly attacked the nominee from quite the oppo-

site direction. Brandeis, he charged, had betrayed his trust in 1913
when the Eastern railroads had petitioned the Interstate Commerce
Commission to permit a 5 per cent increase in freight rates. Instead
of holding firm against any concession to the carriers, as Thorne said
he expected Brandeis should have done, the Boston attorney had
conceded at the end of the I.C.C. hearings that the railroads' net revenues were insufficient. The gist of Thorne's charge was that Brandeis
had helped the railroads grab for profits while masquerading as an
attorney for the public interest.

> The gentleman whom you have under consideration [said Thorne]
> was guilty of infidelity, breach of faith, and unprofessional conduct
> in connection with one of the greatest cases of this generation. . . .
> While acting as special counsel for the commission, Mr. Brandeis
> committed himself to the proposition that a net return of 7½ per
> cent above all expenses, above all taxes, above all interest on debt
> upon the capital stock of a railroad, is inadequate—is "niggardly,"
> using the precise term which he used.

Thorne conceded that the I.C.C. had invited Brandeis as an expert
witness to bring out in the rate hearings all the facts he considered
important. He was not to be viewed by the Commission either a pro-
increase or anti-increase partisan. But, Thorne argued, he had expected as a matter of course that Brandeis should oppose the boost
in freight charges that the railroads sought. What else was he to
think? Brandeis, after all, had sat beside him at the counsel table
when he, Thorne, had represented a group of Western shippers and
state governments opposing the railroad grab for higher profits.
Thorne's side had agreed on a formula permitting a 5 per cent profit
to be paid in dividends to stockholders, and 2½ per cent above that
for capital surplus. Brandeis had been allotted time by the Commission from Thorne's part of the hearing schedule. He was therefore
amazed when Brandeis had accused him of being "niggardly" in the
surplus he was willing to concede to the roads.

Thorne kept returning to his main theme, that Brandeis had
"betrayed" the public interest in expressing his view that roads clear-
ing less than 7½ per cent should be given relief. No one brought up
the matter of the need of railroads to build reserves for capital improvements—the heart of Brandeis' criticism of the New Haven

management. Throwing around multimillion-dollar figures to impress his listeners with the importance of the freight rate issue, Thorne said:

> It is hard to state where it will go to, if you gradually fill up the Supreme Court with men holding that companies earning 7½ and 8 per cent are earning a "niggardly" return. . . . I cannot tell, and you cannot tell, if in the selection of new members of the Court, what will be the result in ten or fifteen years from now by packing the Supreme Court with men with those ideas.

It was approaching ten-thirty at night when Thorne was excused from the witness chair. A rebuttal witness came forward promptly. He was John M. Eshleman, lieutenant governor of California, who had been in on the so-called Five Per Cent Rate Case discussed by Thorne, and on the same side, as a state railroad commissioner fighting against rate advances.

"I shall have to disagree squarely with Mr. Thorne about this particular case and incident," Eshleman said flatly.

> I have never been able to tell why Mr. Thorne felt just the way he did about the conduct of this case; and I have yet to find a single man connected with railroad regulation, up to this time, who agrees with Mr. Thorne's position.

The Californian went on to emphasize that never at any time had Brandeis suggested that the railroads should have been granted the 5 per cent increase they sought, though Thorne sought to make the subcommittee think so:

> Also, I cannot agree with the very strong statements by Mr. Thorne about infidelity and breach of faith and unprofessional conduct in this case.

Brandeis, Eshleman continued, would have surprised him had he not taken a detached view of the rate struggle, since he was retained by the Interstate Commerce Commission for the very purpose of standing aside and viewing the entire situation. Why Thorne alone, of all those interested in rate regulation, held his peculiar view of Brandeis' actions before the I.C.C., and why he ascribed ulterior motives to him before this subcommittee, Eshleman said he simply could not fathom.

The final witness of the first day was Joseph Teal, an attorney from Portland, Oregon, whom Senator Chilton had asked to appear. Some time earlier Teal had helped to prepare Oregon's brief defending its minimum-wage law for women, and knew that Brandeis had worked on the appeal in this case, soon to be considered by the U.S. Supreme Court. The two men did not know each other personally, however. Teal said he was

> very much surprised when I heard Mr. Thorne, whom I know very well and respect highly, had taken the position that Mr. Brandeis had betrayed the public. . . . I was astonished, not only because I do not believe Mr. Brandeis would betray anybody on earth, much less the public; but with my knowledge of him acquired in the way I stated, I could not believe it possible.

Teal suggested the Senators take time to examine Brandeis' brief in the Five Per Cent Rate Case to see for themselves what an impartial statement of the issue it was. Brandeis had suggested many economies that the railroads might effect "running into millions of dollars, such as freight car efficiencies, car-loadings, congestion of terminals, financial economies, fuel economies—one subject after another." And this made sense to him, Teal declared, because as attorney for shippers of heavy commodities like corn, wheat, lumber, and coal he could never see—and Brandeis shared his view—why they should pay in their high freight rates for luxury passenger service, to "furnish cars for ladies and gentlemen between New York and Chicago, with manicures, stenographers, barbers and baths and all that sort of thing without paying for it themselves."

Early in the day, Senator Cummins had led Thorne through his testimony with questions that revealed a predisposition to help the witness build up a case against Brandeis. Later, attempting to recover Thorne's testimony from the damage inflicted by Eshleman and Teal, Cummins told the chairman that he had a question or two. Had not Brandeis, after sitting on the same side of the table with Thorne at the I.C.C. hearing, "simply destroyed the whole case that Mr. Thorne had made?"

The matter of exactly where Brandeis was seated appeared in Cummins' eyes proof of his betrayal of the public. But Brandeis' views on the need for the railroads to practice economy through scientific management in order to make possible adequate surplus—as opposed to profit distributed in dividends—had been brought out through many long days, Teal answered. In fact, Brandeis' economy and surplus ideas were so well known for years that his conclusion should have surprised no one.

The first day's hearing finally wound up at 11:20 P.M. And though the last two witnesses had demonstrated that Thorne was completely alone in his line of opposition to Brandeis, the morning papers carried only the accuser's story. The twin rebuttal was lost in the weariness of a night session.

Gus Karger, at the press table, heard all he wanted of Thorne's testimony and went away laughing inwardly at the pretentions of the Iowa commissioner. He reported to Taft by letter:

> The first round in the fight on Brandeis was a scream. Clifford Thorne, the Iowa reformer, charged "perfidy" and bad faith in the railroad rate case—failing, however, to make much of an impression on the committee. . . . What Mr. Thorne really endeavored to show was that he alone can be regarded as a simon-pure defender and friend of the common pee-pul, his own steadfastness shining out by glorious contrast when compared with the admission by Brandeis that some of the railroads were not obtaining sufficient revenue. Thorne's program has been an ambitious one—involving a senatorship and ultimately, perhaps a Presidential nomination. Only such as he should be left on guard to protect the sacred rights of the people.

"You never deal with a reformer of the Iowa type," Taft replied to Karger a few days later, "that he is not certain to show yellow before he gets through. If what Thorne had to say against Brandeis is all there is, I should not regard it as a very serious matter."

On February tenth the subcommittee spent another hour and a half discussing the 1913 freight-rate case with two more witnesses. One was an I.C.C. staff examiner, the other a private attorney with many years of experience practicing before the commission. Both upheld the testimony of the evening before—that if Thorne considered Brandeis' impartial consideration of the railroads' revenues amounted to a betrayal of the public interest, he was alone in his view.

During the questioning of the two witnesses, several Senators made clear to the roomful of listeners the direction in which they sought to bend the testimony. The previous day Cummins had sought to lead Thorne through his performance as if Brandeis were the defendant in a trial, with Cummins in the role of prosecutor and Thorne a coached prosecution witness. As he had done the evening before, Cummins again tried, though without success, to impeach the rebuttal testimony. Walsh of Montana broke in after Cummins subsided:

> Mr. Chairman . . . speaking for myself at least, and I think that it is the common sense of the committee, that this investigation is for the purpose of developing facts to advise the judgment of the committee concerning this nomination . . . I shall insist that the witnesses be confined hereafter to telling the committee what they know about specific facts affecting the propriety of the confirmation of this nominee.

Senator Clark of Wyoming interposed from the Republican side. Walsh, he suggested, was insisting that witnesses be held too tightly to the rules of relevance as in a trial court:

> I have assumed from the start that this was an investigation and not a trial [Clark objected], that the purpose of the committee was to find out the qualifications or lack of qualifications of the nominee . . . and not to put him on trial for misdemeanors or crimes. Therefore I shall vote that what the testimony of any witness may be shall not be prejudged before he goes upon the stand before the full committee.

While giving semblance of not wanting to put Brandeis "on trial," Clark in effect was arguing that no testimony touching even remotely on Brandeis be kept out of the hearing record. He held the pose of open mind and ears to anything relating to the nominee. Cummins tried to smooth over the disagreement:

> I think we ought not to sit simply for the purpose of receiving opinions respecting the fitness of Mr. Brandeis for the place to which he has been nominated. But we must necessarily be rather liberal with regard to the rules of evidence to be observed. I agree with Senator Clark in this; but we want the truth, and if someone can put us in the way of reaching the truth I think he ought to be permitted on the stand to point the way.

Senator Fletcher broke his silence to urge that witnesses be enjoined "not to state what Tom, Dick and Harry have said to them, to make purely hearsay statements, but shall be confined to what they know."

Chilton said he was certain there would be no trouble about this. Walsh and Cummins said they agreed.

The next witness brought in exactly the kind of testimony to which Walsh had raised objection. Thomas Spelling, a loquacious, self-important attorney from New York City, asserted that he had known Brandeis from an earlier I.C.C. freight-rate case than that of 1913 brought up by Thorne. Brandeis, Spelling charged, had "compromised" in settling the earlier matter, instead of fighting it down to the wire before the Interstate Commerce Commission. According to the legal strategy he had mapped out, Spelling complained, this was all wrong. Further, Brandeis had the impudence to mark up the brief Spelling had sent to him with marginal comments such as *absurd, wholly untenable,* and other remarks Spelling termed insulting. They were in Brandeis' handwriting, all right—Spelling could vouch for that. He rambled on about details of his strategy in the rate fight of years ago.

Cummins tried for several minutes to get more reasonable testimony from the witness. Chilton began to stir in his chairman's seat. Fearing he was about to be dismissed, Spelling proposed to read aloud some material from congressional committees touching on Brandeis' "views on constitutional law."

"Just refer this committee to it, then," Fletcher said testily. "We can read, you know!" So Spelling inserted an 8000-word document into the subcommittee record and reluctantly left the stand.

A thickset man with a neatly brushed brown beard lowered himself ponderously into the witness chair. Name, Clarence W. Barron; residence, Cohasset, Massachusetts; business, farmer. Chilton pulled from "farmer" Barron the fact that he was also "connected with" *The Wall Street Journal,* and two news services, the Boston News Bureau and the Philadelphia News Bureau. It was on account of an editorial entitled "An Unfit Appointment" put out by the Boston News Bureau on Saturday, January 29, that Barron had been summoned.

Barron acknowledged he had written the article. In describing himself as a farmer of Cohasset, a resort town on the Massachusetts South Shore, America's foremost communicator of financial news was modestly masking his brilliant light. Now sixty, Barron had for fifteen years been first editor and then publisher of *The Wall Street Journal* after his marriage at forty-five had put him in a position to control the paper and its parent organization, the Dow-Jones Company. Applying his ideas for humanizing news of the counting rooms and stock exchanges, injecting excitement into the day-to-day business of financial and industrial kings, and speeding the technical processes by which businessmen could learn what was going on, Barron had inspired and built a kind of journalism that had not been known in America before. There was no other paper that could put such a glow on the profits of U.S. Steel as Barron's paper had at the turn of the year.

During his formative years in Boston, Barron had shown boundless energy and a keen nose for news. More recently in New York, with his publishing ventures having grown to the point where they enriched him generously, he adopted the coloration of the tycoons about whom he wrote. Now keeping his weight down to 300 pounds only with great difficulty, Barron led a lavish social life in New York from a suite in the Ritz. There he entertained the successful and powerful, the speculators and the plungers, who were his news sources. For relaxation he had his luxurious yacht and his estate at Cohasset, where he raised prize-winning Guernseys. But these details, which might have explained Barron's views of Brandeis, did not come out at the hearing.

Some years ago, Barron began, Brandeis had warned him to be very careful about anything he, Barron, should print about Brandeis' views in the financial field. Apparently Brandeis believed he had been misquoted or perhaps libeled in a report of a certain legal case. Barron explained that because of this warning he had "employed a firm of lawyers to look up the record of Mr. Brandeis."

CHILTON: Have you and he been enemies?

BARRON: Not at all. I have not spoken with him for thirty years. I mean, there is no occasion for our speaking.

Barron had with him his dossier on Brandeis. He handed copies around to the committee. It came out that the document had been drawn up originally in February 1913, when Brandeis was being considered for Woodrow Wilson's original cabinet—but no one remarked on the timing. Senator Walsh objected that Barron's bill of indictment merely hinted at misdeeds of which Brandeis was guilty in a series of old legal cases, but proved nothing. Where was the proof?

Again Senator Clark opposed Walsh to assert that the committee must listen to everything in order to evaluate the nominee. Chilton, indecisive, poked a few questions at Barron in reference to items he read in Barron's document. The items mentioned the United Shoe Machinery Company and men named Warren and Lennox. He was not a lawyer, Barron replied, and he was not involved in these cases personally, but he had been told all about them. Under questioning directed mainly by Walsh and Chilton, Barron grudgingly gave out a series of names of men who, in his opinion, could enlighten the Senators on the shoe-machinery affair, the Warren will case, the Lennox bankruptcy, the "conspiracy to wreck the New Haven Railroad," and "the life insurance case." Barron's catalogue of cases had a tantalizing ring, like the table of contents of *The Casebook of Sherlock Holmes*. Before Barron left the stand, having hinted at much but producing little that satisfied any of his listeners, his editorial "An Unfit Appointment" was inserted in the hearing record. It declared:

> The nomination by President Wilson of Louis D. Brandeis to the United States Supreme Court is an insult to New England and the business interests of the country. There is only one redeeming feature in the nomination and that is that it will assist to bury Mr. Wilson in the next Presidential election.

The Barron editorial asserted that Brandeis had turned against the United Shoe Machinery Company and helped the government to "prosecute and persecute" the firm because it would not favor his clients, the large shoe manufacturers of St. Louis. The editorial stated further that Brandeis had been responsible for "smashing the credit" of the New Haven and the Boston & Maine, which in turn led to inferior service and higher cost of transportation in New England. Then Barron's article turned from sweeping assertion of Brandeis' remarkable powers to insinuations of his crookedness:

> It is not necessary to uncover the grave of Patrick Lennox or reopen the Warren settlements to show the moral fiber of Louis D. Brandeis and his unfitness for the Supreme Bench. It is only necessary to point to the life insurance scandals where Mr. Brandeis appears first as a public agitator summoning the policy holders and next appears in defense of the life insurance company with its retainer in his pocket.

Mr. Brandeis may be keen of intellect on both sides of cases, public and private, but his record impeaches him on far higher grounds than those of intellectual ability.

Let any Senator at Washington, who thinks the nomination of Brandeis to the Supreme Bench one fit to be made, visit Boston for a day and learn how Brandeis has garnered his wealth.

No one tried to pin Barron down on the precise meaning of his rhetoric. After their sparring match with him, the Senators evidently hoped they could learn more from the men whose names he supplied. The subcommittee dismissed Barron and then adjourned, to meet again in five days.

The next day's newspapers brought word from Boston that a petition of protest against the appointment of Brandeis, signed by more than fifty prominent Massachusetts men, was on its way to Senator Lodge. On Lincoln's birthday Lodge inserted a copy of the message into the *Congressional Record,* then turned the document over to Chilton. The protest read:

> We, the undersigned citizens of Massachusetts, are opposed to the appointment of Louis D. Brandeis to the vacancy in the Supreme Court of the United States. An appointment to this Court should only be conferred upon a member of the legal profession whose general reputation is as good as his legal attainments are great.
>
> We do not believe that Mr. Brandeis has the judicial temperament and capacity which should be required in a judge of the Supreme Court. His reputation as a lawyer is such that he has not the confidence of the people.
>
> For these reasons we express the hope that the Senate will not confirm his appointment.

A. Lawrence Lowell, president of Harvard University, and Charles Francis Adams, lawyer, historian and Treasurer of the Harvard Corporation, were perhaps the most distinguished of the petitioners. Most of the rest, bearing impeccably old-Massachusetts English names like Sargent, Gardner, Grew, Peabody, Thorndike, Bowditch, Putnam, Shattuck, and Coolidge, were middle-aged or elderly bankers, lawyers, and company directors, each with his office in or near State Street, membership in the right clubs, and such forms of recreation as yachting and golf. These were the old grads of Harvard, superior in attitude and tightly knit in social outlook, whose families had known one another for a century or more. They owned much of the property in Massachusetts, and retained it by intermarrying their sons and daughters. To their way of thinking, they were "the people" whose confidence Brandeis did not have.

Edward H. Warren, a professor at the Harvard Law School, stood out from this list as an academic man. He alone of the law-school faculty opposed the Brandeis nomination, as the Boston *Post* had reported some days earlier. Before the University president's protest became known a law-school senior named Shelton Hale, campus correspondent for the *Post,* solicited the views of the eleven law-school faculty members on the nomination. Warren, a heavy-headed man with a thick neck and curly hair, quite understandably nicknamed Bull by his colleagues, merely told the reporter "I am sorry the appointment was made," but would say nothing more.

While one faculty member declined comment, nine professors expressed their approval of Brandeis' nomination and permitted Hale to quote them. Thus Professor Roscoe Pound, who quoted Burke on Lord Mansfield: "His ideas go to the growing melioration of the law by making its liberality keep pace with the demands of justice and the actual concerns of the world." Austin Scott, acting dean of the law school: "He is experienced, wise, constructive and has a passion for justice for all men. I think he is well fitted for the high position for which he has been selected." Arthur D. Hill, who had urged Senator Lodge not to oppose the nomination: "The appointment is an excellent one. Mr. Brandeis is both a great lawyer and a great idealist," qualities which can, Hill added, "make him a great judge." Professor Felix Frankfurter, who knew Brandeis well: "Mr. Brandeis' mind is at once luminous and creative, and a passion for justice is his dominating motive."

Acting Dean Scott, thirty-one, found himself in an embarrassing position when the Boston *Post* headline-writer made it appear that the law-school faculty had passed a formal resolution on behalf of the Brandeis nomination. Professor Roscoe Pound advised Scott to explain away the false impression to Lowell, whose distaste for Brandeis was common knowledge among the faculty. They all knew him, for Brandeis had served for many years on the Committee to Visit the Law School, by appointment of the Harvard Board of Overseers. Scott hastily assured the University head that there had been no official action by the law professors—just an expression of personal opinions. In reply, Lowell acknowledged that Harvard had room for disagreement:

> Individuals are fully at liberty to express the opinions they hold. I have personally recently written to Lodge to say that I think that Brandeis' reputation for character at the bar is such as to unfit him for a position on the Supreme Court.

Whatever unpleasantness Lowell may have anticipated from the law professors' rallying to Brandeis, he must have received a pleasurable glow in reading one note penned from a Philadelphia hotel on February 12:

> *Sir:*
> Your protest against the confirmation of Louis D. Brandeis as Supreme Court Justice will be most potent. It is so pleasing to me that I will celebrate the event by adding to my deed of trust thirty thousand dollars.
>
> *Respectfully yours,*
> HENRY ISAIAH DORR, M.D.

William Howard Taft also wrote Lowell, saying he was "delighted to see that you signed, with others, a protest against the Brandeis appointment." But as father of a recent graduate of the Harvard Law School (Robert Alphonso Taft, first man in the 1914 class), the former President shook his head in bewilderment over the Cambridge professors:

> I cannot understand the attitude of your law school faculty. Ezra Thayer * told me that the bar of Boston did not do justice to Brandeis, in that he thought he was sincere in his announced ideals, but that he said he was entirely without scruple in winning a case at the Bar. It seems to me that he has fooled your law professors into support of him, especially Pound, by becoming very enthusiastic over progress and development in the principles of the law.

While Dr. Dorr and Professor Taft congratulated President Lowell, Senators Chilton and Walsh were hearing from such men as Joseph Pelletier. With a public school and Catholic Boston College background and no corporate directorships or ancestral notes trailing in

* Ezra Thayer had died a few months before the nomination.

glory after his name, Pelletier wrote the Senators from a point of view somewhat different from that of Lowell and his friends. Few of the signers, Pelletier wrote, were known in Boston as being active trial members of the bar, few had had to struggle to attain success, and few were engaged in general practice of law. The signers were

> all estimable men, but almost without exception men of one class and one kind . . . far from representative of the Boston Bar, where we have all races and creeds, whose opinion is worth while and whose standing is beyond question and who are perhaps much nearer to the people than those in the list I have mentioned.
>
> I do not want to accuse anyone in particular but I think I express the notion of the majority of the people of Boston when I say that there is a feeling that the underlying opposition to Mr. Brandeis is more because he is a Jew than that he is unfit by reason of anything he has ever done.

When the subcommittee reconvened on February 15, Walsh took charge at once. Mr. Barron, Walsh reminded the group, had assured them that C. S. Mellen, the former president of the New Haven, could establish that Brandeis had been employed at one time to "wreck" the railroad. A subpoena was issued for Mellen, the Senator continued, in response to which Mellen had telegraphed the committee that he had "no information of any character" that would be of value to the committee, and asked to be excused. Walsh reported that he had wired back to Mellen, asking whether the railroad man had any information that would shed light on the truth or falsity of the charge against Brandeis. Mellen replied in a second telegram which Walsh read aloud:

> I AM ABSOLUTELY WITHOUT INFORMATION AS TO ANYTHING THAT I WOULD BE JUSTIFIED TO TESTIFY UNDER OATH. I THINK IT WOULD BE A WASTE OF COMMITTEE'S TIME AND MINE FOR ME TO GO TO WASHINGTON TO TESTIFY. I AM NOT AT ALL UNFRIENDLY TO BRANDEIS, AND I KNOW NOTHING ABOUT HIS CAREER EXCEPT HEARSAY.

Still, said Walsh, if anyone should want to insist that Mellen appear—. Under the circumstances, certainly not, said Republican Senator Clark. So much for Barron's first source of the truth about Louis D. Brandeis.

Hollis Russell Bailey, a Boston attorney who had known Brandeis and Sam Warren in their Harvard Law School days, took the stand

to explain "the Warren will case" at which Barron had hinted. For
nearly two hours the Senators played question-and-answer with the
witness as he led them through the intricacies of the Warren family
dispute over the paper-mill fortune left by the father of Brandeis' law
partner and classmate. The gist was that Sam's brother Edward had
been dissatisfied over the way Sam had managed things after resigning
from his law partnership with Brandeis to direct the Warren properties. Brandeis had been retained by the family to draw up a trusteeship arrangement on behalf of all members of the family. But Edward
Warren claimed that Brandeis had been favoring Sam's interests to
the detriment of the others. Brandeis said that he had tried to arrange
the trusteeship for the benefit of all concerned—Edward Warren and
the other relatives as well as Sam. He was not simply a protector of
Sam's interests vis-à-vis those of the other members of his family, as
Edward seemed to think.

Bailey, who had represented Edward Warren when the intrafamily
dispute broke out, claimed that Brandeis should not have tried to
represent the entire family. His advocacy should have been of only
one party in a family disagreement. Bailey told the committee: "If
there were conflicting interests he should have advised them to have
independent counsel."

Bailey conceded that after the death of the younger Sam Warren,
the entire matter had long ago been settled by consent in the Massachusetts courts.

"What is the general professional reputation of Mr. Brandeis?"
inquired Senator Clark.

> BAILEY: First, that he is a very able lawyer; that he is a man of keen
> intellect; that he is an able advocate; that he is not entirely
> trustworthy. I think that about covers it.

A bit later Walsh inquired: "When you speak about the general
reputation of Mr. Brandeis in Boston, are we to understand you express the universal sentiment of the bar of Boston?"

No, replied Bailey, he did not want to be understood that way,
because he did not think any reputation is ever universal. Bailey left
the stand having made it plain that he thought Brandeis had been
injudicious in trying too hard as an arranger for all the Warrens. His
words may have hinted so, but he never charged flatly that Brandeis

had been dishonest, or had lined his pockets improperly in connection
with the Warren affair.

A larger issue loomed when Sidney Winslow, president of the
United Shoe Machinery Company, came forward. His attack, which
he read at length, was a strong one.

> I believe that Mr. Brandeis, since he left our company has been
> guilty of unprofessional conduct and of conduct not becoming an
> honorable man. . . .
> Mr. Brandeis has, at the instance of new clients, attacked as illegal
> and criminal the very acts and system of business in which he par-
> ticipated, which he assisted to create, and which he advised were
> legal, and he has persistently sought to injure our business. In so
> doing, his knowledge of our leases and business, acquired while act-
> ing as our director and counsel, has naturally been of value. . . .
> An honorable man, when acting for other clients, would, under
> these circumstances, have been scrupulously careful that any state-
> ments made by him were truthful. Mr. Brandeis, however, has made
> false and misleading statements as to our acts and business. . . .
> The lease system which he has attacked is the same lease system
> which he previously approved of so heartily. . . .

The heart of Winslow's complaint was that Brandeis, after helping
organize the company and direct it for eight years, had changed sides.
In doing so, Winslow thought, he unfairly aided both the government
officials prosecuting United under the antitrust laws and the St. Louis
shoe manufacturers who were challenging the company's tying-clause
lease system. A gentleman, Winslow believed, did not take an insider's
look and then go out and tell.

During the five hours Winslow held the witness chair the dialogue
ranged widely, from fine points on who was in what hotel room when
company policy was discussed to broad matters of government and
company policy. Page after page of documents were inserted into the
record, some from United Shoe Machinery Company proceedings in
the courts, others from company files, still others from the hearings
before the House Interstate Commerce Committee that resulted in
the Clayton Antitrust Act. Brandeis' statements as to the series of
events over several years that led him to change his view of the legality
of the tying clause were included among the mass of documents, but

they were buried. Winslow went on with his testimony as if Brandeis had never explained his views. The point he wanted to make was that the lawyer had been untrue to his old client—Winslow played it over and over like a gramophone record with a stuck needle.

On February 16, new faces appeared on the scene, which by now had been shifted from the dark, crowded room in the Capitol to more spacious quarters in the Senate Office Building. Most important-looking was Austen George Fox, a tall man of sixty-six with a fine reputation in New York as an appeals attorney. He was in Washington, as Senator Fletcher announced in the absence of Chilton, "at the request of and under employment by certain of those who oppose the confirmation of Mr. Brandeis. He suggests that he could arrange the testimony in an orderly way and see to the presentation of the facts supporting the opposition to the confirmation. The committee are willing to have that done in the interest of economy of time." The Committee would ask Mr. Fox, Fletcher added, to file a list of those employing him. It would be a pleasure to do so as soon as convenient, said Fox.

Thus the word was out officially now that those who were fighting the confirmation of Brandeis had hired a high-priced attorney to act as their Washington lobbyist. Never before in American history had a President's nomination of anyone to any office provoked this kind of resistance.

Fox was a Harvard Law School man, energetic, intelligent, active in the law-school association, a member of the Century, City, and Harvard clubs in New York. His office was on Wall Street. Involved in his younger days in committees dedicated to cleaning up corruption in municipal politics, he had run unsuccessfully for district attorney, and thereafter declined political offers. He was by temperament a one-man operator who eschewed trial work to concentrate on appeals briefs and argument before the appellate courts. Fox lived well in his town house at 39th Street and Park Avenue, amid an atmosphere of mahogany and fine silver. His vacations lasted from June to October; his favorite sports were golf at St. Andrews and ice curling, according to the season. Socially and intellectually Fox was at home among the kind of men who in Boston had signed the protest with President Lowell.

On the sixteenth Fletcher also announced the appointment to the

committee staff of George Anderson, an old colleague of Brandeis
in a number of civic campaigns, including that against the New Haven
Railroad's absorption of the Boston & Maine. Fletcher explained
that Anderson's role was "to act for the committee in seeing that the
other side is presented, to the end that the truth may be presented."

From the second day after the nomination it had been clear that
a serious campaign would be waged against Brandeis and that the
Senators would be showered with allegations of his misconduct in
legal matters fought out long ago. What strategy should the administration take to straighten out the distorted picture that the enemies
of Brandeis would hold up? It was finally decided in conferences between Attorney General Gregory, Brandeis' law partners, the nominee
himself, and Norman Hapgood, journalist confidant of both the President and Brandeis, that it would not be wise to summon the prospective Supreme Court member to answer and explain away the accusations. Such a procedure might make the hearings smack too much of
a morals trial. Nor would it be good tactics to have a "Brandeis defender" act in the nominee's behalf; the appearance would still be that
of a trial.

George Anderson, at present the federal district attorney in Brandeis' own city, was therefore given the stature of a committee chief
of staff, assigned to bring out facts to assist the committee members.
And even though every party to the proceedings recognized that
Anderson was in effect the advocate of Brandeis' side of the case,
his pose as a developer of "facts" for the Senators was maintained,
with only limited critical comment from Fox, to the end of the hearings. Introduced by Senator Fletcher, Anderson explained his role
like a character from a medieval morality play:

> I am at the service of the committee. I act under the request of
> the committee, and desire to be explicitly understood that I do not
> appear for Mr. Brandeis or for the friends of Mr. Brandeis, but
> simply to assist the committee by presenting such facts as I have
> knowledge of as a Boston man.

Then, at the invitation of Senator Fletcher, Anderson undertook
a cross-examination of Winslow. Anderson brought out his belief
that the United Shoe Machinery Company was partly responsible for
the undermining of Brandeis' reputation among the Boston bar,
because the company had circulated its own pamphlet attack on him

in 1913. Brandeis had annoyed the United officials because he cited the shoe-machinery company frequently in his testimony before congressional committees preparing the antitrust law that culminated in the Clayton Act. Senator Cummins recalled how deeply Brandeis had impressed him as an antitrust expert at that time:

> He gave a great performance when he talked—the most comprehensive review of the subject which I have ever known, in the course of which he illustrated some of his views by reference to the United Shoe Machinery Company.

Winslow interjected several times that he had not come to Washington in a spirit of vindictiveness against Brandeis—that the committee had asked him to appear, and that he wanted to recite nothing but facts. Yet he seemed to go round in a continuous circle of annoyance that the company lost its best lawyer to the opposition.

A new Senator was at the committee table when hearings resumed the next day. Senator Clark had withdrawn from the Republican side; in his place was John Downey Works, a sixty-eight-year-old lawyer from Los Angeles. Works had made something of a name for himself as an author of legal textbooks; in politics he was known as a reformer. He was rounding out his first term in the Senate, having been elected by the legislature in 1910 as a Progressive Republican. Works was the comfortable-looking type, his smooth-shaven face and silken hair, the rimless glasses and starched collar giving him the air of a benign preacher—except that the firmly inverted curve of the mouth added more than a touch of self-righteousness to the total effect. Like Cummins, he kept one foot in the Progressive camp and had worked closely with La Follette in the Senate. In California, where the voters had a habit of ignoring party labels more than in any other state, Works knew that a politician was a fool to mark himself indelibly as a party man. On the surface, therefore, it appeared that Senator Works might look at Brandeis in a reasonably friendly way.

Edward McClennen, a junior member of Brandeis' law firm, had by this time moved to Washington for the duration. His assignment was to act as liaison man between Brandeis in Boston and his friendly board of strategy in the capital. He was invaluable in supplying Anderson information from the law-firm files, or from his own experience, to counter the accusations of Brandeis' defamers. On the other side was Kenneth Spence, a doggedly determined younger lawyer from New York acting as assistant to Fox. Spence, having introduced himself as the associate of Fox, enjoyed official status before the committee with authority to intervene directly in the hearings. McClennen, however, would speak only when called upon.

Moorfield Storey, a highly respected member of the Boston bar, came to the witness chair on February 17. A historian, Harvard Overseer, once secretary to the great Senator Charles Sumner, and president of the American Bar Association in 1896, Storey at seventy was a man whose opinion weighed heavily. He sparred with the committee briefly, maintaining he did not know why he had been called to Washington. Told that he had been named by Clarence Barron as one who could give prime evidence of Brandeis' unfitness for the Associate Justiceship, Storey said yes, he believed that Brandeis had been retained to "wreck" the New England railroad in the Nineties; no, Brandeis had not been honest in stating exactly whom he represented in his probe of the New Haven; Brandeis had, indeed, dissembled when he claimed to be representing Glavis at the Ballinger investigation when his real client was *Collier's Weekly*. Storey skipped from one issue to another deftly. Walsh wanted to know whether Storey backed up Barron's view "that Mr. Brandeis was employed to wreck the New Haven Railroad."

> STOREY: No. The only other fact I know in connection with this matter is, I believe that I should say to you gentlemen that my name will appear as a remonstrant against his confirmation, and that the reason I did it was because of his reputation at our bar as a lawyer.
>
> WORKS: What is that reputation?
>
> STOREY: . . . that of a man who is an able lawyer, very energetic, ruthless in the attainment of his objectives, not scrupulous in the methods he adopts, and not to be trusted.

Under questioning Storey revealed that in forty years of legal practice he had only been "engaged against Mr. Brandeis in three or four matters." He added: "I have never had any personal quarrel with Mr. Brandeis at all or any difficulty at all. Our public activities or interests have been on different lines." They moved in quite different worlds, legally as well as socially, it seemed. Storey denied a suggestion from Walsh that derogation of Brandeis in Boston may have been inspired by New Haven Railroad people with unusual power in the community. Brandeis had had a bad reputation for many years, Storey said. Since this entire controversy had come up, "I have taken pains to go around and ask a great variety of lawyers the same question that I have been asked here. I found their opinions agree with my own." Would he give some names? Storey declined "to drag them into the controversy. I told them what they said to me would be received in confidence."

Walsh asked the witness to tell the committee a little about the signatories to the Boston protest sent recently to Lodge and spread through the press. Name by name Storey obliged, perhaps without realizing how clearly he was showing the group as a tight little circle from the propertied class. Three of the signers were law partners. Richard Storey was the witness' own son. Mr. Donald represented the United Shoe Machinery Company; Mr. Storrow used to, but had moved over to Lee, Higginson & Company. Others were big men in the world of banking, real estate, mills and factories—most of them wearing the Harvard tie. Storey obviously knew more than he was willing to tell about exactly who drafted the Boston statement and who collected the names. To him the fifty-odd signers were "representative" men in a Boston bar numbering in the thousands.

In one way the appearance of Moorfield Storey was of value to the partisans of Brandeis, in that his testimony refuted that given by Bailey about the Warren will case. "I should have done perhaps very much as Mr. Brandeis did if I had been in his place," said Storey.

> It would have been a matter of caution, however, to have independent counsel, but apparently the family united. . . . There was nothing in the relations between the different members of the family to suggest that there was any divergence of interests, or any reason why they should not act harmoniously, as they did. . . . If I had been in Mr. Brandeis' shoes when that situation came up, I think I would have taken the same course.

How did Mr. Storey, who had served as an Overseer of Harvard for many years, explain the attitude of the law-school faculty favorable to Brandeis' confirmation for the Supreme Court? Senator Walsh wanted to know.

STOREY: Mr. Pound, one of the professors, came here only a few years ago from one of the Dakotas, I think. Mr. Frankfurter is

a young man who came from New York. I think they are not
familiar with the reputation which prevails among the practicing lawyers of Boston. He has always been very courteous
to the school. Mr. Brandeis is an attractive person and he has
been interested in the law school and has helped it, and I fancy
he enjoys the confidence of those professors.

Before Storey quit the witness chair Anderson threw several questions to him in the "Is it not?" and "Did he not?" form, to establish
these facts: that the late Ezra Thayer, dean of the Harvard Law
School, had previously been a partner in Storey's own law firm, and
before that he had beeen employed by Brandeis; that Brandeis had
long been a member of the law-school visiting committee and served
as a trustee; that Harvard had awarded Brandeis an honorary A.M.
degree in 1891 and a membership in Phi Beta Kappa in 1904. Yes,
Storey conceded, all this could be so.

Sherman Whipple, a Boston lawyer for thirty years, active like
Storey in trial work, came to the stand in rebuttal to Bailey. He was
appearing at the committee's request, he said under Anderson's questioning—not at the behest of Brandeis or his friends. Bailey had
been substantially right, Whipple began, in his recital of the facts
of the Warren will matter; but he did not agree that Brandeis had
intentionally framed the Warren property lease so as to favor his
friend Sam over the other members of the Warren family. The witness
ought to know, Anderson brought out, because Whipple was trial
counsel in the case of Bailey's side. None of the Senators questioned
Whipple on his disagreement with Bailey.

Turning now to the "Lennox Bankruptcy case," one of the matters
listed by Barron as deserving scrutiny, the subcommittee was led
through the intricate and tangled affairs of Patrick Lennox, a bankrupt tannery owner, and his son James Lennox. They involved a
bankruptcy agreement under which the assets of the elder Lennox
were put in the hands of a trustee to insure that all creditors would
be paid as much as possible on an equal basis. In this, as in the
Warren will matter, Sherman Whipple had been professionally involved. And though Barron had claimed that in this Lennox case, as
in the Warren affair, a recital of the facts by the men who knew them
would "show the moral fibre of Brandeis and his unfitness for the
Supreme Bench," Whipple did no such thing.

Upon being consulted in 1907 by old Mr. Lennox over his business difficulties, Brandeis had suggested that Edward McClennen, partner in his Boston law firm, be made trustee to protect the interests of everyone involved—including the company employees, the younger Lennox, and the firm's creditors. James Lennox later complained that he was being given short shrift and blamed Brandeis for having deserted his interests as son and heir in favor of those of the creditors. In essence, the situation was just like that in the Warren will affair, with Brandeis maintaining a neutral position of guarding the interests of all parties to the situation. However, Whipple said, Brandeis made a mistake in not making his position perfectly clear to James Lennox:

> I think it is a matter of taste, and I felt then, and I think now, that Mr. Brandeis erred, before I got his point of view. He said: "The paramount duty is to continue the task that I have assumed of seeing to an equitable distribution of this large estate." . . .
>
> He was in love, so to speak, with this idea of looking after everybody concerned and guiding the situation: or, to put it from his own point of view, I asked him, "Whom do you think you were counsel for when Mr. Lennox brought this great estate into your office?" He said he was counsel "for the situation."
>
> He was sincere about it, and it illustrates, to my mind, why you have heard about Mr. Brandeis from the Boston bar some things that you have heard. I think they have misunderstood him. That is my personal opinion, and I think if Mr. Brandeis had been a different sort of man, not so aloof, not so isolated, with more of the camaraderie of the bar, gave his confidence to more men, and took their confidence, said to them when he was charged with anything that was doubtful, "Boys, what do you think about it?"—and talked it over with them, you would not have heard the things you have heard in regard to him.
>
> But Mr. Brandeis is aloof; he is intensely centered in carrying out his own ideas and his own ideals, which I believe are pure, which I believe are high-minded, and he does not, so far as I know, consult with anybody or take them into his confidence, and he will do things of a startling character. Nothing could illustrate this better than this Lennox matter.

Senators asked Whipple about the Boston protestants. He replied: "They are, all of them, very high-minded men. I do not think they are all of them very liberal or progressive men. I think they are conservative, and anyone that threatens or menaces the traditions which they revere, they think is an iconoclast." Brandeis and these men "simply cannot understand each other—they are all too proud to try. . . ."

> WALSH: I want to ask, if I may, to what extent they labor under the invidious influence of their environment?

> WHIPPLE: Consciously, not at all; unconsciously to an extent which I am not able to determine. They breathe the atmosphere of opposition to Mr. Brandeis. As I have said, in my judgment they do not understand him; they do not approve his ideas. They conceive it to be distasteful, but nevertheless a public duty, to prevent his appointment to the Supreme Bench of the United States, where they think his ideas will be harmful to our national interests. I, on the other hand, and a great many others think that just those ideas will be helpful.

Fox, who had been absent in New York for two days, was present when Chilton rapped for order the next morning. He offered the chairman a list of sixty-one names "of the persons at whose request and on whose behalf I am here." A half-dozen had been added since the original Boston protest was made public. A subcommittee of five signers of the remonstrance were retaining him directly on behalf of the larger group. These men, Fox said, included Charles Francis Adams (treasurer of the Harvard Corporation, director of a dozen companies); James D. Colt (lawyer and corporation director); Charles Rackemann, John Noble, and Roger Warner. Senator Walsh commented that Fox did not appear to be very well acquainted with the men who had retained him; he knew a fair number of them personally because they were mainly Harvard men, Fox replied.

The one witness of the morning was Dr. Patrick Lennox, Professor of English at the Catholic University of America. He had been called because Barron had told the committee that Dr. Lennox could give detailed testimony on the bankruptcy case involving his uncle. But, the witness protested, he knew nothing at all about Brandeis, and had never seen him in his life. Chilton dismissed Dr. Lennox a minute later with thanks. Another Barron witness had produced considerably less than advertised.

By the end of the third week in February, the original shock of the Brandeis nomination had subsided and other matters filled the front pages. Yet as the hearings proceeded, those close to the scene let it be known to their friends that the confirmation battle was settling down, like the war in Europe, to a long struggle from entrenched positions. The events of any one day were to be viewed as a limited part of a broader conflict that would move to decision only after a long period of attrition. The opponents of Brandeis were playing for time.

On February 18 Samuel Gompers, president of the American Federation of Labor, was asked by a Boston *Post* reporter for his opinion of the Brandeis nomination. Few of Gompers' associates and few people in the White House knew that Wilson had secretly sounded out the AFL leader for his opinion before offering the Court seat to Brandeis. How did Brandeis stand with Gompers, the President wanted to know. By implication, Wilson was asking whether labor would support him in nominating a man who had argued in favor of the incorporation of trade unions in public debate against Gompers himself. Perhaps the President was also testing how much support the nomination would win from American Jews, since Gompers was acutely conscious of being a Jewish spokesman for a labor movement made up largely of gentiles. Gompers had sent word back without equivocation: Brandeis is the right man for the Supreme Court.

> It is astounding and discouraging [Gompers told the *Post* reporter] the length to which some men have gone in the effort to defeat the confirmation of Honorable Louis D. Brandeis for an Associate Justiceship of the United States Supreme Court. I have kept myself fully informed as to the character of the testimony against his confirmation, and it discloses the fact that it is prompted by either greed or prejudice, and has no real foundation in fact. . . . In the confirmation of Mr. Brandeis . . . the country will be benefited and the Court receive a splendid acquisition.

Brandeis himself remained in Boston, where he went to his law office every day but otherwise withdrew from public activity pending the outcome of the nomination contest. As the weeks passed, his mail brought him one expression after another of good will from people he had never met, as well as from old friends. A letter from the Phi Epsilon Pi fraternity at Dickinson College, for instance, revealed that Jewish college students now looked to Brandeis as a symbol of their ideals and hopes:

> We feel as fellow men and as brothers of the same faith that your elevation was well merited judging from your past deeds. . . . We

have also read with regret of the malignant attacks upon you in regard to your religion; and there being a bond of sympathy between us in this respect, we feel desirous of having your consent as an honorary member of our chapter.

Louis Brandeis Wehle, the nominee's nephew, wrote from Louisville:

. . . You may imagine how constantly you are in my thoughts during these days. You are being subjected to attacks that give you strength in many quarters where you hadn't it before; and your friends are more devoted than ever. . . . Your attitude while the wolves yelp is sublime.

To some of his correspondents Brandeis expressed a relish for the battle, at least in its opening stages. Former Governor Robert Perkins Bass of New Hampshire, a Theodore Roosevelt Progressive and old colleague of Brandeis in antitrust and conservation causes, sent his congratulations to the Supreme Court nominee. "What a commotion the President has started!" Brandeis replied gaily to Bass in mid-February, as Fox, Storey, and Whipple were having at one another's opinions of him in the Washington hearing room. Publicly, however, Brandeis stayed discreetly silent.

Three days of hearings in the third week passed with no major breakthrough by either side. It was a warfare of attack and counterthrust, of charge and rebuttal, witness against the nominee followed by counterwitness—in deep and confusing detail, much of it only vaguely relevant to the fitness of the nominee, through which subcommittee members were compelled to wade by the hundreds of pages as the record piled up. Newspaper reports of the hearings became shorter and less prominent as it became obvious that "the Brandeis case," as the press called it, would go on and on. Until the "case" should go to the jury of Senators, other issues now seemed more important: the great German offensive at Verdun by an estimated 300,000 troops; the sudden resignation of Secretary of War Lindley M. Garrison over a disagreement with the President on preparedness policy; and Wilson's announcement that he would permit his name to be entered in the Ohio primary election, which meant he would run for re-election.

On February 24, the Senators spent an hour questioning Mark Sullivan, editor of *Collier's Weekly* for the past two years since Norman Hapgood had left the post and moved to *Harper's Weekly*.

Fox had asked that Sullivan be called in order to pin down the charge that Brandeis had been secretly retained by the magazine as its attorney in the 1910 Ballinger investigation. He hoped to prove, first, that Brandeis had been well paid for his services to the magazine which had carried the article critical of President Taft's Secretary of the Interior and, second, that Brandeis had somehow concealed his having been retained by the publication and masqueraded as merely the lawyer for Glavis, who had written the article. Senator Walsh immediately spoke up to object that the whole matter was irrelevant. Republican Works countered: we must hear the evidence in order to know if it is relevant or not. Chairman Chilton sided with Works, and told the witness to go ahead with his testimony.

"Everybody" knew Brandeis was acting for the magazine at the time of the investigation, Sullivan protested. Hapgood was the editor then, and had correspondence with Brandeis about it. Works asked for any extant Hapgood–Brandeis correspondence for the hearing record. Senator Fletcher broke his characteristic silence:

> I suggest, Mr. Chairman, that it is most extraordinary and unusual and surprising to call for confidential communications between attorney and client, regarded by every court in every jurisdiction in every civilized country as privileged communications.

At Fletcher's protest, Works hesitated to press the point. Sullivan, apparently not wishing to appear secretive, handed a sheaf of papers to Chilton, saying as he did so that he would like to consult a lawyer.

WORKS: The witness may have that right, of course.

CHILTON: Do you mean before we look at them?

SULLIVAN: I think so.

WALSH: I should think that we should exclude them without looking at them.

Chilton hesitated, then handed the unopened papers back to Sullivan. Walsh turned to Fox and asked him pointedly his opinion on demanding communications between client and attorney. Fox tried to appear on both sides: in general, he supposed it was not the thing to do. But on the other hand, if "the gentleman who is now nominated for this high position, suppressed his connection with a very powerful interest, that would be an important question." Besides, Fox asked rhetorically, what, after all, is a confidential communication? Walsh kept right after Fox, until finally the lobbyist acknowledged:

"On the face of it, if I were sitting in judgment, I should say that, prima facie, they were privileged communications and that no committee or court ought to require them." But he could not resist adding: "Whether, as a matter of fact, they ought to be required I know not."

"It does you credit, Mr. Fox," said Walsh tartly, "to admit there is a public policy involved in the matter."

The hearing then switched to a quite different concern—the part played by Brandeis in the 1907 proxy fight for control of the Illinois Central Railroad. This struggle had pitted one group of directors, of which the late Edward H. Harriman had been the strong man, against another group led by Stuyvesant Fish. The witness on this matter was Waddill Catchings of New York, formerly a lawyer in the offices of Sullivan & Cromwell, a leading corporate law firm. Catchings appeared in answer to a subpoena requested by Fox, who took pains to bring out the fact that he and Catchings had not had a rehearsal interrogation before the hearing.

When he had been with Sullivan & Cromwell, Fox asked, had Catchings not sought the services of Brandeis on behalf of the late Edward Harriman, who was out to extend his railroad empire? The implication again was that Brandeis was operating covertly for a client he would not acknowledge, and that he was lining his pockets richly in the process. Yes, Catchings testified, he went to Boston to ask Brandeis if his firm would undertake the proxy solicitation. But Sullivan & Cromwell, he said, were acting for a committee of directors, not for Mr. Harriman personally. Catchings said he had been warned that the Boston firm would not accept "unless Mr. Brandeis were convinced of the justness of our position. . . . I accordingly had to lay the situation before Mr. Brandeis, and I may say that the hardest interview I had during the whole campaign was with Mr. Brandeis in convincing him of the justness of our cause, so to speak."

Fox felt his witness slipping through his fingers. Catchings was not giving the kind of testimony he had been led to expect. The man must be biased in favor of Brandeis, of course.

Fox: You are a personal friend of Mr. Brandeis?

Catchings: I am not, sir.

Fox: I thought you were.

CATCHINGS: I have never conversed with him on more than half a
dozen occasions.

Fox: So far as your personal relations have gone, they might be
fairly described as friendly?

CATCHINGS: They would be described as a friendly acquaintance, but
only a distant acquaintance.

Fox persisted: "Distant but friendly?" Catchings brought the cat-
and-mouse game to an end by conceding—yes, distant but friendly.

By the time Catchings was dismissed, it had been brought out that
Brandeis, Dunbar & Nutter took on the proxy solicitation in New
England as a normal piece of legal business—not because Brandeis
was secretly trying to assist Harriman in his drive to merge all the
railroads in the United States into one mighty transportation com-
bine. Brandeis was in no way double-dealing his associates in the
fight to retain competition in New England transportation, Catchings
asserted.

Fox still would not let go. He would like to find out from Mr. Alfred
Jaretzki of Sullivan & Cromwell how much of Brandeis' fee came
personally from Harriman. Jaretzki and he were good friends, Fox
added; he would telephone him to find "what the situation is and
what the facts are that he knows, if anything, and if I find anything
I will let you know and ask him to come; otherwise, I am quite content to let it rest. That is the best I can do." The Senators made no
comment.

The hearing next was thrown for two hours into utter confusion
by a recital of the so-called Gillette Safety Razor Company case of
1906, at which Barron's publication had hinted. It turned out to be
one more instance of the falling out of directors in disagreement over
reorganizing a company. Again the witnesses Fox had summoned
proved less than sensational in the production of testimony damaging
to Brandeis. They had opposed him in litigation, the points of con-
tention had long since been settled, and the witnesses would not
oblige Fox with any kind of statement that Brandeis was unethical
or dishonest.

A glimmer of hope that Fox and his backers might eventually
terminate their case lighted the day's record. When Fox asked one
witness to state what he thought Brandeis' reputation to be "as far

as personal qualities are concerned," Anderson interrupted. He had a number of applicants to testify on the other side, Anderson said, and if there were to be any balance at all in the hearings, this kind of testimony could stretch out to most expensive lengths. Senators Cummins and Walsh agreed there should be a limit to the number of character witnesses against Brandeis that Fox might present from this point on. Courts hold it down to six in Iowa, volunteered Cummins. Walsh thought five would be enough. Fox had already presented Bailey and Storey, so Chilton said he would be held to five—not making it clear whether this meant five more or five all told.

On Friday, February 25, Mark Sullivan returned briefly to the witness chair to state that Brandeis was paid $25,000 by *Collier's Weekly* for his services in the 1910 Ballinger investigation which ended the public career of Taft's Secretary of the Interior. Did Mr. Fox have any questions, Senator Chilton asked. No, said Fox. Exit Sullivan. There followed Judge William J. Kelly, member of the Supreme Court of New York, who flatly contradicted Barron's charge that Brandeis had been hired "to wreck the New England Railroad" in a stockholder's suit in the early 1890s:

> JUDGE KELLY: Senator, he was not employed to wreck the New England Railroad at all. . . . The reason he was employed was to show that the New England Railroad was wrecked at that time and to prevent the further distribution of the corporate assets among certain of the directors, sir. That was the object. . . . It was wrecked already, sir—badly wrecked; there is no dispute about that. These things are all of record in the court.

> ANDERSON: You mean it had already been wrecked by these directors for whom Mr. Storey appeared?

> JUDGE KELLY: That was the charge, sir, which was made at the time.

Fox was taken aback when Chilton announced the Senators would sit on Saturday; there was testimony that he wanted to seek out and prepare in New York over the week end. Several times Fox had indicated his disadvantage at not having had time to prepare testimony with his witnesses. Anderson asked whether the committee might be favored with the names of the further witnesses Fox intended to call.

He had a Mr. Youngman here now, said Fox, to speak on the

Warren will case. But he would need time to go over testimony with him. There were also other "cases" to discuss. Further, he hoped that the committee recalled it had allowed him "four more witnesses as to the fact of the reputation of Mr. Brandeis at the Suffolk bar." Two have been heard out of five, Anderson protested; that leaves only three! The number had been left hanging between five and six *in toto,* said Fox. Walsh declared that the record clearly shows a total of five were to be permitted. Chilton did not recall how many had been examined, but he thought the total was to be five. Fox retreated from the dispute, accepting five. Then William Youngman, the waiting and unrehearsed witness, spoke up:

> I am perfectly willing to confer with Mr. Anderson. I came here as the committee's witness, and not on either side. There may be some things I have to say that are favorable to his client. I sought him this morning as soon as I arrived.

Fox was amazed at the frank way the witness he had hoped to use was turning toward Anderson and "his client," Brandeis.

"You sought Mr. Anderson, Mr. Youngman?" spluttered Fox. "Yes, sir," said Youngman. At this point Chilton gaveled the hearing into recess.

First witness the next morning was Norman Hapgood, close friend of Brandeis who had hired him to defend Glavis and *Collier's Weekly* in the 1910 Congressional probe loaded in Secretary Ballinger's favor. There was no concealment of Brandeis' role at the investigation, Hapgood said; in fact, the magazine had published an editorial stating that the magazine had retained him. It was not possible to separate the man who wrote the article, Glavis, from the cause of conservation for which the writer and the publication stood. There was nothing hidden about the *Collier's*–Brandeis relationship from beginning to end, Hapgood stated.

Four long and confusing Saturday hours were then spent in the interrogation of William Youngman of Boston, whom Barron had mentioned as a source of inside information on the Warren will case. Youngman proved to be a better witness for Fox than he had indicated the day before. He had been attorney for Edward Warren, the family member dissatisfied with the way Sam had been running the Warren paper mills under the legal arrangement that Sam had worked out with Brandeis and the others had accepted. The gist of Young-

man's complaint against Brandeis was that "he is on record as producing a sort of chloroform in the form of a legal opinion that put
Mr. Warren's brains and conscience to sleep in equity, in this whole
thing." Sam and Brandeis had taken more money than was fair from
the firm, Youngman said, though he declined to charge either man
with fraud.

> ANDERSON: Then I understand you to mean that you directly charge
> that when the plan was laid out back in 1899, Mr. Warren had
> doubts of its ethical quality, and Mr. Brandeis chloroformed
> him out of these doubts; is that a fair statement?

> YOUNGMAN: No; I object to the emphasis on the *chloroformed.* I
> only used that word to indicate my high regard for Sam War-
> ren's sense of honor and to indicate that Sam Warren had to be
> persuaded, and he was persuaded by Louis D. Brandeis. . . .

> ANDERSON: Then it was this: Sam Warren was a man of a high
> sense of honor, and this plan laid out for the family and con-
> sented to by the family was one which his natural sense of
> honor rejected, but he was persuaded into it by the dishonor-
> able Brandeis?

> YOUNGMAN: That is such an argumentative question I do not think
> I should be required to answer it. I am here to testify to facts.

Chilton tried hard for a concession by Youngman that the Warren will matter might be viewed differently by perfectly honorable
men, like Whipple and himself. After all, had not Youngman and
Whipple been associated in the case? And had not Whipple told the
committee that he found no fault in Brandeis' handling of the Warren
matter so far as ethics were concerned? Youngman would make no
such concession. There was nothing but hard facts in the case, he
insisted. Opinions were beside the point. To him it was incontestable
that Sam Warren was fooled into agreeing to "a scheme that would
give him unreasonable compensation." Youngman's client, Ned Warren, had been short-changed. Brandeis, Youngman's legal opponent,
had master-minded the scheme.

Following Youngman's testimony, ninety pages of Warren will case
documents were added to the hearing record, for the information of
those who would eventually sit in judgment on the prospective justice.
The nomination was now a full month old and stuck in a political
morass.

six

A Lawyer's Reputation

Dear Cabot . . .

I am feeling very blue and distressed over the Brandeis nomination. I understand that the financing of the Democratic national campaign will be assured if he is confirmed, and I suppose he probably will be, but it will be a deplorable injury to the Court, for the man is intellectually acute and morally blind. He has no moral sense.

Elihu Root, elder gray eagle of the Republican Party, appended these somber thoughts to a long letter to his old Senate colleague, Henry Cabot Lodge, shortly after the Brandeis hearings got under way. The Jewish merchants, Root felt sure, were hopelessly Democrats.

Renowned for the keen, analytical turn of mind that had brought him success and wealth through corporation law, Root had long been a dominating influence among Republican leaders, who sought his counsel. He was out of public office now, after sixteen years in the national spotlight as Secretary of War under Presidents McKinley and Roosevelt, T.R.'s Secretary of State, then a United States Senator from New York for a six-year term. Root and Brandeis had clashed bitterly during the Ballinger investigation of 1910. What made the memory especially painful to Root was that the Bostonian had won the plaudits of the crowd for having been on the morally "right" side —and Root cherished his own moral righteousness like fine gold. Against his better judgment, Senator Root had given in to the appeals of his colleagues and served on the investigating committee when he had known that the only wise course was to throw Ballinger to the wolves. In the end, Brandeis had tarred Ballinger and his Senate defenders with the same brush. For that Root could never forgive him.

At the bar Elihu Root was a lawyer's lawyer, honored by his peers this year with the presidency of the American Bar Association. He was respected by many, but loved by very few. Shrewd, cold, endowed with a citric tongue, Root had none of the magnetic personal appeal that caused the masses to follow a William Jennings Bryan or a Teddy Roosevelt. His close-cropped gray hair, brushed severely down all around from the crown of his head, the stony face with its pointed nose, and eyes like a bird of prey gave him the appearance of an ascetic—a monk, perhaps, or a Senator of ancient Rome who lived on a diet of dried figs as he planned the death of a Caesar.

Root saw eye to eye with Henry Cabot Lodge on the issues confronting responsible men in public life, and the Senate had been a somewhat lonely place for the Massachusetts man since Root left Washington early in 1915. As Lodge wrote his erstwhile colleague, the prospect was indeed sad:

> They mean to confirm Brandeis as a party matter. Charges, which have been proved by the records, have been laid before the committee, which ought to prevent any such man from having a place on any bench. Brandeis is an able man but his professional record is very bad, as I look at it, and I think it will be proved up to the hilt; but I do not expect any result from it. Of course the failure of any bar association to make any protest or any resistance, or to send anyone here to present charges as they ought to be presented, makes it much easier for the Democrats to confirm him.

Lodge seemed to have no doubts about the "proofs" of Brandeis' unfitness, even though he had declined to furnish them when asked by Arthur Hill, his friend and personal attorney in Boston. Hill, after all, was a much younger man, without the maturity of judgment of a constituent like John Torrey Morse, who was now seventy-six and had practiced law before Hill was born. Morse wrote Lodge that he assumed every mail brought the Senator protests against Brandeis like his own:

> . . . because I have not yet happened to meet anyone who is his friend. I knew him some twenty-five years ago, when the influence

of Sam Warren got him into the Dedham Polo Club. It was a club of gentlemen, and Brandeis was soon conspicuously left to "flock by himself," with the result that he ceased to frequent the club and his absence was not regretted. . . .

Is it not an extraordinary spectacle that is before the country? A candidate for the Supreme Court on trial, to determine whether or not he is a dishonorable, tainted knave—or rather, not whether he *is* such, but whether he can be formally *convicted* and *proved* to be such; with the understanding that, in the absence of such proof as would call for a condemnation in a jury trial, he is to receive the position! ! Of course he has been clever enough to cover his tracks, and I look to see his vile face, grinning hypocrisy over his judicial gown. . . . I shall despair of the republic, if he gets the place. *Don't let him! ! !*

Lodge continued to receive pleas from both sides. His nephew Ellerton James sent testimony in favor of Brandeis couched in terms that James thought might appeal to the older man. Writing as a close colleague of Brandeis in the Public Franchise League during the fight for control of the Washington Street subway line, James tried to assure his uncle on the score of Brandeis' professional ethics:

In the main his ideas of right and wrong are those of the rest of us but he is a Hebrew and, therefore, of Oriental race and his mind is an Oriental mind, and I think it very probable that some of his ideas of what were fair might not be the same as those of a man possessing an Anglo-Saxon mind.

But the nephew persisted, the man was honest:

I think he would not hesitate for one moment to refuse to act longer as counsel in any case where he became convinced that his client's cause was not just. . . . Contrary to the usual ideas of Jews I do not think the almighty dollar is very attractive to him.

As he had done frequently with others, Senator Lodge assured his nephew that the Senate was free of prejudice:

Not the slightest objection has been made to Mr. Brandeis on account of his race. I have not heard that mentioned here. The only allusions to his race that I have seen have been made by some of his supporters with a view of aiding him and casting odium on those who oppose him.

It had been argued, Uncle Cabot's written lecture to Nephew Ellerton continued, that Brandeis was nominated because it was known in advance how he would rule in a certain class of cases. This was certainly an improper ground on which to name a Justice. Brandeis was said to have rendered public service, but Lodge had rendered much of that sort of service himself. This was common enough. Further, it was hypocritical to announce that one was appearing on behalf of the public, then to take a large fee for doing it. And that, Lodge wrote his nephew, was what Brandeis had done in the Ballinger investigation, which brought him a fee of $25,000. The one point on which the confirmation hung was the nominee's integrity, said Lodge:

> He has been practically tried before a committee of the Senate for some weeks now on a number of very serious charges. . . . There are some people who think that the mere fact that such a trial or investigation is possible ought to be a disqualification for the Supreme Court of the United States. Nothing like it has ever happened in our history. . . .
> My own impression is that the Democrats would confirm him unless he was actually in the penitentiary. I do not say this at random, because they have confirmed a number of men to various offices who have been convicted in court for various offenses from one to four times.

Lodge continued to suggest in every letter in which he thought it might be useful that the bar associations should take action to oppose Brandeis. He did not know that certain leaders of the bar had for some time been quietly organizing under the stimulus of George Wickersham, who had nursed a special detestation for Brandeis since the Ballinger investigation of 1910. As council for *Collier's* and Glavis at that time, Brandeis had proved that Secretary Ballinger and Attorney General Wickersham had prepared for President Taft's signature the document that whitewashed Ballinger's handling of the disputed Alaska coal lands before Taft had even considered the facts. To Ballinger, Wickersham, and Taft, this was a normal administrative procedure, the kind to which busy public officials must resort to get their work done. But Brandeis had made it appear that the entire business smacked of fakery and deceit. Ballinger was out of political life now, and Taft was somewhat neutralized as a teacher of law

and lecturer on public affairs. But Wickersham was in law partnership on Wall Street with Taft's brother and still politically active.
He, more than anyone else involved in the Ballinger fiasco, thirsted
for revenge.

Wickersham called on Elihu Root to phrase a statement of protest
against the nominee, hopefully to be signed by men who had been
leaders of the legal profession as presidents of the American Bar Association. Root, the incumbent A.B.A. president, readily complied.
Wickersham sent Root's statement to Taft, who had served as Bar
Association president three years before. Delighted at the initiative,
Taft sought out the venerable Simeon Baldwin, A.B.A. president in
1890, professor of law at Yale, state judge for fourteen years, then
twice governor of Connecticut after reaching seventy. Baldwin was
willing to sign the Root letter but suggested an even stronger wording. Taft agreed with Baldwin and asked Wickersham to get Elihu
Root's approval of the change. Then, with three names that really
carried weight, Wickersham could canvass the former presidents of
the American Bar Association, including Alton Parker, the Democratic nominee for President in 1904. Taft conceded to Wickersham
that the protest might not defeat the nomination, but he felt it a
duty:

> I think we owe it to ourselves and to the Bar not to be supine,
> growling under our breath and whispering in the closet. We should
> speak out.

Then, referring to the pro-Brandeis views of the law professors at
Harvard to whom he had confided the legal training of his son Robert,
the former President expressed his vexation:

> The thing that angers me most is the attitude of the Harvard Law
> School people. I have thought that was the best law school in the
> world, and I still think so, but I have thought so because I have
> regarded the faculty as uniting advanced progressive ideas in respect
> to the law with sanity and common sense. Frankfurter has evi-
> dently been hypnotized by Brandeis and has legged around to get
> signatures.

Two weeks later Taft was writing to Gus Karger:

> The Brandeis evidence is revealing a professional crookedness—
> for I can call it no less a word than that—in Brandeis which will

make it an indelible stain on Wilson's Administration if he is confirmed. . . . Nothing could be more damning than the effort of Sherman Whipple to explain Brandeis' action in the case with respect to which he was called as a witness. His Shoe Machinery business, his New York and New England business, and this case that Sherman Whipple described, would be enough to suspend him from the Bar before an impartial court; and yet he is to be promoted to the highest Bench.

I think the Jews have a right to complain that the first man selected should be of such a character.

Karger, an old Washington hand, observed the hearing with detachment. "Unless something of unquestionable character is brought out," he informed Taft, the public would not see proof of Brandeis' unfitness—just a difference of opinion on the ethics of the legal profession. "Mr. Brandeis' case is being conducted by a committee of friendly tendency," Karger wrote.

Taft, whose hopes distorted his judgment, took issue with Karger: Any lawyer in America would be shocked to see elevated to the Supreme Court a man guilty of using "subterranean methods, the chief one of which is that of concealing his relation to his real client." If the wedge now dividing Wilson from some of his Democrats in the Senate could be driven a little deeper, Taft wrote, the nomination of Brandeis might be prevented. On March 2 Karger replied matter-of-factly:

The Brandeis hearings are going on, but nobody pays much attention to them. The subcommittee, it seems, will vote three to two in favor of his confirmation.

At the other end of Pennsylvania Avenue from the Capitol, Woodrow Wilson found that he could scarcely spend a day without the Brandeis nomination's being brought to his attention. Those who had cried out in such surprise at the nomination were, Wilson knew, really masking their anger. His real friends were with him. Several of them had anticipated his choice of Brandeis for the Court, had urged it on him, and so had strengthened his determination to risk the storm. Attorney Henry Wing of Charlestown, Massachusetts, for example, had proposed naming Brandeis on the ground that "an American of the future is needed now," that the United States was "evolving a composite nation," and that Brandeis, rather than being biased and sectarian, was a man "of autonomous mind."

Representative William Kent of California, a political independent and a progressive who had already pledged his support to Wilson for the 1916 campaign, wrote to the President before the nomination reached the Senate, saying that no one in the country was better known than Brandeis

> for clear-headed, forward-looking, constructive statesmanship. . . . You know, as well as I do, that the Supreme Court is the real living Constitution and therefore see clearly the necessity of having on the bench men with a vision of improving average human conditions, which is the end and aim of democracy. . . .
>
> I know of no appointment that would more surely rally to your support the thoughtful independent vote of the country.

Wilson drew a deep measure of satisfaction from both Kent's estimate of the nominee and the political effect of the nomination. He heard in similar vein from Amos Pinchot, a New York lawyer active in the Progressive Party:

> I understand that you are considering the advisability of appointing Louis Brandeis to the bench of the Supreme Court. . . . Such an appointment would be a large service to the country, and a credit to yourself and the Democratic administration.
>
> Two years ago, I would not have said this, although I believed then, as much as I do now, that Brandeis would make a sound and strong judge. But I think that at that time the country would not have been ready for his appointment; for the wisdom of the things he has said and done had not then been proved as it is now. Then, it might have been considered an appointment a little ahead of the times; now, the public has caught up with Brandeis, has accepted him and is deeply grateful for his work. We see Brandeis now as a man who has been fighting rather an uphill battle, the sane usefulness of which has been justified by events.

Wilson left Washington on a speaking tour of the Midwest on the evening of Friday, January 28, after dining at the home of his son-in-law, William McAdoo. Brandeis was present, with several members of the Supreme Court and a number of cabinet members. Everyone in the room was acutely conscious of the angry stirring of emotions the nomination had caused that afternoon, Wilson most of all. Later, as his train rolled westward on a swing that would touch Chicago and St. Louis, the President was kept in close touch with the progress of his Supreme Court nomination through telegrams dispatched from the White House to his secretary, Joseph Tumulty. The mail that steadily piled up in Washington furnished evidence that for the American people, perhaps more than the President had realized at first, the man he nominated had become the personification of a quality, a movement, an ideal. Many spoke of his intelligence, as did a California real estate broker: "He is honest, able and has a head filled with the highest quality of brains."

A Rhode Island warehouse operator described Brandeis as a kind of heroic public avenger ready to fight in the people's defense:

> The railroads fear him because he understands their modern ways of getting around the law. . . . I believe such a man as Mr. Brandeis is just the man to represent the poor public. The monopolies have already too large a representation.

Could he become a fair-minded judge after having been a committed advocate for many years? A Philadelphia attorney, David Wallerstein, put his answer in a double negative. Brandeis, he told President Wilson, was not committed to unfairness: "Mr. Brandeis has not got a set of opinions ready made, favorable to the extension of the use of the Fourteenth Amendment to prevent and destroy progressive legislation."

A testimonial to Brandeis' judicial capabilities came to Wilson from a conference of employers and union representatives in the New York dress and shirtwaist industry:

> We know Mr. Brandeis' judicial ability. He has been for three years the presiding judicial officer of our supreme court in the dress and waist industry, as chairman of the board of arbitration, under our existing peace protocol, and in that office has shown a firm grasp of difficult and complex industrial questions, and an application of the judicial mind and manner which mark him as the modern lawyer and modern judge. We congratulate the nation on the wisdom of your choice.

Wilson did not need telling, as many of his correspondents did, that Louis Brandeis on the Supreme Court would be spokesman for fresh ideas, for today and tomorrow rather than for yesterday. A Cincinnati notary exulted to the President:

Thank God I have lived to see the day, when a man can be appointed a U.S. Supreme Court judge who has not been a corporation lawyer all his life. For years it has been the rule only to appoint corporation lawyers to federal judgeships. From a Roosevelt Republican, God bless you!

Wilson may have been somewhat startled to observe how many interests Brandeis was supposed to "represent" on the Court—progressive political thought, the public, the poor, even organized labor, as some enthusiastic union officials let the White House know. "This is the first recognition of organized labor in this important department of our government," declared a letter from a committee of the Order of Railway Conductors, instinctively seeing Brandeis as railway labor's ally against management.

From Indianapolis, the United Mine Workers of America convention voted to send a hearty commendation to the President through Secretary-Treasurer William Green. From Brooklyn and St. Louis and San Francisco and a hundred other places where union men gathered, commendations flowed in to the President's office. The Macon, Georgia, Federation of Trades applauded "the action of the President in the appointment of a true friend of the working class as a member of the Supreme Court of the United States."

The evidence continued to mount that Brandeis had a hold on the popular imagination that Woodrow Wilson had not seen before in response to any of his appointments. What depth of feeling that Brandeis was the workingman's friend lay beneath a letter like that on plain paper, pressed with the seal of the Central Council, Clarksburg, West Virginia, A.F. of L.:

> Mr Presedint at the lat regular meeting of Trades Council. a resoluatition was passed approving your nomenatition of attorney Brandies for Supreme Court Judge. Labor is Hartiley in favor of Mr Brandies and wont forget any favors when the oppertunity presents itself I have been instructed to write Both of our Senators regarding Mr. Brandies. whitch I have done. hoping this is some little encouragment
> I remain Sinceirley yours
>
> ANDREW HESTER *Sec.*

Merely being sympathetic to organized labor was enough to cause many union men to look on Brandeis as a "representative" of the trade union movement on the bench, even though he had never belonged to a union. But it was not stretching a point at all to say that he represented the Jewish Americans, even though he never attended religious services. Brandeis had not really felt he was part of the Jewish ethos until he was mediating the 1910 garment-industry dispute in New York. Here he found that Jewish employers and union officials, across the gulf of their bitter class enmity, shared a common ethic that derived from their allegiance to the moral laws of Moses. From his recognition that he, too, shared this moral heritage, Brandeis proceeded to a deep involvement in Zionism when the outbreak of war caused an immense refugee problem which Americans were called upon to help solve. It was as an activist in the movement to help suffering Jews in Europe and the Near East that Brandeis became nationally known to his own people for the first time—when he was in his mid-fifties. And the President was fully aware when he was weighing his choice that Brandeis was now a prominent spokesman for the Jewish community, whatever his past record as a thoroughly assimilated American whose Jewish origin was unknown to many associates.

Wilson knew when he settled on Brandeis that this would be the first nomination of a Jew to the Supreme Court, and that this fact alone would cause difficulties. To most Americans, Jews were people apart, whom one knew about by way of comic caricatures on the music-hall stage, with exaggerated noses, baggy pants, and hilarious accents. If one happened to know a few Jews in business or in college, he did not know them very well. Although one or two were in the House of Representatives, there were none in the Senate or places of the highest social distinction.

There was an assumption that the Supreme Court should "represent" the nation, in religious make-up as well as geographic origin. Wilson had therefore quietly checked up on the religious affiliation of the Court members. White and McKenna were Catholics, he knew; Holmes was a Unitarian by family tradition who never attended church; Day and Van Devanter were Methodists, Hughes a Baptist, Pitney an Episcopalian, and McReynolds a member of the Christian Church. Sprinkled through the lower federal courts were a few men who were not Anglo-Saxon Protestants, particularly judges with German names in the Midwest and Irishmen in New York, but they were greatly outnumbered on the federal bench. A Jewish judge was quite a rarity at any level in the system.

THE JEWS OF THE UNITED STATES INDEED APPRECIATE YOUR LOYAL
AMERICANISM AND BROAD TOLERANT SPIRIT IN SELECTING THEIR
GREAT LEADER TO THIS AUGUST BODY AND WILL FOREVER REMEM-
BER THIS MEMORABLE EVENT.

Thus David Lourie wired the President immediately on hearing of
the nomination in Boston, where he was one of the most energetic
younger leaders in Jewish welfare work. Many others spoke in terms
as broad.

Men of education and the semiliterate, rabbis and fraternal-society
leaders, along with Jews speaking only for themselves from full hearts,
told Woodrow Wilson of their joy in his act of recognition. A rabbi
in Lynn, Massachusetts, felt called on to mix thanksgiving and praise
with practical politics:

> Your nomination of Mr. Louis D. Brandeis . . . was received
> by the Jews of this city with great joy and enthusiasm. The Jewish
> people at large may congratulate itself on the fitting tribute you
> paid to one of its best sons. We cannot help thinking that at this
> hour of intense woe and unspeakable anguish, there is one blessed
> spot on God's footstool where the Jew is duly appreciated.
>
> The Jews of Lynn, I assure you, Sir, will never forget the man
> who has done so much to alleviate Jewish suffering and to reflect
> glory on the children of Israel.

Gentiles conscious of the Jewish issue in the confirmation struggle
wrote approvingly to Wilson, prefacing their messages with "I am
not a Jew," or "As a native American, I—" Publicly and in his
correspondence Wilson acted as if there were no such thing as lines
of religious demarcation among the American people. Yet he revealed his concern with the religious issue with studied casualness in
conversation in St. Louis on the morning of February 2, the final
day of his Midwestern speaking tour. Wilson that day attended a
breakfast meeting of the convention of the U.S. Chamber of Commerce, sitting next to Clarence Howard, president of the St. Louis
Business Men's League. Howard, an old friend of Brandeis, wrote
the nominee shortly afterward that he and Wilson "had quite a talk
about you and he spoke so beautifully of you—your work and
Christian character and all. When I see you will gladly tell you many
interesting things. Knowing all will work out OK."

While conservative interests were generally hostile to Brandeis because they thought him a radical, the President heard from a number who saw the Brandeis appointment as a step to conserve the Court. They hoped it would blunt the kind of radical attack on American institutions represented by recent agitation for the recall of judges. A Michigan judge told the President:

> I think the real interest of the privileged classes themselves is best conserved by a Supreme Court the membership of which fairly represents every substantial school of political and economic thought. The appointment of Mr. Brandeis was therefore a very fine stroke of policy.

Along with the praise, Wilson was just as quickly the target of criticism, as he fully expected he would be. From New York:

> The nomination has shocked the country and the present Justices must feel a sense of degradation. . . . The writer would suspect the decisions of any court on which this agitator was seated. No objection to a Jew, but don't like this professional sensationalist who represents the soap box Washington Square outdoor spouters and not a clean American sentiment.

From Los Angeles: "Appointment insult to present members Supreme Court. Recall it."

From Boston: "If you really knew what he is, you would not have suggested him."

From Pittsburgh: "Even the influential Jews in Pittsburgh are sore, and the better class of laboring men claim the Democratic Party will lose more votes than it can ever gain in catering to the worst element in America."

From a Brooklyn physician:

> I am much surprised to learn that you have recommended a Hebrew for the Supreme Bench. I feel if you knew the unfavorable comments that the writer has listened to in the social clubs and the public places you would reconsider the matter. There are a great number of the Democratic party that feel as I do.

In contrast, the President's secretary, Joseph Tumulty, brought him one especially cheering letter he had received as the nomination hearings were about to start. Amos Pinchot, who had anticipated the nomination, called it the best news for the United States I've heard in many years. Incidentally it, in my opinion, goes far toward eliminating the Colonel from the list of presidential possibilities; for, although I don't think the appointment was political, Brandeis will pull a strong oar for Wilson in Wisconsin, Minnesota, South and North Dakota and other Roosevelt strongholds. It took courage and sense to make this appointment and I take off my chapeau to the President.

I have been violently assailed down town and in this club * on account of my admiration for Louis and my belief that the appointment proves the existence of a personal God. . . .

When the sixty Boston lawyers made public their sweeping condemnation of Mr. Wilson's nominee, the signature of President A. Lawrence Lowell caused a considerable stir in the Harvard community. Whether he liked it or not, the Harvard president personified the institution he directed; when he spoke, be it ever so routinely, he was spokesman for the mystical entity that embraced everything connected with Harvard. Mark A. DeWolfe Howe, editor of the *Harvard Alumni Bulletin,* found himself acutely embarrassed, since the nominee was a prominent Harvard Law School graduate noisily opposed by a powerful group of Harvard alumni, among them President Lowell. For three weeks, while the nomination was news in journals from Oshkosh to Medicine Hat, there was no word in the alumni weekly of the honor that had come to one son of Harvard, or of the indignation of his Harvard opponents. Finally, almost a month after the nomination, the *Harvard Alumni Bulletin* broke its silence by printing a long letter from Frederick Coburn, class of 1891. Of course, Coburn's letter stated, President Lowell and the others had a perfect right as citizens to petition against the confirmation of Brandeis; but it was

> maliciously phrased in such a way as to injure the professional standing of the person against whom it was directed, and without one word of proof, one statement of fact, in substantiation. . . .

Harvard students, meanwhile, were taking an interest. On the evening of February twenty-third a petition addressed to Senator Walsh urging a favorable report on Brandeis was circulated in Memorial Hall. Five days later it was sent to Washington, bearing 713 signatures of Harvard students. Accompanying it was a letter from M. P. Mc-

* The Metropolitan Club of Washington.

Nair, a member of the senior class, stating that the petition he had drawn up with several friends

> was called forth primarily by the action of A. Lawrence Lowell, President of Harvard University, in signing the petition against Mr. Brandeis calculated to injure his personal and professional reputation. . . . The impression was spread abroad that Mr. Lowell's action was representative of Harvard sentiment on this matter. Therefore a large number of Harvard students, graduate as well as undergraduate, have signed this pro-Brandeis petition with a view to counteracting this impression.

Lowell, meanwhile, was receiving his own letters of protest from Harvard alumni. Stiles Jones, class of 1888, expressed his shock that the Harvard president "should join the clamor of the privileged and predatory interest of the country in defaming the reputation of this great lawyer and citizen." And even though Lowell had confessed to Senator Weeks some days earlier that he could not substantiate his case that Brandeis was guilty of unscrupulous behavior as a lawyer, the Harvard president replied to Jones:

> The objection relates to his professional reputation for integrity. I believe strongly that no man ought to be put on the Supreme Bench of the United States who has been unscrupulous in his legal practice; and that Mr. Brandeis has that reputation among the more honorable members of the Suffolk Bar is undoubted. I was for seventeen years myself in practice at that bar, and certainly my opinion of his professional reputation depends on personal acts, and has nothing whatever to do with his opinions on social and economic subjects.

Once more, then, the viewpoint expressed by Lowell's friends at the hearings in Washington—that a nominee for the Supreme Court should enjoy a spotless reputation for professional integrity. The credentials of his critics need not be examined, nor should proofs to back up their opinions be asked. For are they not, according to Lowell, "the more honorable members of the Suffolk Bar"? One does not question the motives of such men.

It was easily understandable that the Harvard student petition was directed to Senator Walsh in the mistaken belief that he was chairman

of the hearing subcommittee. In the opening weeks Walsh had seemingly taken charge of the cross-examination of hostile witnesses, and
his name appeared in the newspaper accounts with far greater fre-
quency than Chilton's, or any of the others. As the hearings proceeded,
Walsh sensed that if the nomination were not to be buried under a
barrage of adverse testimony, organized by an experienced attorney,
backed by a national movement of moneyed men with access to the
press and to many Senators, it was up to him to lead the fight. Chilton,
a tired man suffering from glaucoma, did not have the kind of tough
alertness required to match wits with Fox and his witnesses day after
day. Fletcher, though his vote could be counted on, did not care
enough about the nomination to exert himself. The two Republicans,
though not old-line stand-patters, had clearly shown their partisan
hostility to Brandeis.

Walsh had proved his intelligence and toughness in Montana long
before coming to the Senate. An attorney specializing in compensation claims, he had won the enmity of the Anaconda Copper Mining
Company, the dominant industrial power in the state, through his
advocacy of the rights of the working man. Walsh did not become
active in politics until he was past forty-five, but the broad following
he had built from his law practice, his reputation for fearless honesty,
and his progressive economic views matching the demands of the
times led him quickly to the Senate. Here—amid aged, obese, and
tired men—he stood out. His erect carriage, high forehead, and sweeping black mustache reminded the viewer of the bold sheriff in the cow-
boy movie—personifying the vigor of the Great West whence he
came. In Washington, Walsh's blue-gray eyes bored into a witness
under interrogation, the firm voice carried his meaning with precision,
just as it had in convincing countless juries in Helena and Bozeman
and Butte.

As soon as the nomination was announced, Walsh became the
target of communications pro and con because of his position on the
Judiciary Committee. A Boston stockbroker named William Fitzgerald, active Democrat and director of several corporations, wrote
Walsh at length as a fellow Irishman who should not countenance
such an unmerited invasion of the Supreme Court:

> The fact that a slimy fellow of this kind by his smoothness and
> intrigue, together with his Jewish instinct, can almost land in the

Cabinet, and probably on the bench of the Supreme Court of the United States, should teach an object lesson to men who believe that for the future generations manhood should be the test . . . rather than showing that shysters can reach the goal. . . .

P.S. I believe in the recognition of the Jews as well as Irish if they really represent.

To this Walsh returned an invitation to send in information or facts "if there are any facts, pointing to a want of professional or personal integrity in the nominee." When a close friend wrote the Senator from Montana that Brandeis "left an unpleasant impression with me," Walsh did not hesitate to question whether his correspondent might not be "just a little warped by reason of racial prejudice." Walsh added that he himself kept an open mind in regard to the charges against Brandeis, but stated that "if these claims are not sustained I am for him."

When the Wall Street form letters of protest reached him, Senator Walsh invited the writers to back their opposition with "some facts showing the unfitness or unworthiness of the nominee." Albert Seibert, counselor-at-law of 49 Wall Street, was virtually alone in trying to supply a reason why the Senator should vote against Brandeis. But Seibert rested his case on the same shifting sand of "reputation" used by A. Lawrence Lowell:

It cannot be that you would regard any failure of proof as to the charges made against Mr. Brandeis as establishing his fitness for the high office to which he has been nominated. It is, I think, generally recognized that Mr. Brandeis is totally lacking in the judicial temperament, which should be an absolute prerequisite in any judicial officer. . . .

A Justice of the Supreme Court of the United States should be such as to be above the breath of suspicion. He should not be a lawyer against whom charges affecting his professional conduct have been made and have failed of proof, but he should be a lawyer against whom no charges affecting his professional or personal conduct have been at any time made.

Walsh was a skeptic with those who were too sure of themselves. As an old foe of the vested interests in a part of the country that in his lifetime had seen the worst of vigilanteism, corrupted legislators, bribed jurors, and bought judges, Walsh knew how to look for the

fire of personal interest at the source of smoke. When a storekeeper
wrote from Helena that Brandeis must be the wrong man for the
Supreme Court because every true Westerner knew that Bostonians
were all to be distrusted, Walsh replied: "Brandeis is fiercely hated
and ardently admired. It becomes exceedingly important that the
source of either commendation or condemnation be scanned with
suspicious scrutiny."

It was precisely this element in the investigation that came forth
when the hearings went into their fourth week on February 29. Fox
presented a witness in his late fifties named Edward Hutchins, a
Boston lawyer and director of several corporations, who said he had
known Brandeis since law-school days. What is Brandeis' reputation
at the Boston bar? asked Fox. That he is a lawyer of great ability,
but not straightforward, responded Hutchins. Fox handed over to
Chairman Chilton several statements backing up Hutchins' view of
Brandeis, signed by a number of Massachusetts lawyers. No one mentioned the fact that they were worded exactly as the original Boston
lawyers' protest had been phrased. These signers are "men of standing," are they not? Fox asked. Certainly, Hutchins replied.

Anderson took the list and ran down it, name by name. This one,
he asked Hutchins, was opposed to Brandeis in an insurance case,
was he not? Others fought Brandeis in the Old Dominion Copper
litigation, didn't they? In a few minutes the "men of standing" were
standing out as men who had been Brandeis' opponents in the courts,
and usually the losers.

When Senator Works asked Hutchins just what he meant when he
described Brandeis' conduct as "not straightforward," the witness
could not recall a single example from his nearly forty years of observ-
ing Brandeis in Boston. He could only cite the Ballinger investigation
in Washington, when, he said, Brandeis claimed he was representing
Glavis when he was really being paid by *Collier's Weekly*. That, declared Hutchins, was not being straightforward. Of course, the witness
wanted it understood that he was only estimating for the committee
what other Massachusetts lawyers thought of the nominee. As for
himself, declared Hutchins, "I have had no experience which would
lead me to suppose that Mr. Brandeis, from anything that I had with
him, litigation or otherwise, was untrustworthy."

Anderson cut in. While on the subject of reputation, he would like
to read the Senators a letter sent him by Arthur Hill, a Republican,

Harvard man, and former district attorney in Boston, now teaching at the Harvard Law School. It was a long and thoughtful letter, which Hill had composed with respect for the feelings of his intimate friends like Henry Cabot Lodge. Socially and politically, Hill belonged with the Boston protestants, and with the conservative senior Senator to whom they had sent their message. Yet Hill was young enough (forty-six) to be able to judge the nominee with a detachment that older men found impossible. His letter frankly conceded that Brandeis had made enemies:

> There is little question that he is not generally popular with the bar, and among a considerable proportion of lawyers here he has the reputation of not being a man with whom it is pleasant to deal in business matters, and one who is unscrupulous in regard to his professional conduct. Just how far there is any solid foundation for such a reputation it is extremely difficult to say. . . .
>
> I believe that the reputation to which I have referred is not founded so much on anything that Mr. Brandeis has done as it is on other causes. He is a radical and has spent a large part, not only of his public, but of his professional career, in attacking established institutions, and this alone would, in my judgment, account for a very large part of his unpopularity. It would be difficult, if not impossible, for a radical to be generally popular with Boston lawyers, or to escape severe adverse criticism of his motives and conduct. . . .
>
> The fact, too, that Mr. Brandeis has been the object of constant attack, and in particular of a very skillful and long continued press campaign by Mr. C. W. Barron, has probably increased the feeling against him; for such advertising inevitably produces effect, by mere repetition, upon people who are not conscious of its influence. When you add to this that Mr. Brandeis is an outsider, successful, and a Jew, you have, I think, sufficiently explained most of the feeling against him.

Anderson continued to read Hill's letter—paying tribute to Brandeis' devotion to unpaid public service, his simple mode of life, his disdain for amassing a fortune. Then the writer cut to the heart of the matter: the fitness of the prospective Justice on trial before this jury of Senators:

> He has acquired an unusual grasp of those social and economic conditions which underlie many of the most important questions

with which the Supreme Court will have to deal. I believe he will bring to the consideration of these problems not only great legal acumen and deep sympathetic insight, but a power of careful analysis and an ability to see facts and law in their larger relations, which will make him a great judge.

There was no challenge from Fox or Spence at the counsel table, nor from the Republicans in the Senators' chairs, to this testimony in favor of confirmation. What could one say in rebuttal to such a candid analysis both of the nominee and of the viewpoint of his detractors? Hill, a Republican, was standing on his home ground— Harvard and Boston. If anyone had the right to examine the motives of the anti-Brandeis petitioners, this man did.

Charles Choate came to the stand, under subpoena by the committee. Clarence Barron had stated that Choate could explain how Brandeis had first helped the New Haven Railroad "wreck" the New England Railroad, then had later undermined public confidence in the rich and powerful New Haven. The gist of Choate's testimony, after nearly two hours of sparring, was that although Brandeis' analysis of the railroad situation twenty years earlier had been generally correct, the sad events that overtook the New Haven were just "the things that have happened to develop."

The hearing veered back to the Ballinger investigation of 1910. Kenneth Spence, right-hand man to Fox, inserted material from the Senate majority report that had whitewashed Ballinger, asserting that Brandeis had seduced a confidential clerk into telling his boss' secrets to his enemies. The case against Ballinger and Wickersham had been clinched when Frederick Kerby, Ballinger's shorthand clerk, came to Brandeis and revealed that the two cabinet officers had prepared the Taft memorandum backing Ballinger at a considerably later date than the public had been told. Tortured in his conscience between his duty as a confidential secretary and his obligation to serve the public interest honestly, Kerby had decided to give his story to the press, then tell what he knew to the investigating committee.

Now, six years later, Spence tried to twist the facts about, and suggested that Brandeis had somehow sought out Kerby and played Svengali to Kerby's Trilby. But Senators Chilton and Fletcher forced Spence to acknowledge that it had really been the other way around— that Kerby had sought out Brandeis. Fox intervened in a rambling way to point out that although Brandeis had not been found guilty of "absolute wrongdoing, to the extent that any discipline could be imposed," this Supreme Court confirmation was quite special, and for that perhaps the honorable Senators would want to keep the Kerby business in mind. He was suggesting here, as he had often before, that this might not be a solidly black mark on Brandeis' record, but it was an unseemly gray.

Thirty-two days had now passed since the nomination had reached the Senate. Fox said he still had some documents to present on the Protective Association, and a man named Pillsbury would be in tomorrow. Anderson, aware that some of the Senators were wearying of these minutiae of the past life of Louis Brandeis, asked "whether Mr. Fox proposes to call any more witnesses except Mr. Pillsbury."

Yes, said Fox. He had a Mr. Francis Peabody, plus certain others to testify to Brandeis' reputation. "We could call a great many," Fox added, and some may be a bit slow because they are men "somewhat advanced in years." Chilton proposed that they be asked to send in statements. Fox said that he was willing, but his clients might prefer to appear in person. Senator Works, never in a hurry, suggested that Anderson might want to cross-examine them. Fox quickly picked up the signal: true, it might be better to bring the men from Boston, even if it should require waiting.

Chilton observed wearily: "Some of these days we will have to say we are through, you know."

Anderson decided to have it out on Fox's clearly exposed design to stretch out the hearings just as long as possible:

> I do wish, Mr. Chairman, that in view of Mr. Fox's remark when he came in here about bringing order out of chaos and marshaling the facts and witnesses, that we should proceed speedily and determine the matter. I was conscripted by this committee out of a peaceful home . . . and am glad to serve this committee . . . but it is rather due to the committee and to the country and to the court . . . that we get through. He was to put on one more witness, I believe.

"Mr. Fox, what do you say as to that?" asked Chilton.

Fox turned peevish: "I am rather tired of hearing my brother Anderson talk about himself being conscripted for service by this committee. He was here as friend of Mr. Brandeis, to see how Mr.

Brandeis' interests got along, and sat with his counsel, and that is what he is here for now."

Senator Fletcher remarked this was not the question. Did Fox have any other witness outside the Messrs. Pillsbury and Peabody?

"I do not think there is any other witness, with one exception," Fox replied, "but I do not think I ought to state we will close."

Albert Pillsbury, sixty-six, had practiced law in Boston for more than forty years, served in both houses of the legislature and as attorney general for the Commonwealth, and was now a senior director of several banks and charitable societies. He had known Brandeis, though only slightly, since the nominee had first come to the Boston bar. Would Mr. Pillsbury please state what Brandeis' reputation had been? Fox asked.

> PILLSBURY: His reputation, as it has come to me, is that of a very active, adroit, and successful business lawyer; a man of unbounded audacity; a man, if you wish to go into questions touching integrity—a man, I should say, of duplicity.
>
> FOX: Of what, sir?
>
> PILLSBURY: Of duplicity, double-dealing; a man who works under cover, so that nobody ever knows where he really is or what he is really about.

Anderson drew on his long memory of legal struggles in Boston, plus material supplied him by McClennen. Had Pillsbury, he inquired, not been opposing counsel to Brandeis over the issue of municipal control of the Boston subway? And over the application of the Westminster Chambers, a Boston hotel, to build higher than the permitted limit? And the valuation of gas company stocks during the Consolidated Gas Company fight? Pillsbury just could not recall. He then quickly slanted off to attack Brandeis' motives in public cases: "Mr. Brandeis has appeared very often in the character of a friend of the people and has very often been reputed to be under pay."

Was he being paid, or was he only reputed to be? Chilton asked.

> PILLSBURY: Reputed to be.
>
> ANDERSON: Have you any instance of that that you are ready to state to the committee?
>
> PILLSBURY: Nothing whatever. I know nothing about the facts.

Then the witness would not claim that he knew positively that Brandeis had ever secretly taken money from the interests he pretended to be fighting? No, Pillsbury said firmly, he made no such claim. This was just "part of his general public reputation, as it has come to me."

Who were these men whose thoughts on Brandeis Mr. Pillsbury had come from Boston to relay to the committee? Senator Works wanted to know. Pillsbury regretted it, but he just could not give out their names, lest they be "open to the position in which my signing the remonstrance has put me." No one asked Pillsbury just what this position was, and the names were not pursued.

Fox came next to the Equitable Life Assurance Society matter, to which he had alluded cryptically for some days. Documents proved, Fox said, that Brandeis changed his tune according to who paid him. First Brandeis was hired by certain insurance policyholders to file a bill of complaint against the company for mismanagement. He delivered an impassioned speech before the Commercial Club of Boston, assailing the irresponsible management of the company. Then the following year he represented the Equitable as counsel, "taking a position at one time precisely contrary to the position taken later, not only as regards the legality, but the morality." McClennen would discuss this affair when he reached the witness chair, Anderson assured the committee.

Then Fox, having neither witnesses nor new issues at hand, asked Chairman Chilton if his clients in Boston might choose the one remaining character witness he was permitted. Fox named four men, assuring the chairman that the final witness as to Brandeis' reputation would be from among the group. The Senators agreed.

"Those are all the witnesses Mr. Fox has?" Anderson queried hopefully. Fox responded that he was "not making any promise." At some point, persisted Anderson, "there must be an end."

Edward McClennen finally took the stand after having sat in the hearing room for days on end. Employed in Brandeis' law firm since his graduation from Harvard Law School in 1895, McClennen said he was fully conversant with all the matters brought up in the hearings so far. Moreover, if certain cases had not been perfectly clear in his memory when first mentioned, Brandeis and his other Boston colleagues had sent him the documentation with which to answer the charges presented by Fox and his witnesses.

McClennen made short work of the Equitable Life affair. The Brandeis firm, he explained, had done some legal work in Boston for a New York law firm which represented Equitable. The festering insurance scandals of 1905 brought a group of big Equitable policy-holders to the Brandeis office to see if he could save their investment. Brandeis agreed to do so and gave his services without charge, because he regarded this as a public matter. As part of his advocacy he delivered speeches and wrote articles attacking the gross mismanagement permitted under lax state insurance laws. His message was one of reform, both self-policing within and regulation by state government. By the end of 1906, when a major part of his program had been achieved, Brandeis was given a vote of thanks by the policy-holders' committee. End of the affair. . . . Fox had no questions, no counterargument. Neither did the Senators. The picture of Brandeis the crusader being bought off by the insurance company seemed to have popped like a soap bubble.

Now the case of the New York & New England Railroad, which had been absorbed by the New York, New Haven & Hartford in the Nineties. The charge against Brandeis, hinted at by Clarence Barron and expanded upon by Moorfield Storey, was that Brandeis had brought a suit against the New England Railroad ostensibly on behalf of a man named Goldsmith, but that his real clients were certain big stockholders of the New Haven. Their plan, according to the charge, was to harass the smaller road with the Goldsmith litigation, force it into receivership, then pick it up for a bargain price.

Not only was Brandeis no party to anything of this kind, said McClennen, but he had left the Goldsmith case in June 1893. Whatever happened afterward he learned only from the newspapers, for he was out of it. He had never been in on any wolfish New Haven plot to use Goldsmith to feed on the New England Railroad. The charge, said McClennen, had no truth in it.

Fox broke in, objecting that McClennen was only a law-school student at the time, so how could he give competent testimony on this matter? By studying the record, including the Brandeis law-office diaries, as well as by asking people who were there, McClennen responded. That's quite another thing, Fox grumped. But no one questioned McClennen's summary of the New England Railroad affair or argued from any of the previous testimony to refute his statement.

The March 1 hearing opened with a renewed plea from Anderson for an early finish. He had wired four men in Boston to come give their impressions of Brandeis' general reputation, Anderson said, but he would be glad to have them submit letters instead. He turned to the committee: "Is there hope, reasonably grounded, of completing today?"

Chilton laughed off the question as too iffy for a reply. Senator Cummins of Iowa, who had been fairly quiet since the appearance of his witness Thorne on the opening day, put in his bid against haste in closing. Then Senator Works observed that of course the nominee's side must not be hurried. Messrs. Anderson and McClennen, he said, "ought to be given every opportunity to produce any evidence desired."

Sixty-seven-year-old Stephen Gregory of Chicago, a former A.B.A. president, came forward. No, he answered Anderson, he was not related to Attorney General Gregory. Brandeis' reputation, the witness stated, "is excellent as a lawyer of ability and character." But, Fox asked, this was a "general reputation" from a thousand miles, not a local reputation in Boston, wasn't it? Quite true, said Gregory; he did not know Brandeis as a close neighbor at the bar.

McClennen returned to the stand and filled the rest of the day with the details of the United Shoe Machinery Company case. Anderson fed him questions for hours, apparently recognizing this as the stickiest part of the combined campaign to defeat the nomination. But amid all the testimony and insertion of documents into the hearing record, the picture was essentially unchanged for those who had heard it all before. Brandeis had advised the company in its early years, had severed connection with it, and later had sought justice for a plaintiff against it in the courts. Anderson said he wanted it made perfectly clear that Brandeis took no payment for this latter service, because the burden of the charge against him, starting with Barron, was that Brandeis had mercenary motives in switching sides. Again, when the Anderson-McClennen dialogue was wound up, there were no challenging questions from Fox or Spence, none from Senators Cummins or Works.

Francis Peabody, one of the signers of the Boston lawyers' protest and the final character witness to be presented by Fox, took the witness chair on March 2. He responded readily to Fox's inquiry as to Brandeis' reputation as a lawyer: "I think he is considered as a conspicuously able man; but, on the other hand, his reputation is that he is not always truthful, that he is untrustworthy, and that he sails under false colors." Fox had no further questions.

Anderson then brought from Peabody the fact that he and Brandeis had been opposed to one another in the 1907 struggle for control of the Illinois Central Railroad between the groups of directors headed by Stuyvesant Fish and Edward Harriman, and also had taken different sides in the New Haven fight to absorb the Boston & Maine. The Senators should understand, Peabody said, he had been quite friendly with Brandeis in the old days, meeting him often on the bridle path when they were both members of the Dedham Polo Club. But then "it seemed to me that he made almost a practice of concealing the identity of the client by whom he was employed, which struck me as disingenuous and not entirely honorable."

The witness then rambled awkwardly into a touchy subject no one else had broached: "I found the opinion very prevalent in Boston that Mr. Brandeis was doing a fine thing in the Ballinger case in acting for Glavis, who seemed to be a friendless man of his race, a Jew, who had been turned out." The revelation that he was paid by *Collier's Weekly* changed that prevalent opinion. Gratuitously, Peabody carried the Jewish-concealment theme to the Illinois Central proxy fight:

> Although it made no particular difference to me in any way, yet, until within a number of years, I did not know that he was a Jew. I would say that that had not been disclosed until a few years ago. That made no difference as far as my opinion of him goes, except as it was made prominent and before that had not been known.

Peabody had ventured on ground where none in the room wanted to stay, so the innuendo in his remarks was left unchallenged.

The floor was now open to witnesses with good words for the nominee. Newton D. Baker, recently mayor of Cleveland and still president of the National Consumers League, presented a memorial praising Brandeis for his work on behalf of industrial justice. The attached names were those of public-spirited citizens and officials in New York, such as Oscar Straus, Charles R. Crane, Rabbi Stephen Wise, and Florence Kelley; editors Paul Kellogg of *The Survey,* Norman Hapgood of *Harper's Weekly,* and Walter Lippmann of the *New Republic;* labor officials and manufacturers in the garment industry where the Brandeis arbitration system had fended off strikes for six years; and social workers like Frances Perkins, who had gone out and collected the names of the others at the instigation of Paul Kellogg.

Baker was followed by Henry Moskowitz, clerk of the board of arbitration covering the New York garment industry. He had watched Brandeis act in a judicial role since 1910, the witness said: "If there is one characteristic of Mr. Brandeis' thinking, it is his capacity to see both sides; it is his capacity not only for judicial statement, but for judicial thought." Only a man with this quality could have brought peace to a strike-torn industry, said Moskowitz.

A switch back to Brandeis' home ground with Asa French, president of the Norfolk County Bar Association, for eight years United States attorney in southeastern Massachusetts. The reputation of Louis Brandeis? French did not mince words:

> I have never heard it assailed or questioned by an impartial critic —that is, by anyone whose opinions or interests have not been antagonized by Mr. Brandeis. May I say that we have what I may call an aristocracy of the Boston bar. . . . They are high-minded, able, distinguished men. But they cannot, I think, consider with equanimity the selection of anybody for a position on the great court of the country from that community who is not a typical, hereditary Bostonian.
>
> Among the rank and file of the Boston bar and the Massachusetts bar, so far as I know them, Mr. Brandeis has, in my experience, the reputation of being a man of integrity, a man of honor.

Joseph Walker of Brookline, lawyer and practical politician, former speaker of the legislature, put a bold dollar sign on the reason for Brandeis' unpopularity with the elite: "I think it was that public service that Mr. Brandeis rendered beginning in 1906 with the gas matters, that stirred up a great many financial interests against him in Boston." Walker ticked the interests off—owners of the overvalued gas-company stocks and of New Haven securities, factory owners unwilling to reduce their working women's hours, and bankers anticipating the take from a captive Boston transit system.

During the next five days of hearings, omitting only Sunday, March 5, McClennen held the stand, introducing documents and explaining the other side of one case after another that had been cited in the attack on Brandeis. Each centered either on the allegation of wrongdoing by Brandeis the attorney toward his client or his former client, or else involved a claim that he had concealed his true client or true motive. Page after page from court records, congressional committee hearings, office memoranda, letters, and other documents were handed to the committee clerks for insertion in the hearing record until it seemed that nothing more could be said. Still the questions on minutiae of Brandeis' personal history as a lawyer kept coming, and patiently McClennen tried to answer them, or provided the response the following day after taking time off to study his library of reference or obtain documents from Boston.

Through it all a close observer had the impression of a burlesque dialogue in which one party repeatedly misconstrued what the other was saying. The Louis Brandeis presented by Fox and his witnesses was a devious shyster, an image which they projected repeatedly by alleging dishonest behavior in particular legal cases over the past twenty years or more. In so doing they seemingly did not listen to the refutation witnesses, who addressed themselves to those very issues in defense against the charges. Nor were they impressed by the mass of documentation inserted in the record by McClennen at Anderson's request. As for the positive record of Brandeis, brought out by those witnesses who were trying to picture the nominee as a man preeminently fitted for a seat on the Supreme Court, the attackers hardly deigned to look upon it.

Thus, the Fox case was to direct the Senators' attention to the United Shoe Machinery Company, the Warren will, the Lennox affair, the "wrecking" of railroads, the switching of interests and—above all —the smoke-haze of distrust murking Brandeis' professional reputation in Boston.

Anderson, on the other hand, was forced to play two themes: one defensive, against the Fox charges, the other positive, extolling the virtues and the solid achievements of Louis Brandeis. At only rare intervals, as in the detailed, thoughtful letter from Arthur Hill, in the blunt oral testimony of Joseph Walker the professional politician, and the more sophisticated language of Asa French, did the defenders of Brandeis point to the tainted motives of his attackers. Brandeis, they said, had angered men of power and property who therefore fought him now. But they did not go so far as to tell the subcommittee the full truth—that such people considered Brandeis a menace to the grand old way of life enjoyed by generations of men of wealth and position in Boston. In him the privileged saw the personification of everything that had been cutting into the profit system in recent years—antitrust laws, the income tax, labor agitation, restrictions on female labor, federal and state controls over what had once been the freedom to do business undisturbed.

It was therefore in the light of Brandeis' long record of working in a dozen ways to increase the social cost of doing business that Boston's most conservative gentlemen instinctively reacted against his nomination as a Supreme Court Justice. Brandeis stood on the opposite side of the fence from them on virtually every social issue. To place such an unrelenting opponent on the bench was, to them, an outrage. Any person so biased in his thinking against the established order that he mouthed rabble-rousing terms like "the Money Trust" and "the Money Power"—such a warped, twisted personality, with all his shrewdness, could never be a fair judge.

As the hearings trailed on toward their close, Fox tried every possible tactic to drag them out. On March 4 he asked Senator Chilton in his customary loquacious way whether it might be possible to have a quorum of the five Senators present at all times. The Senate was busy, Chilton replied, and members did occasionally have to be in two places at once. All Judiciary Committee members could read the record, he said. Senator Works came to the support of Fox, but said he would not make an issue of the quorum.

In midafternoon, having finished cross-examining McClennen on the Lennox bankruptcy affair (in which Brandeis had declared himself "counsel to the situation"), Fox asked the chairman's permission to catch the four o'clock train for New York. He and Spence hoped over the week end to find a couple of fresh witnesses on the Lennox matter, he said. No one offered any protest, so off Fox went hunting.

A brief hearing on March 6 was devoted to a new charge against Brandeis that had not yet been raised: the nominee had been a liquor lobbyist twenty-five years before! A clergyman named James Cannon, lobbyist for the Anti-Saloon League, brought in documents to prove that Brandeis had been the spokesman, back in 1891, for the Massachusetts Protective Liquor Dealers' Association before the state legislature. Cannon was not saying anything for or against Mr. Brandeis, but simply pointing to the record. Sooner or later the prohibition issue would come before the Supreme Court of the United States, and it would not be wise to put on the Court a man already committed. Had Cannon any indication, Senators asked, of Mr. Brandeis' views on

liquor laws during the past twenty-five years? No, said Cannon, he
and his Anti-Saloon League colleagues had searched, but they had
found nothing. The hearing record, thanks to Cannon, was now thicker
by eighteen pages of fine print.

The final three witnesses brought in by Fox also proved to be less
than sensational. They waded through a morass of detail on the Lennox bankruptcy case without either sounding any serious charge
against Brandeis or adding anything new. It was the same old question—could one attorney honestly represent all sides in a trusteeship,
or should he be advocate for only one party? McClennen then plodded
through a question-and-answer refutation of miscellaneous parts of
the Lennox, United Shoe Machinery, New Haven Railroad, and Old
Dominion Copper Company cases to which by this time no one had
the energy to listen with great attention.

Finally, at noontime on March 8, Spence declared: "That is all we
have to submit, Senator." Fox added with finality: "So far as we are
concerned, we are at rest." Anderson at once followed with his own
declaration that "we think we have put in enough."

So, with the chairman expressing his wearied thanks to Fox and
Spence on the one side and to Anderson on the other, Chilton gaveled
the hearings to their end, forty days after the Brandeis nomination
had reached the Senate floor. No one at this moment could foresee
the political complexities that would drag out the case of Louis D.
Brandeis more than twice again as long until it was finally resolved.

seven

The Summing Up

Brandeis will undoubtedly be confirmed, and I think this will be done by a very large majority vote. . . .

I know Brandeis as I know very few men, and my respect for him has been increasing during the last three years. He is a man who cares nothing for money, and for the last twenty years his lifework has been standing for personal liberty as against property rights.

He is a radical, but one radical in nine is not a bad thing on the Supreme Bench. His appointment will strengthen the confidence of a vast number of American citizens in that court and in the judiciary generally. His rejection would fortify many men in the mistaken belief that no one but reactionaries and persons attached to large interests can go on the Federal Bench.

From a political standpoint, which is of course one of the last things to consider, the appointment is excellent.

So wrote Attorney General Gregory in early March to Robert Lynn Batts of Austin, Texas. Batts was Gregory's personal investment counselor, who in 1914 had prosecuted the antitrust suit brought by the government against the New Haven Railroad and was familiar with Brandeis as an expert on railroad finance. Although Batts considered Brandeis "a very big man, and a very good man," he had confessed to Gregory that he doubted the wisdom of naming a person so controversial to the Supreme Court.

As the Attorney General was predicting the confirmation of his "radical" friend Brandeis, with the hearings concluded former President Taft was becoming anxious about what had happened to the protest he had signed with Elihu Root, Simeon Baldwin, and, hopefully, other former presidents of the American Bar Association. He had just returned from Boston University, where he had delivered a series of lectures on legal ethics, when he received a complaining note from Louis A. Coolidge, the United Shoe Machinery Company treasurer. Judging by the enclosed clipping from the Boston *Post,* Coolidge wrote Taft, the former President had spread the unfortunate idea in his lectures that he did not believe a lawyer's attitude toward corporations bore any relation to his mental honesty. The *Post* suggested that this meant Taft was weakening in his opposition to Brandeis. This was not so, was it? Coolidge asked.

Not at all, Taft replied. He had signed an A.B.A. presidents' protest against Brandeis as not a fit man to become a member of the Supreme Court, and added reassuringly: "I never had said anything in his favor . . . I did say some things in the lectures condemning counsel who failed to disclose their real clients, and some other unethical practices I condemned, in respect to all of which I had Brandeis' methods in mind."

Coolidge paid a quick visit to Washington just after the subcommittee hearings closed on March 8, and on his return sent Taft an optimistic report, based vaguely on unnamed informants:

> I was interested in Washington to find that the evidence laid before the committee had impressed a good many people who had hitherto been ardent supporters of Mr. Brandeis and who had no previous conception of the character of the case against him.
>
> One very eminent lawyer of his own faith whom Brandeis had asked to come to Washington to help him out, told me that he had been staggered by the evidence and was thinking of notifying Mr. Brandeis and his friends that he could no longer stand with him.

Taft received a less hopeful report from Gus Karger. At the close of the hearings March 8, the Cincinnati correspondent observed:

> If the testimony there adduced had concerned Elihu Root, friend of the corporations, today he would be denounced from coast to coast and his associates would seek to disbar him; it's different in the case of Louis D. Brandeis, friend of the people. "We have the votes," as Senator Stone once said. At any rate, there will be delay—and sometimes the unexpected does come to pass.

Taft echoed Karger in bemoaning the double standard in justice. Poor Root would indeed have fared ill "if they had proved against him what they have proved against Brandeis." March fourteenth found Taft writing to George Wickersham, inquiring anxiously about the Bar Association protest he had signed a month earlier with Root, Simeon Baldwin, and the others: "I had assumed that it would have been published long ago. Lowell, whom I saw in Boston, was anxious to have it published. I presume we cannot defeat the confirmation, but I think we ought to go on record."

As Taft wrote, the subcommittee hearings were being reopened at the request of Fox, so that he might submit further testimony. Before he did so, Fox stated, he had "a communication" he would like to read to the Senators:

> The undersigned feel under the painful duty to say to you in their opinion, taking into view the reputation, character and professional career of Mr. Louis D. Brandeis, he is not a fit person to be a member of the Supreme Court of the United States.

The signatures were those of Taft, Baldwin, and Root, plus those of Francis Rawle, Joseph H. Choate, and Moorfield Storey. A letter with the same sense, but differing slightly in wording, came from Peter W. Meldrim. Of the seven signers, six were former presidents of the American Bar Association, and Root was the incumbent president. Holders of the highest honor the legal profession had in its power to bestow, these were men eminent not only in law but also in their family connections, in government, business, and scholarship. Baldwin, now seventy-six, was a teacher and author who had served as president at various times of the American Historical Association, the American Political Science Association, and the American Social Science Association, had been chief justice of the Connecticut Supreme Court and governor of the state.

Moorfield Storey, now seventy-one, was a historian, had served as secretary to Senator Charles Sumner, carried on an active law practice, and had for years been president of the National Association for the Advancement of Colored People. Joseph H. Choate was one of the distinguished elder statesmen of the New York bar, who had served Presidents McKinley and Roosevelt as Ambassador to the Court of St. James and represented the United States at the Hague peace conference in 1907. He had written biography and history, and in his later years termed himself a diplomatist rather than an attorney. Francis Rawle, a Harvard overseer and patrician, practicing law in

Philadelphia, was a legal scholar and member of the American Philosophical Society. Peter W. Meldrim, only Democrat among the seven, had sat in both houses of the Georgia legislature and been mayor of Savannah while building a lucrative law practice in that city.

The fact that such a group of distinguished attorneys had joined to protest the appointment seemingly added the weight of the legal profession to the case against Brandeis. No such rallying of the leaders of the American bar had been seen in the capital before, on any issue. Word of this latest blow against the nominee carried to the four corners of the country by front-page headlines, simply because it was struck by men of such eminence.

An editorial in the St. Louis *Globe-Democrat* was typical of those who saw this as the Voice of Authority:

> The protest seven former presidents of the American Bar Association have filed . . . cannot be waved aside with an epithet. All are great lawyers, who realize the significance of their act. . . . Any intimation that they are moved by racial prejudice is absurd. . . . Jewish blood has been an asset in the case of Mr. Brandeis. Nor can the protest be ascribed to "the interests." . . . All these men are known to the bar of America and have been given the highest honors in their profession, in their several states and in the nation.

As he had from the beginning, Brandeis issued no comment in response to the latest attack on him. Reporters had long since learned that the prospective Supreme Court Justice would provide them no news. He went to his office each day, but was seen very little in court and not at all in legislative hearing rooms or on the lecture platform. Part of his time in the office since early February had necessarily been spent in retrieving from the files documents for McClennen and Anderson to use in refuting the assertions of the parade of witnesses in Washington.

Shortly after the Taft-Root protest was read in the hearing room, George Anderson was writing to Senator Walsh from Boston, pinning to each of the bar leaders a particular motive for trying to bring about the rejection of Brandeis by the Senate: Taft because of the Ballinger investigation; Root by having been one of the Senators assigned to the Ballinger whitewash committee and having been confounded by

Brandeis' defense of Glavis and *Collier's Weekly;* Choate and Meldrim being ultraconservatives devoted to the defense of propertied interests; and Baldwin, "showing a mind as strongly opposed to all progressive, humanitarian legislation as there is in this country. . . . Doubtless an honest and high-minded man, he is so constituted as to believe legislation such as Mr. Brandeis has advocated destructive to the foundations of our government."

Had the A.B.A. presidents' protest been analyzed more carefully than it was at the time, a few facts might have emerged to shadow the claims made for it as the voice of leadership of the American bar. No one pointed out that the seven presidents who signed were only a minority of the sixteen living A.B.A. presidents, whose signatures Wickersham had assiduously pursued. Missing, for example, was the name of Jacob M. Dickinson, who had served Taft as Secretary of War for two years after a long career as attorney for railroads in Nashville and Chicago. In January Dickinson had earnestly pressed Taft's name on Attorney General Gregory as the right man to fill the Supreme Court vacancy, and he had instigated Tennessee lawyers of both political parties to petition Wilson on behalf of the former President. Later, on seeing the nomination go to Brandeis, Dickinson had written to his Senators disapproving Brandeis for lack, he believed, of the judicial temperament. But despite George Wickersham's entreaties, Dickinson would not lend his name to the A.B.A. presidents' protest; members of the profession would understandably resent it, he told Wickersham, because the signers appeared to act "representatively" for the A.B.A. in a controversial matter.

Taft had also hoped, though without success, to secure the name of Alton B. Parker, New York lawyer and former judge who had been the Democratic candidate for President in 1904. It was understandable that the petition did not appeal to Frank B. Kellogg, a former bar association president who had prosecuted the Standard Oil trust under Theodore Roosevelt and won his President's accolade as "the best trust buster of them all." And it was obvious that Stephen S. Gregory of Chicago, who had sympathized with organized labor and reform movements, was friendly to Brandeis. He had, in fact, proved this by coming to Washington to testify in the nominee's favor. But it was less clear why leading railroad counsel like Frederick W. Lehmann, whom President Taft had made Solicitor General of the

United States, and George Peck of Chicago, or a Harvard man like Edmund Wetmore, now in his eighties, should hold back from signing the Taft-Root remonstrance.

In this petition, as throughout the entire Brandeis affair, age had its significance. Of the seven A.B.A. presidents who came out against Brandeis as "not a fit person" to join the Supreme Court, only Taft was younger than the nominee. Choate was eighty-four; Baldwin, Storey, and Rawle were in their seventies; Meldrim was sixty-eight. The characters of these men had been formed, their values established, before the social ferment of the late 1870s, the big immigration wave, and the coming of trade-unionism had changed the face of American society. Like most of those who led the campaign to reject the nomination of Brandeis, these A.B.A. leaders were largely men whose methods of thought were of the nineteenth century. They had never quite accepted the twentieth, with its requirement that lawyers adopt a fresh outlook. There was some crossing of the age line in both directions, but as a general rule, those who actively championed the confirmation of Brandeis to the Court, like Norman Hapgood, Felix Frankfurter, Walter Lippmann, and George Anderson, were under fifty. The principal opponents, on the other hand, were mostly in their sixties or older.

Gus Karger was doubtful, as he wrote to Taft, that even the A.B.A. leaders' protest would do much good:

> I believe that it has had a profound effect on the few real lawyers in the U.S. Senate, some of whom are rather shamefaced about it. But I doubt whether it will have the effect of really changing votes. I think already the lines are drawn and a partial poll of the Senate shows 58 votes in Brandeis' favor, with more in prospect, if the question of confirmation shall be brought to a vote.
>
> The only way to defeat Brandeis' nomination, in the opinion of those with whom I have talked, is to keep the Senate from voting on it, and that cannot be done unless a Senator should claim his personal privilege. . . . Lodge is bitter in his opposition, but he can not very well raise the personal question in the case of a Supreme Court appointee.

Taft in reply seemed almost resigned to losing the battle:

> I did not suppose that our protest would accomplish anything, but I felt it a duty that my conscience required me to discharge to pro-

test publicly against Brandeis' appointment. I think it is a blow at the Supreme Court, which I cherish as a kind of sacred shrine, to have a man whose reputation is shady in respect to the ethics of his professional practice, to be put on the Bench. I did it with full knowledge that Brandeis' particular forte is in the muckraking business, such as he showed in the Ballinger Case and his attempt to revive the issues in that case is no surprise.

Now that Taft's name had come out into the open as a combatant in the anti-Brandeis ranks, he knew he must expect the unpleasant Ballinger affair to be drawn back into the public print, with all its attendant innuendo of scandal about his administration. Louis Coolidge in Boston sensed at once the risk that Taft courted by exposing himself to the hostility of the Brandeis crowd, so he congratulated the ex-President on having selflessly performed a public service. And still he sang a tune of optimism:

> It took courage for you and the others to sign the protest, for it must have been done with the full consciousness that it would expose each one of the signers to the venomous attacks of Mr. Brandeis' friends. Some of the newspaper comments already indicate the lengths to which they are ready to go; but the general effect has been striking. I have been interested to hear many men who have hitherto supposed confirmation was inevitable say since the publication of your protest that they believed the nomination would be rejected.

Although the reading of the denunciation of Brandeis by the Bar Association presidents on March 14 required only two minutes, it took the headlines away from the two-hour discussion that followed. This concerned Brandeis' relations with the Old Dominion Copper and Smelting Company, which had been hinted at for weeks as a skeleton in the Brandeis closet. Fox and Spence first presented a written account of the Old Dominion matter, slanted to show that Brandeis had played a wily part in the company's history. Then they brought in William F. Fitzgerald, a Boston stockbroker who had at one time owned a large block of Old Dominion stock. In rehearsal with Fox at the Willard Hotel before going to the Capitol, Fitzgerald had supplied Fox with a quotation, allegedly from the lips of Brandeis, that sounded most damaging to the Supreme Court nominee. When the management of Old Dominion was negotiating with a much larger

firm, the Phelps-Dodge Corporation, a proposed merger with one of
its subsidiaries, Brandeis was alleged to have said: "Fitz, you had
better come over on the other side. That's where the big money is.
I have got on the bandwagon, and you had better do the same."

The import of these words, as Fox relayed them to the subcommittee, was that Brandeis had changed sides from the smaller and
weaker firm to the side offering a big payoff, and he was offering
Fitzgerald a chance to join him.

Senator Walsh began cross-examining the Boston broker to separate his memory of the facts from Fox's reconstruction of them. By
the time Walsh was through, a quite different picture emerged—that
Brandeis, as counsel to the weak firm in financial difficulties, was
advising its directors to merge with the better-financed company solely
to protect its stockholders' investment. Fox intervened in an attempt
to rescue some testimony harmful to Brandeis, but he was discon-
certed to find that his own witness would not oblige.

"Perhaps," said Fitzgerald, "I have given the wrong impression of
it. I would say Mr. Brandeis was conserving my interests in telling me
to get on the bandwagon, and that my money was there by having a
concern that could finance and handle this mine, which was exceptionally rich."

Somewhat later Fox inquired whether Brandeis had not meant by
"getting on the bandwagon" that Fitzgerald ought to join him in shifting his allegiance from Old Dominion to Phelps-Dodge. Fitzgerald
flatly denied such an import to the words: "I do not mean in any way,
shape or manner to suggest that Mr. Brandeis was working for the
Phelps-Dodge interests, or conspiring or doing anything in that way,
because I know he was not."

"No," Fox mumbled hastily, "I did not mean to imply that."

Walsh excused the witness forthwith. Edward McClennen was invited to occupy the witness chair Fitzgerald had just vacated, should
he want "to add anything to what he has heretofore said on this subject." Brandeis' junior partner tried to run quickly through the high-
lights of the Old Dominion merger affair without becoming bogged
down in the petty details that would drag the matter out for days, as
had been done with the Lennox bankruptcy, the Warren will, the
United Shoe Machinery, and other topics on which the hearings had
lingered. Walsh indicated to McClennen that this latest item in the

anti-Brandeis catalogue was not worth too much time: "Exercise your judgment about it, bearing in mind that the more protracted this is, the less likely it is that it is to be read by anybody except the committee."

From his side Senator Cummins added a bit of comfort: "I hope it is not improper for me to say that Mr. Fitzgerald's testimony did not make the slightest impression on me."

Senator Walsh had long since become wearied of the way in which Fox, and his assistant Spence, were chasing every conceivable will-o'-the-wisp in the hope of injuring the reputation of the nominee and of dragging out the hearings. In caustic words Walsh reminded Fox, and his listening fellow Senators, that six days ago everyone presenting testimony had declared he was finished. Anderson had returned to Boston. Then the committee had met on Saturday at the special request of Fox, solely to consider what the prosecutor of Brandeis alleged was "new evidence" on the Old Dominion case. They had given Fox his fresh chance. Now Fox was insisting on their waiting until tomorrow to hear a man from Boston named Edward Warren, on what topic no one seemed to know. There must, Walsh protested, be an end to this. After all, the committee had counted on Fox, who had been hired to present the case against Brandeis, to take charge of his side of this controversy. If anyone more had anything important to say he should have got in touch with Fox or the subcommittee staff by now.

Fox expostulated stubbornly: Would the committee really "shut out" a witness? Was this important public issue "to be closed"? Senator Works in his mild manner again played the role of pacifier, again on behalf of Fox. We cannot know for sure, Works said, whether this new testimony that Mr. Fox wants to present is material or not until we hear it, "but I still think if there was any important testimony offered here the committee should receive it." Grudgingly, Walsh agreed to hear Warren the following morning.

It was Charles Sumner Smith, however, who first took the witness chair the next day, to testify to the fees that the Brandeis law firm had been paid in the settlement of the Old Dominion Copper Company affairs—more than $200,000, based on a percentage of the award in a drawn-out suit on behalf of the company. There was no charge of dishonesty, just evidence of the high fee. Then William Youngman returned to the stand. He came "in rebuttal," he asserted, to what he

termed McClennen's misstatement of the Warren will affair more than
a week earlier. It was clear as daylight now that Fox was using every
bit player in his troupe to keep the show running. Walsh exploded:

> SENATOR WALSH: I wish you would bear in mind, Mr. Youngman,
> that we are not trying the Warren case.
>
> YOUNGMAN: No; we are trying Mr. Brandeis. I appreciate that.
>
> SENATOR WALSH: We are trying to find out what delinquency, if any,
> is chargeable to Mr. Brandeis.
>
> YOUNGMAN: Exactly; and when I get to my next step here, which
> shows. . . .

Walsh, unsupported by the weak Chilton, gave up for a few minutes, then tried again: "You will pardon me if I say that you gentlemen who have been in these lawsuits seem to wander off into the
trial of the lawsuit rather than the matter that the committee is more
directly concerned in." Youngman rambled on for another hour,
under questioning from Fox.

The final witness against Brandeis, Edward R. Warren of Boston,
turned out to have no connection whatsoever with the Warren family
will affair. Nor was he the Harvard Law School professor, Edward
H. Warren, who was the lone teacher in the school to object to the
Brandeis nomination. The Warren now in the witness chair had been
associated with Brandeis in the Public Franchise League in Boston
and had differed with him over the solution of the city's gas problem
in 1905. Warren's attack against Brandeis paralleled that Commissioner Clifford Thorne had launched at the opening of the hearings
six weeks before—that Brandeis had reversed himself, turning against
the public interest in favor of the special interests. As Warren put it,
"Mr. Brandeis has a wonderful magnetism when he speaks . . . and
he carried those men right off their feet. There was not time for them
to give the proper deliberate thought to that matter."

What obviously irked Warren was that the other League leaders
had endorsed the compromise gas bill that Brandeis proposed, leaving
Warren in a one-man minority. One of his colleagues who had second
thoughts about the compromise bill had asked: "Wouldn't it be possible to open this question again?"

Clearly recalling the experience with bitter humiliation, Warren told the Senators: "I remember Mr. Brandeis' reply, which I shall never forget, and I can remember these words, he said: 'Don't cry-baby.' "

McClennen took but a few minutes in reply to this new assault on Brandeis from a man who felt himself wronged and hurt, long ago. He inserted into the committee record a copy of the detailed letter the nominee had written to Warren on the very day that the decisive meeting of the Public Franchise League had taken place. In it Brandeis outlined precisely what had occurred at the meeting, and invited Warren to consider carefully the terms of the proposed compromise gas bill, "and let me know if you find any of them not entirely clear." Warren could not recall having received the letter—but acknowledged that he must have, since it was a carbon copy. McClennen said he had nothing more to contribute on the matter.

Fox then conceded: "We have nothing further, Senator." Walsh, in the absence of Chilton from the hearing room on other business, gaveled the hearings to a close for the second time. Brandeis, the nominee, had never appeared in the hearing room. But thirteen hundred sixteen pages of record, dissecting his professional life as far into the past as his enemies cared to go, were now ready for the printer. Any Senator with sufficient interest might search through them for guidance on the fitness of Louis D. Brandeis to sit on the Supreme Court.

In its ponderous fullness, the record of the Senate hearings tended to obscure the gist of both the case for the nominee and that against him. Yet the opponents had succeeded in two respects. First, they had brought in so many documents and witnesses in their campaign to block the confirmation of Brandeis that they had made a certain impression by the sheer volume of their efforts. Their case, some press commentators noted, had "taken weeks" to present. On its face, this made the opposition appear to have a "long list" of complaints against the nomineee, to have "many instances" to cite, going back "through many years." Certainly, said those the opposition had impressed, there "must be something to it," or else the nomination would have gone through routinely.

The second objective of the opponents had become obvious as February turned into March with the subcommittee still tied up in the hearings: to seize every possible opportunity to delay. Every week gained at this stage would put off the decision of the subcommittee;

this in turn would help postpone action by the full Senate Judiciary Committee with its eighteen members, and subsequently a Senate vote. In fattening the record with material touching on the behavior of the nominee ten, fifteen, and twenty years earlier, Fox and Spence, consciously aided by Senators Cummins and Works, and perhaps unconsciously by Chairman Chilton, were making it more plausible to plead for time at a later stage. For no Senator mindful of his duty in this great and important matter (as Fox kept stressing it was) could skim through this record in a day or two.

The friends of Brandeis, fighting defensively most of the time, had swung to the attack on few occasions. There were the strong letters of Asa P. French and George Anderson, among others, which pointed an accusing finger at the detractors of Brandeis. Professor Felix Frankfurter at the Harvard Law School had worked hard with former Governor Robert Perkins Bass of New Hampshire to stimulate letters in Brandeis' favor, aimed both at the subcommittee and at the presss. ("We need to yell what the issue is, no matter what the outcome may be," Frankfurter wrote Bass, pressing him to further efforts.)

The partisans of Brandeis missed their best chance to document the nominee's present approach to the law and the role of judges in giving it life. None of them thought to insert into the hearing record the text of the address Brandeis delivered at a meeting of the Chicago Bar Association on January 3, a few hours after Justice Lamar had died. This talk was printed under the title "The Living Law" in the *Illinois Law Review* of February 1916, while the subcommittee hearings were in progress.

In the past half-century, Brandeis had reminded his Chicago audience, public respect for law had been waning, and there had taken place a shifting of the people's longing from legal justice to social justice. This was to be expected, Brandeis said, when the industrial revolution had greatly affected men's daily lives while the law in large measure remained blind to the changes, as if the relations of factory worker to the corporation that employed him were still those of English villager to landlord.

"Has not the recent dissatisfaction with our law as administered been due, in large measure," asked Brandeis, "to the fact that it had not kept pace with the rapid development of our political, economic and social ideals?"

He declared that conservative judges had misused the Fourteenth Amendment to freeze the status quo:

> Where statutes giving expression to the new social spirit were clearly constitutional, judges, imbued with the relentless spirit of individualism, often construed them away. Where any doubt as to the constitutionality of such statutes could find lodgment, courts all too frequently declared the acts void. . . . The law has everywhere the tendency to lag behind the facts of life. . . . Small wonder that there arose a clamor for the recall of judges and of judicial decisions. . . .

But lately, Brandeis continued, attacks on the courts had abated, primarily because federal and state courts had swung in the other direction, following the upholding of the Oregon women's ten-hour law in *Muller* v. *Oregon*. Brandeis had modestly not mentioned his own premier role in winning the Muller case or the other victories for social legislation following closely in its path.

"The struggle for the living law has not been fully won," Brandeis continued. He pointed out that the 1905 Lochner ruling by the Supreme Court had not been expressly overruled and that the Court "showed by its recent decision in the Coppage case the potency of mental prepossessions." Thus, although "the living law" had won its Gettysburg, it had not yet brought its opponents to a final Appomatox.

"What we need is not to displace the courts," Brandeis concluded, "but to make them efficient instruments of justice; not to displace the lawyer, but to fit him for his official or judicial task." Lawyers should be taught not only how corporations are formed, but how investors, management, workers, and consumers think and behave in an urban, mechanized society. Lawyers so trained can educate the judges by properly presenting their cases with a broad outlook, Brandeis declared.

> Intense specialization [in the law] must continue. But we can correct its distorting effects by broader education—by study undertaken preparatory to practice—and continued by lawyer and judge throughout life: study of economics and sociology and politics which embody the facts and present the problems of today.

This address on "the living law" should have been Exhibit A in the case made by Brandeis' friends; yet no one brought it to the

Senators' attention. Instead, most of their time was spent in rebuttal of the charges brought against him.

So complex and unwieldy had the case become that Fox and his colleagues realized they must put their side in more manageable form if they were to convince many people that Brandeis should be rejected. They required a hard-hitting digest that would convey the villainy of Brandeis at a glance. In the latter part of March, therefore, Fox and Spence circulated summaries of their case against the nominee on a wholesale basis, using legal directories as mailing lists so uncritically that copies were received by Senators friendly to Brandeis, like Walsh, and such members of Woodrow Wilson's official family as Solicitor General John W. Davis and several members of the cabinet. Fox and Spence, in a hurry to cultivate opinion at the grass roots before the subcommittee would have time to issue its opinion on the hearings, circulated an article clipped from *Leslie's Weekly* which they called "a brief summary of *some* of the charges" against Brandeis, and promised in a covering note that "the testimony will be fully reviewed in a brief which we shall submit to you within the course of a few days." The *Leslie's Weekly* article, its partiality transparent as an open window, asked:

Is Brandeis Fit for the Bench?—then followed with a provocatively loaded question: "Has the advocacy of popular causes by Louis D. Brandeis been merely a cloak whereby he has covered unprofessional practices which have netted him a large fortune?" The article took up each of the charges briefly, in wording which begged condemnation of their target, without a hint of the rebuttal adduced at the hearings. It ended with the coy and somewhat paradoxical suggestion that the Senators could be counted on to examine the charges carefully, then to overlook the sins of Mr. Brandeis and confirm him.

Another widely circulated propaganda piece was the product of Thomas C. Spelling, the frustrated New York lawyer who had complained that Brandeis once had marked up his brief with such notations as *untenable* and *ridiculous*. Spelling's product was a four-page leaflet entitled "In re Nomination of Louis D. Brandeis—Summary of Charges." It was an attempt to explain what the shouting against Brandeis was all about, and listed the nominee's offenses as follows:

First: that Brandeis was charged [by Thorne] in the 1913–1914 Five Per Cent Rate Advance Case of having schemed to deprive the shippers of the chance to make their own final argument before the Interstate Commerce Commission, then conceded their case to the railroads.

Second: that in the Ten Per Cent Rate Increase Case of 1910–1911 Brandeis had needlessly conceded away the public interest to the railroads' demands, and had acted beyond his legal authority.

Third: that he had used the prestige and special knowledge gained from his former position of influence with the United Shoe Machinery Company to persecute the company in later years, and had reversed his view of the legality of the company's leases to his own gain.

Fourth: that he had dissemblingly served the interests of powerful, hidden parties bent on wrecking the New York & New England Railroad, concealing the identity of his true client.

Fifth: that in the Ballinger investigation he had concealed his employment by his real client, *Collier's Weekly,* and that "by unfair methods he acquired and made available as evidence the confidential knowledge of Ballinger's private secretary."

Sixth: that he was inconsistent in aiding the Harriman interests win a proxy fight for control of the Illinois Central Railroad in order to tie it to his Union and Southern Pacific network, while simultaneously fighting the New Haven's attempt to merge with the Boston & Maine; also that he denied working in Harriman's behalf, and that he "subsequently severely assailed and criticized Harriman."

Seventh: that in the Lennox bankruptcy case he had played both sides, leading James Lennox to believe he was acting as the firm's counsel while he was assigning its assets to his own law partner for distribution to the bankrupt's creditors—and that his law firm had taken $43,852 as fees from the insolvent estate.

Eighth: that in the Warren estate matter "having for a law partner the senior heir over whom he exercised a controlling influence, he used his confidential position and connection with conflicting interests in the estate largely to the pecuniary advantage of said senior heir and himself, in the form of attorney's fees and fraudulent diversion of funds."

Ninth: that in the legal struggle for control of the Gillette Safety Razor Company Brandeis had master-minded a scheme whereby one clique of stockholders had ousted another group, even including some of the clients of the Brandeis law firm.

Tenth: that Brandeis in 1905 had assisted in organizing the protective committee of policyholders of the Equitable Life Assurance Society and had severely criticized the company management, then in 1906 had turned around and defended the company against a suit in the Massachusetts courts.

Eleventh: that in 1902 and 1903 he had helped Fitzgerald take control of the Old Dominion Copper and Smelting Company through a proxy campaign, then carried through "secret methods for financing the re-organized company, at variance with the purpose for the accomplishment of which he had been employed."

Twelfth [more a conclusion than another charge]: "that his legal attainments and reputation as a member of the legal profession are not such as justify his being considered for so exalted a station as Associate Justice of the Supreme Court."

The twin themes running through the Spelling document, as through the article in *Leslie's Weekly* and the "Summary of Charges" that Fox and Spence mailed out, were Brandeis' secrecy and his inconsistency. Brandeis, they emphasized, was a trickster. Even should one succeed in finding what the man was really after, he was likely to squirm out of one's grasp like an eel and show up on the other side. Always he had a mercenary motive for behaving as he did.

Although Fox had listened day after day to the explanation of one of these charges after the other, and though he had himself conceded that some points advanced by witnesses did not seem supported by the facts, and even though he had frequently declined to attempt to confute rebuttal witnesses brought by Anderson, he nonetheless used the Spelling leaflet and the *Leslie's Weekly* article in his mailing campaign. It was as though the hearings had never been held, for these attacks on Brandeis could have been written before they opened. In his mailings, Fox did not even hint that a single charge against Brandeis had been answered.

Fox's strategy in this case was the same he had pursued in his appeals work in the New York appellate courts. He had advised law students to pick one strong point and concentrate everything on it, rather than to scatter their shots. If they could drive into the judges' heads just one strong argument to uphold a case, they should not weaken it by confusing, lesser issues.

The one point about Brandeis at which Fox had been driving for weeks was that the best people in Boston did not trust him. This cardinal fact was as plain to Austen Fox as any propositon could be. If the full import of the mistrust of nominee Brandeis could be borne home to the Senate, the country could be spared the unpleasant spectacle of Associate Justice Brandeis on the bench. For surely, Fox thought, Senators in their right minds could not vote to confirm a man in whom the better class of attorneys in his home city had no trust.

It was therefore of only secondary importance to Fox that each of the twelve issues raised at the hearings be categorically proved— or any of them, for that matter. A Senator might dismiss the Warren will, the Lennox bankruptcy, the New England, New Haven, and several other matters from his mind. It was important only that he be impressed with one issue, such as the Brandeis *volte-face* in the United Shoe Machinery Company case, and conclude from it that the man was a scheming double-crosser. To this end Fox had bent his full efforts by bringing to Washington as many "witnesses as to reputation" as the hearing schedule would allow.

When the *Harvard Alumni Bulletin* broke its silence about the Brandeis controversy just as the hearings closed, Fox was delighted to read in it President Lowell's defense of his right to join with the Boston lawyers in their protest. "It is an odd thing," Fox wrote the University president,

> . . . that the fact of a man being considered fit for the office which you fill should be held to disable you from expressing, in public form, a protest against the purpose of putting on the bench of our greatest court a man who can, justly, be even suspected of having a defective standard of professional ethics.
>
> I thought it a great honor that your committee asked me to represent it in a matter of such far-reaching importance—a "debt to our profession" which I was very glad to be able to try to discharge.

Yes, it was odd, Lowell replied, that of all people he should have to claim liberty of speech for himself, when he had been fighting for that very right on behalf of Harvard professors during the past two years:

The Brandeis case is to me a very painful one, because I have long believed him untrustworthy, while he was still a lawyer for corporations, before he began attacking them.

Some time I should like to have a talk with you about the popular psychology of these things—the way in which men who have a great reputation as reformers over the country are singularly apt to be thought defective in character in their own state. The disregard shown, by many intelligent people in the Brandeis case, for character as a qualification for the Bench is to me discouraging; but, being an optimist, I believe it to be only temporary.

By March 23rd Fox was sending a hopeful note to the Harvard president:

> I have reports to the effect that our work may produce results. Three Democrats on the Judiciary Committee are said to be unwilling to vote for confirmation. If this be true, and *continue* to be true, . . . there will be an adverse report. In that event, confirmation will be difficult.

While the five-member jury in the Brandeis case was considering its verdict, those who had taken part in the hearings would have found it difficult to measure from the press how persuasive they had been. For the hearings had offered to both sides just the evidence they needed to confirm their visceral reactions to the Brandeis nomination. Publishers and editors had adopted a *parti pris* for or against Brandeis from the outset, much as they stood staunchly for or against the protective tariff. The middle ground of neutrality was slight indeed. As the hearings had rolled on, the press stood substantially on the fixed ground it had first adopted.

The hearings had barely got under way when Taft received a clipping from Gus Karger showing that the Washington *Times* required no further evidence to prove Brandeis unfit for a seat on the Supreme Court. Has the career of Mr. Brandeis, the *Times* asked itself,

> . . . with his tempestuous, passionate, vindictive personal attitude, wholly against anything and everything bad or good, on the side opposed to him, and his enthusiastic, fiery, and unqualified personal attitude, wholly in favor of his own side, to the inclusion of anything and everything, the bad as well as the good—has that career proved his unfitness to sit in the highest tribunal of the land? . . .

Can he see a thing straight, or can he see a thing only with the eyes of personal prejudice, antagonism and hatred? If he cannot see a thing except as he wants to see it . . . he ought not to be a judge . . . for any cause which calls for a dispassionate weighing of the facts and a sure determination of the right.

Nobody who has studied the career of this man thinks there is any such judge or the possibility of any such judge in Louis D. Brandeis.

While Karger sought to buoy Taft's spirits with this condemnation of the Justice-designate, Woodrow Wilson was receiving evidence of support from his friends and followers. The Los Angeles *Morning Tribune* and *Evening Express,* progressive papers owned by E. T. Earl, rejoiced that

. . . the appointment of Louis D. Brandeis gives the Supreme Court of the United States its first thorough-going radical. . . .

Throughout his whole career Louis Brandeis has been the aggressive champion of the rights of the plain people. . . . It is good to think that there will be at least one judge on the Supreme Court bench who sets humanity above all else and who will interpret the Constitution in terms of manhood rather than of property.

In Stockton, California, the *Record* spoke to the issue of "judicial temperament" with great perception when the hearings were in their final week:

There is probably no man on the present Supreme Bench who has more than a small fraction of Brandeis' acquaintance with the living and thinking of the 85 per cent of the American people who earn their way in humble station. There is probably no man anywhere who looks at law, at government, so understandingly from the standpoint of the greatest good to the greatest number.

This temperate valuation of Brandeis as a potential judge came from the same newspaper that five weeks earlier had melodramatically hailed the nominee as a modern St. George and a gladiator for the people, rolled into one:

. . . Brandeis is a mighty man in heart and brain. . . .

Brandeis has delighted to pit his talents against the encroachments of trust privilege. At more than one investigation and hearing he has stripped the pretenses of justice from veneered wrong and

revealed an insensate creature that has nourished its porcine system
on the sweat and blood of men, women and children. And, with a
thrilling eloquence that sounds like an echo of the ringing words
of an Isaiah, from whose race he comes, Brandeis has demanded
consideration for the bodies and souls of the toiling victims.

He has stood in the arena of industrial strife and held his thumb
high over the prostrate form of his brother man. . . . No student
of history can mistake the meaning of the first man of the Brandeis
type coming to Supreme Court honors.

The *Nation,* weekly magazine of opinion, was one of the few
publications to evaluate with some care the evidence brought out at
the hearings. At the outset the *Nation* disapproved the nomination,
but its opposition to Brandeis was restrained. A man "of his temperament, and of his record as an intense and often bitter advocate"
might eventually achieve the judicial attitude, said the *Nation,* but
"his connection with many cases or agitations" certain to come before
the Supreme Court for decision, would surely force his disqualifica-
tion because of "the ardor of his advocacy." Further, it was a pity
that the President should take such an obviously political step in
order to attract to him the Jewish voters, the labor unions, and Teddy
Roosevelt's Progressives:

> Even the Colonel may be imagined asking himself why he never
> ventured so bold a thing as putting a great radical into the Su-
> preme Court. Bold, indeed, the President has been. It is another
> question whether he has been wise.

When the battle over confirmation had been joined, the Washington
correspondent of the *Nation* warned his readers that the possession
or lack of judicial temperament was the one issue by which Brandeis
should be weighed. A profile of Brandeis, signed pseudonymously
"Tattler," was the work of Francis E. Leupp, a Republican by
instinct and family tradition, whose beau ideal in public life was
Henry Cabot Lodge. Leupp willingly conceded to Brandeis brilliance
and disregard for money; but he presented it as an obvious fact also
that a "propagandist" such as Brandeis could not possess judicial
capacity. It was indeed a pity, the columnist said, that "the President
should have chosen this particular time to throw a bone of conten-
tion in among the multitude of citizens whose support, regardless
of conventional party lines, he is soliciting in the crisis our foreign

relations have reached." The President could have nominated Brandeis as "bait for the Hebrew vote at the coming election," as a move to attract "the now disorganized remnant of the Progressive party," or in order "to procure for the cause of 'social justice' a hearing in the private councils of the judges." But whatever Wilson's motives, "Tattler" continued, "Mr. Brandeis cannot be sneered out of the field; his enemies will have to fight him with the weapons of reason, and not of contempt or innuendo."

Several weeks later, as the hearings drew to a close, the *Nation* sought, as few publications did, to evaluate the evidence. It judged the Warren will, the Harriman proxies, and the Equitable Life as matters that had "been either disposed of or made negligible." The one charge that had been strengthened by the evidence, the magazine said, was that of Brandeis' dealings with the United Shoe Machinery Company. His course, the *Nation* concluded, "was not only in clear violation of professional ethics, but was marked by a shiftiness and lack of moral delicacy which are hurtful to his reputation." The feeling against the nominee among members of the Boston bar weighed heavily in the judgment of the *Nation,* though it acknowledged that Brandeis was certainly not "a monster of duplicity." It cited the explanation by Sherman Whipple of Brandeis' being aloof, isolated, and "self-centered in carrying out his own ideas." But Whipple's human explanation of the feeling against Brandeis, the *Nation* concluded, "does not prove his fitness for the Supreme Court."

In contrast to the *Nation,* the new liberal weekly *New Republic* stated from the very outset that Brandeis had proved by his life's work as a lawyer that he, above all others, was trained for Supreme Court service. The magazine's view was stated in an unsigned editorial written by Professor Felix Frankfurter of the Harvard Law School, who had known Brandeis for a dozen years and was even now preparing to take Brandeis' place in defense of the Oregon minimum-wage law before the Supreme Court. One public benefit of the controversial nomination, the law teacher pointed out, was that it had started discussion of what the Court means in American life. Basically the Supreme Court's job, Frankfurter wrote, "is to define limitations of power," which at present revolve about the commerce clause and the Fourteenth Amendment and their application to the realities of a modern industrial democracy. Frankfurter continued:

To the consideration of these very questions Mr. Brandeis has
given his whole life. To their understanding he brings a mind of
extraordinary power and insight. He has amassed experiences enjoyed by hardly another lawyer to the same depth and richness and
detail, for it is the very condition of his mind to know all there is
to be known of a subject with which he grapples.

The *New Republic* editorial asserted that a man who could bring
peace between labor and capital in the anarchistic garment-manu-
facturing industry, as Brandeis had done, "has that balance of head
and heart and will which constitutes real judicial-mindedness." True,
he might not always be amiable in a fight, and some people might be
honestly convinced he had wronged them. The old charges raised
against him have never been proved, the editorial declared, yet his
friends welcome their being examined by the Senate committee because "they believe that no man's career can stand as much scrutiny
as his. They want the insinuations crystalized, examined and disposed
of, so that the nation may begin to employ this man who has at once
the passion of public service and the genius for it."

From time to time as the hearings progressed the *New Republic*
tried to interpret the jumble of testimony in the committee room, but
it was impossible to clarify every point. At the end, the liberal weekly
declared:

All that any supporter of Mr. Brandeis would ask is that people
read the testimony. His opponents have had every conceivable opportunity to present every bit of evidence, rumor and suspicion that
could be found to throw an unfavorable light upon him. . . .
The advocates of Mr. Brandeis have not done what they might
so easily have done, started a counter-attack upon Mr. Brandeis'
enemies. . . . Had they felt less sure of themselves, they could, for
example, have put President Lowell, Mr. Taft and Mr. Root on the
stand and cross-examined them mercilessly to show that no one of
these gentlemen has any exact knowledge on which to base his
suspicions.

The *New Republic* put its finger on the basic inconsistency of the
campaign to defeat Brandeis in discussing what it termed the leitmotif of the charges: that he had frequently been guilty of double-
dealing:

He is supposed to be a man who is at once violently partisan for his client, yet disloyal to him. He is supposed to be without the "judicial temperament," and at the same time inclined to be on both sides of a case. Those who attacked him seemed unable to agree on whether he is a ruthless partisan, or a man who is not partisan enough. But they concentrated finally on the belief that he is not the absolute partisan of his client.

The editors of the *New Republic* did not know it at the time, but William Howard Taft was on the point of launching a libel suit against the weekly on the strength of its indictment of him for having signed the A.B.A. protest. One would have supposed, the *New Republic* had observed, that Taft was ill qualified to judge Brandeis because the Boston attorney had "caught him in what is perhaps the most deplorable episode in which a President of the United States has been involved." The censor of Brandeis' manner and morals was reminded "that he antedated a public document in the Ballinger case, that he deceived the public in regard to his action, that he tried to conceal his deception with a falsehood." It was Mr. Brandeis, the editorial said, "who demonstrated to the country Mr. Taft's immoral procedure in a disreputable incident."

The former President consulted his old Attorney General, George Wickersham, and Wickersham's partner Henry Taft about a suit, but the skittish Wickersham counseled his chief against pursuing the issue in court:

Certainly neither you nor I thought we were doing anything wrong in formulating the facts we had found in the documents we had before us on September 11th, 1909, and the conclusions we reached, in the form of a memorandum and recommendations actually written after that date, but bearing the date on the day you promulgated your decision. It remained for the sophistry of a Brandeis to put an immoral construction upon it. I was pilloried . . . at the time for my share in it, and called by every vituperative epithet applicable to a liar and forger.

But at the present time I think nobody but a bunch of Hebrew uplifters of the same stripe as Brandeis would dream of repeating the criticism. Frankly, I should not for one moment seriously think of dignifying them by a libel suit. . . . The paragraph in the *New Republic* is vicious and abominable. But it won't hurt you one whit, and unless made the subject of a lawsuit few will see it and still fewer be impressed with anything but disgust at it.

Wickersham then shifted from his rage against the "Hebrew uplifters" of the *New Republic* to the cardinal issue—the chances of blocking Brandeis' confirmation:

> Fox tells me that he is very hopeful of preventing Brandeis' confirmation; that only two Republicans—La Follette and Clapp—will vote for him, and that several Democrats will vote against him. He says the Republicans are confident of being able to prevent it coming to a vote unless they are sure of defeating him. It is however a disgusting fact that while many Jews privately criticize the nomination as unfit, none of them will put pen to paper to say so.

Taft replied that Wickersham's advice against a suit "is probably the correct one, though I confess I would like to try out the matter and inflict a substantial verdict on the entire contingent running the magazine." But he shook his head sadly over the optimism of Fox, saying he wished he could be as hopeful. A few days later Taft wrote Wickersham that he had looked over the Ballinger investigation record again and was pleased to see that it contains "an assurance by the majority of the committee that there was nothing discreditable in the whole matter either to you or to me. That is as far as the committee thought it necessary to go."

As the days of waiting stretched on, Taft found it impossible to banish the shade of Brandeis from his thoughts. The newspapers told him in late March that Brandeis had been chosen honorary president of a national conference of Jewish leaders in Philadelphia, which planned a great convention of Jews to be held in Washington later in the year. Although Brandeis since his nomination had withdrawn from every public activity, the urgencies of the war impelled him to carry on his work for Jewish welfare and Zionism. Taft could see his swift rise to leadership only through political eyes.

"I am really sorry for this," Taft wrote to Gus Karger. "I should not be at all surprised if our worthy President had something to do with it in calling on other prominent Jews to help him to use this to secure confirmation."

Karger did not reply to Taft's speculation on the long hand of Wilson meddling in Jewish affairs, but he seconded Taft's regret:

Your opinion of the Philadelphia gathering of Jews and the purposes of Brandeis is shared by the great body of reform Jews in
America. The Philadelphia gathering was participated in largely by
the orthodox, many of whom wore their hats in the hall, as they
would in the "shool."

The fight is between Stephen Wise and Brandeis on the one
hand, and Jacob Schiff on the other. Wise is about as radical as
Brandeis and the movement is a Zionistic one. The "Congress" is to
be held in Washington, and there, in the name of Judaism, they
will demand their rights and redress of wrongs. I fear that it will
take the guise of a class movement, and will do the Jews in America
a great deal of harm.

Fifteen days after the subcommittee had closed hearings, Taft
could not hold himself back longer from writing to Senator Lodge
to urge him to carry on the fight, whatever the committee should
report. He slid into the subject by first congratulating Lodge on his
latest essay on Charles Francis Adams, then came to his true purpose
in writing:

I also take this opportunity to express to you the satisfaction that
I have in hearing that you expect to make a strong stand against
the confirmation of Brandeis. In the last ten years of bitter attack
upon the courts and the exploitation of various nostrums and
hostility against our social order, it was to be expected that under
an opportunist President, such as we now have, some traits of the
hysteria would appear in the personnel of the Supreme Court.

I am an optimist, and therefore even Brandeis' elevation to the
Court and taking part in its decisions will not discourage me. Still
it is an evil and a disgrace that ought to be avoided. I sincerely
hope that you will make your opposition and that of the other Republicans who are with you, and such Democrats as have courage
to take the same view, emphatic enough so that even if unsuccessful, it shall impress itself on the country.

The protest signed by the A.B.A. presidents was initiated by Wickersham in response to Lodge's call for support from the bar, Taft
stated. Now he would like to know from the Senator "how the matter
stands in your opinion." Karger and the New York press gave him the
impression that Brandeis would be confirmed, yet Fox seemed to
hope that the Senate Judiciary Committee would make an adverse

report because of the disaffection of some Democrats. "I am afraid Fox is too hopeful," Taft concluded.

Lodge replied in the tone of one who stood far above the battle:

> As to Brandeis, all you say is entirely true; but my own opinion is that he will be confirmed because the Administration is behind him and the Democrats will stand by the President. There will be, of course, a good deal of discussion, but I fear that the result will be what you anticipate.

Taft had brought up the Jewish issue to Lodge as if it loaded the dice unfairly in Brandeis' and Wilson's favor:

> As there is an element of racial support for him, it takes on the peculiar form that was to be expected. There is no opposition to Brandeis because he is a Jew, whether fit or not. There are many Jews who know that he is altogether unfit, but they have not the courage to speak out and seek to stem the current of that racial feeling that it is so easy for him to set moving. I observe that his friends have pulled the wires so as to make him the President of a great Jewish Congress, all for the purpose of bringing the political pressure of the Jews upon the issue of his confirmation.

Of course, Lodge replied to this part of Taft's letter, "as you say, there has not been the slightest opposition to him because of his race. That has been brought forward only by those who favor him. The entire opposition centers on the question of his personal and professional integrity."

As Lodge and Taft were exchanging their disclaimers of prejudice, Brandeis in Boston and a young friend in New York were experiencing its subtle manifestation. Richard Whitney, secretary of the admissions committee at the Harvard Club of New York, wrote to Brandeis asking him to withdraw his proposal of Henry Hurwitz, class of 1908, for membership, "owing to the fact that there was great opposition to the candidate in the committee." The Harvard Club of New York was hardly a tight little organization of personal friends, since it had about 4000 members. In most cases a Harvard tie was the only ticket of admission required. Yet Whitney gave Brandeis no reason why "great opposition" should arise from his proposal of Hurwitz' name. Brandeis might have interpreted the rejection as a slap at himself as sponsor of the prospective member; or it might be that the committee resented Hurwitz for being "aggressively Jewish," since he had founded the Menorah Society as a student at Harvard, and now edited the *Menorah Journal,* dedicated to the advancement of Jewish culture and ideals. Perhaps it was the combination of Hurwitz and Brandeis that Whitney and his committee could not bear, even though the eminent Charles Eliot, former president of Harvard, was one of the consulting editors of the *Menorah Journal,* along with Brandeis.

"You are evidently a victim of my enemies," Brandeis wrote to Hurwitz, notifying him of his rejection by the Harvard Club. "I suppose there is nothing to do but to withdraw your name, which I will do as soon as I have your approval." Resentfully, Hurwitz gave up.

At about the same time the Harvard Club of New York was barring Brandeis' candidate from admission to membership, a series of behind-the-scenes political events were taking place that would solidify the Republican opponents of the nominee. On the evening of Wednesday, March 29, Justice Charles Evans Hughes opened his door to admit Henry L. Stoddard, editor of the *Evening Mail* of New York, a Roosevelt intimate, and a 1912 Progressive leader. Since the turn of the year, Hughes had felt increasing pressure from Republicans that he leave the Supreme Court and accept the Presidential nomination. He alone, they argued, could unite a party that had split in 1912. The Justice had said repeatedly that he was completely out of politics, but still his admirers would not leave Hughes alone. Now, with the nominating convention just nine weeks away, he felt that he must talk with someone, so he consented to a private interview with Stoddard. Hughes may not have known, though he easily could have surmised, that Roosevelt's political manager, George Perkins, had urged Stoddard to seek the interview to determine Hughes' real intentions.

The Justice told Stoddard that he would commit an act of disloyalty to his colleagues on the Court by resigning now. The Court was short-handed and overburdened with work. Not only was the Lamar seat empty, but Justice Day was still feeble from a recent illness and McReynolds as a former Attorney General was unable to sit in a number of cases to which the federal government was a party. Yet as Hughes talked on, stressing the reasons why he would not resign from the Supreme Court in midterm, Stoddard noted the one primary fact that had changed from previous political disclaimers by the Justice. Hughes did not forswear acceptance of the nomination if it should come to him in June. He said that he would not resign now, but he did not speak of the matter of acceptance later.

The jurist summed up his posture with an oracular remark: "I shall remain silent until the end."

On Thursday, Perkins in New York received a detailed memorandum from Stoddard on the Hughes interview, and immediately went into conference with Roosevelt. On Friday, March 31, five of the most important Republicans in the United States met for a quiet luncheon. Roosevelt and Elihu Root, who had not spoken to each other since their bitter parting at the 1912 GOP convention, came together at last. Also present were Senator Henry Cabot Lodge and General Leonard Wood, who fancied himself a man-on-horseback political leader. They met at the home of Robert Bacon, who had been Secretary of State and then ambassador to France in the Roosevelt and Taft administrations after serving as a partner in the J. P. Morgan banking firm, where he had been a close colleague of George Perkins. When news of the conference got out, the conferees assured reporters that they had talked only "national defense and preparedness." But no one in the country believed such a group could have avoided discussing the coming Presidential campaign and the need to heal the 1912 breach with a candidate who could defeat Woodrow Wilson. They all could see that the gulf that had divided regular Republican from Progressive four years ago had narrowed to the vanishing point. The war was to be waged on one front against Wilson and everything he stood for.

The day after the Republican leaders conferred in New York, Brandeis was stirred from his near-seclusion in Boston to receive an astounding proposal. It came from Henry Morgenthau, who had recently returned to the United States after resigning as Wilson's ambassador to Turkey and was eagerly throwing his energies into the advance work of Wilson's campaign for re-election. A mixer and doer who thrilled to be at the center of big decision-making and the raising of political funds, Morgenthau sparked with inspiration for *coups* and startling approaches to political problems. The impasse over the Brandeis nomination, the subcommittee having been out for two full weeks without a decision, was for Morgenthau intolerable. Hastily he sent a message to Brandeis in Boston: he had a brilliant stroke to propose—where could they meet? Brandeis suggested New

London as mutually convenient, and there the two conferred on April 1. Morgenthau's hasty diary recorded the gist of their interview:

> I met Louis Brandeis at New London and discussed with him the advisability of his declining to be Supreme Court Judge and run for Senator in Massachusetts against Lodge, as that would give him a chance to vindicate before the world as to the charges made against him before the Judiciary Committee, and also urged upon him that he will have a much greater opportunity to fight for the rights of the people and oppose interests in the Senate than in the bench where he would have to have four associate judges side with him before an effective decision could be reached.

Brandeis listened quietly, then asked Morgenthau if he would divide the proposal into two questions: first, his declining the Court nomination, and second, the matter of running for the Senate. Morgenthau balked at this; under no circumstances should Brandeis decline the associate justiceship if he would not run for the Senate. Morgenthau's diary noted that he had scored something less than a triumph of persuasion: "He promised to take it under prayerful consideration." The two then discussed Zionism among other topics before they parted.

Shortly afterward Morgenthau confided to his journal that Woodrow Wilson did not want Brandeis to step down from the Supreme Court nomination because he was "certain" to be confirmed. Yet, should he fail of confirmation, the President added, "it would be a good thing for him to run." A little later Morgenthau got word from Brandeis that he would stick it out with the Supreme Court nomination.

The suspense from the Judiciary Committee came to an end on Monday, April 3. Senator Chilton announced that his subcommittee had approved the Brandeis nomination. The vote, which was strictly along party lines, had been three in favor to two opposed. The subcommittee report on its way from the Government Printing Office was a thick one in four parts: one signed by Senators Chilton and Fletcher, a concurring but separate report from Senator Walsh, and two strongly worded, lengthy adverse reports from Senators Cummins and Works. The next round would be fought out in the full Senate Judiciary Committee.

eight

Delay in Committee

In his report to the Judiciary Committee, Senator William Chilton offered his colleagues a guide to the thick volume of testimony that he knew they would not take the time to read:

> The nominee whose name is before us now has been an active, forceful quantity in his city, state, and country. He has enjoyed a large, lucrative law practice almost ever since he was admitted to the bar. He has been . . . a public speaker and lecturer with pronounced views, and with exceptional powers for impressing those views upon the public; the unpaid counsel of labor organzations, protective associations, and other civic bodies; the paid counsel in many of the most important legal contests before the courts and other public tribunals; an arbitrator in strikes and labor disputes; and the special counsel of the Interstate Commerce Commission.
>
> Such a man, so prominently active in public and private life . . . is bound to have been engaged in contests before the courts and before legislative bodies more or less bitter; and he would indeed be a human prodigy if he had not aroused some bitter antagonisms. It is in evidence that there was a systematic campaign of advertisements to injure him in the estimation of the public.

Approaching the evidence in the case of Louis D. Brandeis from this perspective, Chilton summarized the charges against Brandeis, then dismissed them one by one as proving nothing against the prospective Justice on trial. The allegation that Brandeis consciously advised and assisted Sam Warren in a breach of trust in fraud against his brother "is wholly unfounded," declared the subcommittee chairman. "In order to condemn Mr. Brandeis for anything done in this whole matter one must emphasize every suspicion and minimize the prominent facts shown by the weight of the evidence."

Chilton required several thousand words to explain the complex United Shoe Machinery case. The most significant fact, he concluded:

> . . . is that Mr. Brandeis voluntarily and with no prospect of profit to himself gave up his connection with a profitable client as soon as and because he became convinced that the policy which it was pursuing, and would not change, was wrong. Four years later, and again without desire for profit for himself, he gave his assistance to the effort to stop what he believed would be the future and increasing effect upon the community of that wrong policy.
>
> It may well be asked, "How long does an employment mortgage the lawyer's conscience?" After all, what "private information" was divulged? I can not see that there was any.

The West Virginia Senator expended some 4000 words in explanation of the tangled affairs of the Lennox tannery. He documented the part played by Brandeis in them as in a graduate thesis, giving page references in the hearing record for Senators who might want to consult the lengthy sourcebook. In summary, the subcommittee chairman declared that "the events in this case were due entirely to the fact that the debtors went back on the plan to which they agreed and under which the matter was taken up, namely, to devote their property fully and without hesitation to the payment of their debts. They were never deserted in any way."

So went Chilton's majority report, through charge upon charge. On the New York and New England Railroad matter: "I can find neither reason nor excuse to justify anything but an unequivocal vindication of the nominee from this charge." The Gillette Safety Razor case: "nothing to criticize . . . at any point." The Illinois Central Railroad proxies and Brandeis' alleged ties to the sinister monopolist, E. H. Harriman: "anyone looking at the evidence . . . could not fail to dismiss this charge as wholly unsupported." Thorne's cry of "betrayal" in the Five Per Cent Rate case: "in my opinion this charge is without any merit whatsoever. . . . Mr. Brandeis performed his duty fully and with due regard for all parties and counsel interested, and for the commission which retained him as their counsel." The Equitable Policyholders' Protective Committee—Chilton saw no conflict between Brandeis' work for the policyholders and for the insurance company in specific cases.

As to Brandeis' "wrecking" the New Haven Railroad, Chilton declared that "this charge is without foundation. . . . He investigated and made public the financial condition of this railroad . . . was bitterly assailed for this . . . the correctness of his position is now generally conceded. This extensive work was done without compensation." The appearance of Brandeis in the Ballinger investigation as attorney for Glavis while under payment by *Collier's Weekly:* "Those interested knew the situation then as well as they do now. This incident has nothing in it detrimental to the nominee." Brandeis' use of information obtained from Frederick Kerby, the Interior Department stenographer, in the Ballinger investigation: "In neither interview did Mr. Brandeis urge him to make the disclosure or offer him any inducement. . . . There are no limits to suspicion, but there are rules of evidence. . . . Shall we ignore the proved facts and indulge a suspicion in order to condemn the nominee? I cannot." And so it went with the rest of the sixteen topics the subcommittee chairman examined.

Most of the nominee's opponents, Chilton reported, "have been erroneously influenced by the advertising campaign carried on against him." To illustrate the character of the campaign, Chilton cited an article in *The Wall Street Journal* that convicted Brandeis as a liar and crook in the Lennox case, then besmirched the miscreant with a subtle touch of anti-Semitism and anti-German feeling. Brandeis on the bench, *The Wall Street Journal* had sneered, "puts the United States before the world below even the present standards of his Teutonic ancestors."

Chilton declared that the subcommittee had followed every lead furnished by Clarence Barron, publisher of the *Journal,* and found "absolutely nothing to reflect upon Mr. Brandeis' character as a man or lawyer." He dismissed peremptorily the suggestion that doubt concerning the ethics of the nominee should by itself block his confirmation. "If that theory shall obtain," Chilton argued, "then it is possible, by a campaign of slander, to bar the best men and the best lawyers in the country from the judicial office. I am not willing to indorse a campaign of slander." Senator Fletcher of Florida, the chairman said, agreed with his report.

The Chilton statement was not strong enough for Senator Walsh, because it did not expose the tangle of motives that prompted the bitter assault on the nominee. The hearings had laid open the past life and conduct of Louis D. Brandeis for examination. Now, Walsh believed, it was time "to bring to mind some idea of the atmosphere breathed by those who speak in disparagement of him."

Walsh pointed out that Bigelow, who had clashed with Brandeis in the Old Dominion Copper Mining Company case, eventually was forced to pay more than $2,000,000 to Brandeis' clients:

> It was bad enough to be required to give up $2,000,000, but to be branded as having misappropriated so much of the property of the stockholders who had been induced to come into a corporation organized by him was a grievance that very naturally rankled. It is altogether probable that Mr. Bigelow would not express himself in complimentary terms concerning Mr. Brandeis if he were moved to speak of him.

Senator Walsh cited several of Brandeis' public campaigns, each of which brought him into conflict with powerful forces of great wealth and influence, each leaving behind its residue of bitterness against him. Walsh also ran through several of the private cases, finding no fault in Brandeis' conduct in them that would warrant rejecting his nomination. The Senator then summed up with vigor:

> The real crime of which this man is guilty is that he has exposed the inequities of men in high places in our financial system. He has not stood in awe of the majesty of wealth. . . .
>
> He has been an iconoclast. He has written about and expressed views on "social justice," to which vague term are referred movements and measures to obtain greater security, greater comfort, and better health for the industrial workers—signifying safety devices, factory inspection, sanitary provision, reasonable hours, the abolition of child labor—all of which threaten a reduction of dividends. They all contemplate that a man's a man and not a machine.

Here at last Senator Walsh exposed the crux of the case against Brandeis: that he personified a fearsome threat to the current rate of profit—to the dividend system unrestrained by social law. None of his opponents had said this openly, because it was the the kind of thing men found embarrassing to put into words. Nor had any observer other than the plainspoken Walsh put the gist of the anti-

Brandeis sentiment into one simple proposition. Yet as Walsh looked back over everything that had been said in nearly ten weeks since Brandeis had been nominated, all the diverse parts seemed to click into place. Brandeis put the social imperative above the requirement that an investor reap the highest possible profit. He fought consistently and effectively for the sorts of measure that had steadily reduced the dividend rate that men of property enjoyed a generation ago. To those who saw his activities as subversive of their traditional way of life, Brandeis was a force for evil. His public work was, to them, a social crime.

Walsh could not agree with those who argued that only the uncontroversial should sit on the Supreme Court:

> It is easy for a brilliant lawyer so to conduct himself as to escape calumny and vilification. All he needs to do is to drift with the tide. If he never assails the doer of evil who stands high in the market place, either in court or before the public, he will have no enemies or detractors or none that he need heed.

The minority views of Senator Cummins contained no hint of the underlying motives of Brandeis' enemies. Caught in a vise between his past as a quasi-Progressive foe of big business on the one hand and his ambitions for the Republican Presidential nomination on the other, Cummins was embarrassed by the Brandeis nomination. His public conduct seemed to put him in the pro-Brandeis camp; the two had both been close to Robert La Follette in philosophical and economic outlook, and they had come into contact in the broad movement to control the abuses of monopoly. Yet in a Presidential election year, with Charles Evans Hughes still an enigma and bitter resentment against Roosevelt still eating at the heart of the GOP, Cummins was repairing his political fences. Since the Brandeis struggle had taken on the aspect of a partisan matter waged along strict party lines, Cummins the candidate decided early in the contest that he had no choice. He must align himself with his party, and so use the Brandeis nomination issue to inflate his prestige with the conservative Republicans whose support he was courting. He therefore had to join them in opposing Woodrow Wilson on every available ground until the national convention, nine weeks away.

Cummins' report condemning the nomination was strained from

start to finish. It leaned most heavily on Clifford Thorne's complaint that Brandeis at the Interstate Commerce Commission hearing had betrayed the public in favor of the railroads' grab for higher freight rates. Brandeis, the Senator said, "made an admission which destroyed any hope of defeating the claims of the carriers. Sitting as a judge rather than as an advocate he thus practically decided the suit in favor of the railroads." To Cummins the conduct of Brandeis "seems utterly indefensible. He was an attorney for the public." If his action was not betrayal, the Senator declared, "then I confess I do not understand either common morality among men or the ethics of the profession to which Mr. Brandeis belongs."

Cummins ran quickly through several other cases, finding fault with Brandeis in some, dismissing others. In the United Shoe Machinery case, "a due regard for professional propriety would have prevented Mr. Brandeis from accepting employment from anyone to attack his former client." In the Lennox affair, his presiding over the distribution of a bankrupt company's assets to creditors made him "hostile to his former client"—"to me it is an unseemly spectacle. . . . I am bound to condemn the whole transaction." In the Ballinger investigation, Cummins stated, "it was his duty to state openly and frankly to the committee" his employment by *Collier's Weekly*. . . . "Mr. Brandeis failed to recognize his plain obligation." In the Warren will case, Cummins objected to Brandeis' attempt to represent everyone in the dispute.

Most of the other charges, however, Cummins dismissed as not reflecting on the nominee. He had great admiration for "the strength of his mind and the scope of his knowledge," the Senator protested, and sympathy with Brandeis' sociological and economic opinions. "I cannot, however, even seem to approve his course in many of the matters" brought before the subcommittee. For this reason, said Cummins, the nominee "has lost the confidence" of so many lawyers and citizens "as to vitally impair his usefulness as a Justice of the Supreme Court."

Senator Works of California came to the same conclusion as Cummins, but he needed three times as many pages to justify his view. They revealed a studied effort to be fair, the tone was restrained, but the verdict was nonetheless a downturned thumb.

Brandeis, Works decided, had not done "the fair thing" to his colleague Clifford Thorne in the Five Per Cent Rate Case before the

I.C.C. His course in the United Shoe Machinery case had been "far from commendable," revealing a lack of "a due sense of the proprieties." Brandeis had not observed the canons of the bar in having been "employed by Mr. Lennox to protect his interests and failed to do so." Further, it was "an impropriety" for Brandeis to have "concealed" his being paid by *Collier's Weekly* when he defended Glavis in the Ballinger probe. And he made the "grave mistake" of not resigning from the Warren will case when two members of the Warren family found themselves at odds.

Works dismissed a couple of the charges as worthless, but found a distinct black mark against the nominee for having represented Massachusetts liquor interests in the 1890s. In the righteous tones of the political Prohibitionist, Works denounced Brandeis' long-ago arguments for reasonable liquor laws as "paid-for sentiments in the interests of a business acknowledged by all thinking people to be injurious to the public welfare." Brandeis had sold his advocacy "on a great moral question," the Senator said.

Even more stoutly than had Cummins, Works declared his sympathy for the economic and social views of Brandeis. But the nominee, he said, deservedly acquired the reputation of being "intolerant and offensive in his methods," has "defied the plain ethics of his profession," and "disregarded or defied the proprieties." This reputation, the Californian concluded, "stands as a strong barrier against his confirmation." Works wound up his forty-six-page outline of the case with the Caesar's-wife argument President Lowell of Harvard had set out at the end of January, and to which Austen Fox had given his best efforts:

> A man to be appointed to the exalted and responsible position of Justice of the Supreme Court should be free from suspicion and above reproach. Whether suspicion rests upon him unjustly or not his confirmation would be a mistake. . . . He is of the material that makes good advocates, reformers, and crusaders, but not good or safe judges.

The publication of the subcommittee report on April 3 moved the Brandeis nomination to a new stage with a new cast. The Senate Judiciary Committee had eighteen members, ten Democrats, and eight Republicans, who would decide whether or not the nomination of the prospective Justice should be reported favorably to the Senate.

The subcommittee hearing record and report bulked a fat two and a half inches, a formidable amount of reading for busy Senators with many duties other than rendering a decision on Mr. Wilson's Justice. If the full committee should follow the tactics of delay that had become obvious in the subcommittee, there was no telling when it would vote.

The approach of the Presidential campaign was dulling the critical faculties of the insurgent Republicans. Party unity was in the air. Those on the progressive fringes of the party in days past might have drunk from the same font of economic liberalism with Brandeis; but this year they were partisan blood-brothers with Henry Cabot Lodge, Elihu Root, and Taft. If all eight Republicans within the Committee would oppose the confirmation of Brandeis, then it was imperative that not a single Democratic vote be lost. Should just one Democrat vote with the Republicans, the Committee could not report the nomination to the Senate with the backing of a majority. In that event, there would be a tremendous encouragement to disgruntled Democrats in the Senate to break away from the President and defeat his nominee on the Senate floor. They remembered that a handful of determined Senators had twice frustrated President Cleveland when he had tried to fill the vacancy left by Justice Blatchford, and the only way Cleveland managed to break the deadlock was to nominate a man from the Senate itself, who was now Chief Justice White.

The responsibility for the Brandeis nomination passed from Chilton to Senator Charles Allen Culberson, a handsome and cultured Texan now nearing the end of his third six-year term. Formerly a vigorous lawyer and political leader, Culberson was now an ill man who suffered markedly from paralysis-agitans. For the past five years this ailment had caused the Senator's hands and jaw to tremble intermittently, although there was no apparent impairment of his mental powers. Now the attacks were more frequent. Culberson could open his mouth and speak a sentence or two marred by considerable stuttering, but it was out of the question for him to deliver a speech of any kind. And while his colleagues deferred courteously to Culberson's handicap, the chairman was physically incapable of strong committee leadership.

Culberson had good reason to fear the outcome within the committee, as he knew by way of the cloakroom gossip that began buzzing from the hour Wilson's nomination had been read out in the Senate.

He was not the kind of man to buttonhole members of his committee and he certainly considered it out of order to do so while the matter was before the subcommittee. Though he resented the President's having concealed his choice until it was a *fait accompli,* as a loyal Democrat who had to face the voters for re-election along with his national party leader, Culberson knew where his duty lay.

His was a committee filled with strong men jealous of their prerogatives. Of the nine other Democrats, three had already approved the nomination. Beyond them, only young Senator Henry Ashurst of Arizona was a certain vote for Brandeis. Culberson could not be sure of any of the remaining five. Senator Lee Overman of North Carolina, a veteran politician now in his third term as U.S. Senator, had once been a railroad president. That fact alone might easily predispose him against a Yankee attorney whose whole public life bespoke regulation of railroads and other utilities. When the nomination reached the Senate back in January, newspapermen quoted Overman as being "astounded" at the name of Brandeis. He would say no more at the time.

Next in committee seniority among the doubtful members was James A. O'Gorman of New York, a routine Tammany Irish politician, with red hair and a goatee. O'Gorman was presently at odds with Woodrow Wilson over patronage matters—the postmastership of New York City among them. Never really at ease in Washington and the Senate, O'Gorman was planning to retire this year so that he might return to his beloved city of New York, where he would not be beholden to his party chief in the White House. But so far he had kept his plans to himself. At this point, O'Gorman was feeling his freedom from party obligation and inclined to be rambunctious and difficult toward a President who this year needed the Senator's loyal support in New York perhaps more than O'Gorman needed him.

Handsome Jim Reed of Missouri posed a different problem for the committee chairman. A brilliant and colorful orator of the old school, with the kind of platform charm that swept crowds into his train, Reed was gauging his actions now on an intensely political basis. Silver-haired, fifty-four, and at the peak of his influence after his emergence from the bitter factional feuds for which Missouri Democrats seemed to possess bottomless energy, Reed was already looking ahead to capturing the Presidential nomination in 1920. He was therefore inclined to play a waiting game on the disputed Brandeis nomination and not make a move until he was certain which course would be the shrewd one. So Jim Reed could not be counted on for an early commitment to enourage the others.

Chairman Culberson had received no indication from Senator John Knight Shields of Tennessee as to his stand on the Brandeis matter. The final Democrat on the committee roster, Hoke Smith of Georgia, was also unpredictable. If anything, the fact that neither Shields nor Smith faced re-election in the fall tilted the scales somewhat against their feeling obliged to uphold the President.

On the Republican side of the committee table, Culberson was confronted by eight men from whom he might barely hope to get one vote to confirm Brandeis. That possibility was extremely thin, since Cummins and Works had already voted to reject. The best hope now lay with William Edgar Borah of Idaho, the stony-faced Boise lawyer who had built something of a reputation as an independent who would not be collared. If anyone had the character to stand up and tell his party leaders not to meddle with his vote, Borah seemed to have that quality. He was known as a foe of monopoly, which he melodramatically identified for his mountain-bound following of ranchers and small-townspeople as Satanic and Eastern. What Borah would do would depend on whether he saw in Brandeis a foe of Wall Street like himself or an Eastern city slicker of evil intent.

If Culberson dared hope for a possible break in the GOP ranks with Borah, he could expect nothing but the most grim opposition from tough old Knute Nelson of Minnesota, who had presided over the Ballinger investigating committee five years earlier. Nelson had been enraged by Brandeis' success in diverting the proceedings from their purpose through his persistent questioning of Ballinger. It was virtually an act of retributive justice that Brandeis should now be under examination by a committee on which Nelson was sitting.

Politics were simmering close to a boil as the nomination reached the Senate Judiciary Committee in early April, every public man anticipating the forthcoming election campaign. Taft in New Haven felt his blood pulse with the excitement of the season as he corresponded with Charles D. Hilles, serving in his twin capacities as chairman of the Republican National Committee and as Taft's personal investment counselor. The ex-President turned easily from a discussion of the most desirable bonds for safe investment to arranging with Hilles that Senator Warren G. Harding of Ohio be slid into the chairmanship of the Chicago convention in June. Harding had placed Taft's name in nomination in 1912; he was a safe man who would stand firm against any maneuvers by the Progressive supporters of Roosevelt to try to stampede the convention. Austen Fox reported to Taft with his wonted optimism that "it looks now as if Brandeis might be defeated in the full committee." Fox added that Nicholas Murray Butler, president of Columbia University, had reported to him "that in the Middle West there is an outcry against the nomination, expressed openly, and in private letters to Senators." Young Robert A. Taft reported to his father from Cincinnati that "Mr. Wickersham came out last week to deliver a lecture on Preparedness, and Uncle Charlie had him to dinner, where he told us of the view of the Supreme Court on the appointment of Brandeis, and seems to think that he might not be confirmed."

The Supreme Court was very much on Taft's mind the next week when he finally brought himself to pen a letter he long had delayed —a passionate and personal appeal to Justice Charles Evans Hughes, whom Taft had put on the bench, asking the jurist to understand the extraordinary circumstances that required his leaving it to accept the Republican nomination for the Presidency. Several times in the past Taft had praised Hughes for refusing to leave the bench for a new venture into politics.

"I believe myself to be as anxious as anyone to keep the Supreme Court and Supreme Court Judges out of politics," Taft wrote, "but there are few general rules of policy, not involving moral considerations, to which circumstances of the country's need may not justify an exception." A united Republican Party was the need of the hour, Taft continued, to rescue the country from the Democrats, which he termed "the organized incapacity of the country." No other candidate would be able to unite the party and win against Wilson—not Elihu Root, nor any of the others qualified to be President. Roosevelt, with all his thunder about seizing the nomination and his sneers at Hughes as "just another Wilson with whiskers," would loyally support Hughes once nominated. With a reunited Republican Party behind him, Hughes would surely win, Taft asserted.

Reflecting on his appeal the next day, Taft recognized he had written to Hughes in purely political terms. He promptly sent a follow-up message, approaching his quarry from another angle:

> After mailing my letter last night, it occurred to me that there were certain phases of the matter I had not touched. . . . Of course, if you accept the nomination, your resignation must follow

promptly and an opportunity for Wilson to fill your place. His selection of Brandeis does not give hope that he will strengthen the Bench by another appointment though I think his experience with Brandeis will make him somewhat anxious to propitiate the many whom he has shocked by that appointment.

But if his filling one vacancy is to be reason for not resigning, think of the vacancies he is likely to fill if he is reelected. He can almost destroy the court.

Should Hughes decline the nomination, Roosevelt would take it, Taft went on, with the result that he would quite likely pull the country into the European war and break up the Republican Party. Taft saw even more to the menace of Roosevelt:

His appointments to the Bench might include such men as Hand and Seabury and Draper * of the Pennsylvania Law School, supporters of the Recall of Judicial Decisions that I fear would be in many ways quite as bad as Brandeis.

Taft probably did not appreciate the discomfort Wilson's nomination of Brandeis had caused the fighting Colonel of Oyster Bay, who might perhaps have named Brandeis to the Supreme Court himself. Roosevelt did not sanctify the Court as Taft did, nor was he a reactionary like Lodge who regretted the passing of the nineteenth century. Roosevelt and Brandeis were personally acquainted on a most pleasant basis. As early as 1907 Roosevelt had asked the Boston lawyer, on the strength of his study of the New York life insurance scandals, to draft a model insurance law for the District of Columbia. On other occasions Brandeis had called on Roosevelt at the White House to discuss such matters as the regulation of stock brokerage and invoking the antitrust laws against the New Haven Railroad. After leaving the White House, Roosevelt had urged Felix Frankfurter to take up a legal career in New York public service like that Brandeis was following in Boston. Roosevelt knew how strong a Progressive Brandeis had been early in 1912, when Brandeis stumped the Midwest in an attempt to win the Republican nomination for Bob La Follette, and he felt the loss keenly when the Boston lawyer had chosen Wilson in preference to him during the 1912 campaign, and had helped Wilson to win.

Now, however, Roosevelt had lost interest in domestic issues: the

---

* Learned Hand, Samuel Seabury, and Dean William Draper Lewis. Undoubtedly Taft made a slip in misnaming this close friend of Roosevelt.

one overriding consideration was the war and America's preparation
to enter it. Roosevelt and Henry Cabot Lodge in their frequent
correspondence at this time seemed to vie in expressing the greater
anger over the spinelessness of those who would not face up to the
war issue. Their past differences over domestic politics were buried
now. Shortly after the Brandeis nomination, Lodge could not refrain
from protesting to Roosevelt over the iniquity of the Colonel's 1912
followers:

> The worst crowd we have to deal with are the so-called Progres-
> sive Senators. . . . They are not supporters of preparedness; they
> are friendly to Brandeis, and we can hardly count on them for any-
> thing. . . . I do not know how others feel but I know my own de-
> testation of this Administration goes beyond anything I ever expected
> to feel in politics.

Roosevelt in these weeks consistently encouraged Lodge to step
up his attacks on Wilson's pose of neutrality in the war. But he
avoided answering Lodge's oblique solicitation of a statement opposing Brandeis. This Lodge definitely wanted, to use in bolstering
opposition to Brandeis among his liberal-leaning Massachusetts
friends such as Arthur D. Hill. And although the Senator asserted
in his letters to others that he "knew" Roosevelt was opposed to
the confirmation of Brandeis, Lodge never got from the former
President an open statement to this effect. The closest Roosevelt
came was to point out to Lodge the sad picture of poor, deflated
Taft in New Haven, who had been trailing along after Wilson's note-
sending foreign policy. "Taft is not a very important man," Roosevelt
wrote to Lodge, "but he has done some real damage by his consistent
backing of Wilson—and after all he does not get the Supreme Court
and sees it given to Brandeis."

Ironically, Taft urged Justice Hughes to accept a Republican
draft for the Presidential nomination with the argument that otherwise Roosevelt might appoint men even worse than Brandeis to the
Supreme Court. Yet Henry Cabot Lodge, who detested Brandeis,
had been trying to secure the Republican Presidential nomination for
Roosevelt. The Brandeis nomination made Hughes less a threat,
Lodge had written to Roosevelt in February:

> Borah . . . and I, too, have had some pretty direct information
> that Hughes would not take the nomination, that he has said he

would not be the first man to bring the Supreme bench into politics, and it is pretty generally believed that the nomination of Brandeis has strengthened his determination in this respect.

This belief was dissipated when Hughes indicated to Stoddard at the end of March that he would accept the nomination at the end of the Court term. In his determination to drive Woodrow Wilson from office, Roosevelt was willing to subordinate all his differences with the stand-patters of 1912, against whom he had directed the main thrust of his campaign. Since these GOP regulars stood solidly against Brandeis, and since the need of the hour was the reuniting of the Republican Party, the natural affinity Roosevelt felt for Brandeis as a symbolic figure of the progressive movement was suppressed.

Roosevelt therefore remained officially as silent as the Sphinx throughout the Brandeis struggle, even though the issues it involved were those that had put fire in his eye and strength in his arm through most of his career as a national figure. Had he lifted his voice just once, he might have encouraged a few Progressive Republicans in the Senate to declare themselves for confirmation. But Brandeis had emerged as Woodrow Wilson's man, a red rag enraging the Republicans against the man in the White House. The Roosevelt of 1916 could not utter a word that might be interpreted as approbation of the President, in even the most tiny particular.

"What a swine Wilson is!" Roosevelt scrawled in postscript to a typical fire-and-brimstone note to Lodge, in the weeks of preconvention maneuver while the Brandeis struggle continued.

Taft was by temperament incapable of the emotional commitment to the Wilson-hatred that gripped Theodore Roosevelt. While the Brandeis matter was pending within the Senate Judiciary Committee, Taft in a Chicago speech commended the President's most recent note to the German government. Wilson sent a personal note of appreciation for this public support; Taft returned his own thanks for Wilson's courtesy. Such an exchange of courtliness, even on the formal plane, would have been impossible with the raging Roosevelt.

In April the Supreme Court battle settled down to watchful maneuvering, attrition, and delay. The temporary absence of certain Senators from Washington at times gave the advantage first to one side, then the other. But it was soon apparent that except for Borah, the Republicans would vote solidly against the nomination, if they all

were present. Yet neither the partisans of Brandeis nor his opponents
were certain on any one day what the result would be if a committee
meeting were held and a vote taken. Just so closely did Senators Reed,
Shields, Overman, O'Gorman, and Smith hold silence on their views.
When a committee meeting was held, it was easy for one or two
members to postpone the issue for a little while longer:

> Mr. Chairman, I have not yet had time to consider all the evi-
> dence in this hearing record. . . . It is a record of unusual length,
> Mr. Chairman. . . . I must ask the Chairman to postpone a vote on
> this nomination because my colleague, Senator ———, is unable to be
> here. . . . I must leave the city next week. . . . I shall have an-
> other committee meeting on that date. . . .

So it went on for weeks, first the Republicans delaying, then the
Democrats, neither side sure of itself. The lack of a strong chairman
compounded the effects of the multilateral filibuster which could no
longer be hidden from the outsiders. By the end of the month Gus
Karger was reporting on the delay tactics to Taft:

> The Brandeis nomination is still sewed up in committee. An
> effort was made to bring it up today, but it failed. If the proponents
> of Mr. Brandeis can force a vote, the committee, it is understood,
> will report in his favor by a majority of one. The filibuster continues,
> however, and there is some prospect of preventing action at this
> session.

Two days later:

> The Brandeis case is still dragging along. In committee it hinges
> on one vote, and the probability is now recognized that the com-
> mittee will throw his name into the Senate without recommenda-
> tion. That will encourage a stronger fight and may throw it over,
> although Brandeis still has enough votes in the Senate to win if a
> vote can be forced.

Karger reported that Senator Hoke Smith still wanted to "think it
over." Taft took this as a bad sign for the opposition:

> I am not hopeful about the Brandeis matter, although my prayer
> is earnest that he be rejected. When Hoke Smith wants to think, it
> means he wants to count votes, and in counting votes and in re-
> viewing his own welfare, I presume that the balance is in favor
> of Brandeis. The country's welfare never occurs to Hoke.

As the committee held the nomination in its hands without action, Fox and Spence mailed out their anti-Brandeis brief to all parts of the country. It contained charges against Brandeis without regard to the replies offered at the hearings. Lists of lawyers, editors, and other public-opinion leaders were used indiscriminately, apparently without concern for the cost. But the authors failed to appreciate the psychological effect on the recipient, outside the rarefied atmosphere in which they habitually moved, of a mailing bearing a return address at 60 Wall Street, New York. Had it come from any address but Wall Street it might have been more welcome to the typical American lawyer who resented "the Street" as a symbol of the Money Trust. One attorney in Fargo, North Dakota, mailed the form letter and brief he had received to Senator Walsh, to let him know just what was being sent to members of the bar. Walsh replied that he had already received similar evidence of the mailing campaign from many parts of the country, including one from his home office, addressed to "Thomas J. Walsh, Esq., Helena, Montana." He separately notified Attorney General Gregory, who was becoming alarmed at the "systematic propaganda, evidently substantially financed" that the mailing by Fox and Spence

> . . . is important chiefly as it indicates that there is a well-financed campaign on. Possibly the argument of the gentlemen named may affect the minds of some people who have no better means of ascertaining the truth. Both Senator Works and Senator Cummins declared before the committee with ill-disguised contempt that the thing is utterly worthless.

BRANDEIS AND THE DYNAMITERS was the provocative headline on another mailing, intended to stimulate a whispering campaign, sent out by Joseph D. Holmes, a New York dry goods manufacturer. It purported to show that Brandeis was tolerant of murderous bombers and therefore "eminently unfit, with his evident bias of mind, to be a member of the Supreme Court of the United States." The leaflet quoted a statement he had made in 1911 apropos the confession by the McNamara brothers, radical trade-union officials, that they had been responsible for the bombing of the Los Angeles *Times*. Actually, Brandeis had termed such bombings "unpardonable crimes." But he had gone beyond expressing indignation over them to suggest that thinking Americans should seek out the causes for the social

unrest that led men to perpetrate such horrible acts in the hope
of improving the condition of the wage-earners. Brandeis suggested
that when trusts became too big for the law they became contribut-
ing causes for crimes of this kind.

In mid-April Senator Walsh and Attorney General Gregory both
became disturbed by anonymous reports that seemed to be influencing Senators against Brandeis on a matter that had never come before
the subcommittee: the nominee's views toward the federal Constitution. Walsh thought it would be wise for Gregory to obtain a document from Brandeis to answer them.

Gregory to Brandeis, April 12:

> In a conversation with a Senator on yesterday he said that he had
> heard in the cloakroom of the Senate that you had stated you did
> not believe in a written constitution. . . . Subsequently, another
> Senator said he had heard that you had on some occasion expressed
> yourself to the effect that nine Judges of the Supreme Court could
> not be restrained from responding to a demand of the people by a
> Constitutional restriction.
>
> Will you kindly let me know whether you entertain either of the
> views alluded to above or have expressed such views? I may wish to
> show these Senators your reply.

Brandeis to Gregory, April 14:

> Would it not be possible to follow up such statements to their
> sources and find out who it was who originated them? They must
> have originated in deliberate lies.
>
> I have not only not said any such thing, but not said anything
> which anybody could have distorted into such a statement. My views
> in regard to the Constitution are, as you know, very much those of
> Mr. Justice Holmes.
>
> It was sufficiently trying throughout two months of the hearings
> to have lies and misrepresentations spread in regard to me without
> the opportunity of being heard by the Committee and the public,
> but to have these lies circulated privately after the hearings are
> closed seems to me not in accord with American conceptions of fair
> play.

The Attorney General promptly saw to it that both communications reached Walsh, for use when and if needed. The Senator, in
acknowledgment, said that the shadowy figures smearing Brandeis

as an anticonstitutionalist probably "will confine themselves to private discussions and intimate communication. I shall keep the letters for reference should an occasion arise when it might seem important to refer to the matter."

Henry Morgenthau was constitutionally incapable of keeping out of the Brandeis case, even after his scheme to pit Brandeis and Lodge against each other in the Senate race had fallen through. Busy all spring lining up Democatic contributors for Woodrow Wilson's re-election campaign, Morgenthau on his fund-raising errands also pleaded the cause of Brandeis' confirmation wherever he thought men who could influence Senators were to be found. He asked Brandeis to call with him on President William A. Day of the Equitable Life Assurance Society and on Frank A. Vanderlip, president of the National City Bank of New York, hoping, perhaps, to build a backfire in the fields of finance against the propaganda of Austen Fox. Nor did Morgenthau neglect spiritual leaders, for he spent considerable time conferring with Dr. Felix Adler, professor of ethics at Columbia University and founder of the New York Ethical Culture Society. Adler was stirred into action, as an entry for April 28 in Morgenthau's diary reveals:

> Professor Adler called me up and told me that there was trouble about Brandeis' confirmation. I told him . . . a favorable editorial would appear on Saturday in the *World,* and promised to call up Colonel House, which I did. House told me that he had already been informed and had taken such steps as he could, but he seemed to think that they might be unsuccessful as the Democrats had admitted that they were responsible for the filibuster and that Hoke Smith was uncertain.

Colonel Edward M. House, Woodrow Wilson's man of confidence, had served the President as an intimate adviser in many capacities. Early in 1913 when Wilson was choosing his original cabinet, House had blown cold on the idea of including Brandeis, whether as head of the Justice, Commerce, or Labor Department. He had none of the great enthusiasm for Brandeis that warmed the blood of his fellow Texan, Attorney General Gregory, and it was perhaps with the memory of the way his advisors had smothered Brandeis in 1913 that Wilson had decided not to confide in his staff over the Supreme Court appointment.

The very afternoon that House expressed his pessimism to Morgenthau, a spirited discussion erupted in the Senate chamber. Shortly after luncheon Senator Ashurst of Arizona was resting on a sofa in the cloakroom when a friend came through the swinging doors to inform him that Senators Sutherland and Brandegee, both Republican members of the Judiciary Committee, were planning to take the floor and "give you hell." In keeping with the chivalric rules of the Senate, they sent warning to the target of their attack. Ashurst quickly entered the hemicycle and took his seat. Across the chamber, George Sutherland of Utah was standing by his desk in the front Republican row. The Senator from Arizona, Sutherland complained, was reported in the Washington *Herald* of this morning to have left the previous day's Judiciary Committee meeting "in a perturbed state of mind" over the "acrimony" attending the discussion of Brandeis, "after telling the Republican members of the committee that they were deliberately filibustering against a report of the nomination." Nothing of this kind had occurred, protested Sutherland: "No Republican Senator is responsible for not having an immediate report made on the Brandeis case. On the contrary . . . the Republican members are quite ready to vote upon it at any time."

Ashurst quickly disavowed the inaccuracies about "acrimony" in the *Herald* article. In his next breath he affirmed that he had said, and still believed, that the Republicans were filibustering against the Brandeis nomination until after their national convention in June. Senator Clark of Wyoming objected that Ashurst himself had not been attending the committee meetings regularly.

"Unlike some other members of the Judiciary Committee," Ashurst shot back, "I do not pretend to deliberate when my mind is made up!"

Henry Fountain Ashurst was a remarkably agile, articulate man, gifted with a phenomenal recall for quotations and historical facts, which he could pour out at will in a flow of golden rhetoric. Tall and darkly handsome, Ashurst was relatively young at forty-one in a body of elders and he consequently exerted special effort to bear himself with sophisticated courtliness. Because Arizona had been Indian territory a scant five years before, known as a land of sun and desert, cattle and cactus and Indians, he adopted in compensation the pose of a polished slab of the sunburned Southwest, the rugged man of the outdoors who could outdo the cultivated East on any social or intellectual ground. And because he bore within him the Western predisposition against the Eastern Money Trust that rigged the prices of cattle, metals, and freight service against Arizonans, Ashurst was delighted that an enemy of Wall Street was going to the Supreme Court. That Brandeis was a Jew was all the better, because the history of civilization had proved to Ashurst's satisfaction that the Jews were the smartest men on earth.

Almost from the day Wilson had sent Brandeis' name to the Senate, Ashurst had told newsmen that he would vote to discharge the committee if the nomination should be delayed there. Now, three months later, he was confronted by irate Republicans with the charge that it was the Democrats who had delayed a vote on the nomination. Further, said Senator Clark, it was an impropriety for any member to tell newspapermen what had occurred at an executive session of a Senate committee. Ashurst at once thundered forth his declaration of independence:

"I deny here and now that I retailed what took place. . . . I said what I thought, and I should like to see the color of the person's hair who can imprison my thoughts!" Then Ashurst seized the opportunity, which his opponents unwittingly handed him, to sound a rallying cry to the nation in behalf of Brandeis:

"I can well understand the perturbation, indeed the astonishment, that must have greeted the Republican Party when the name of such a man as Louis D. Brandeis was sent in to be a Justice of the Supreme Court!" he cried.

"If the nominee had been a man who all his life had been steering giant corporations around the law, there would have been a yell of approval from the Republican side. But there having been sent in the name of a man who has consecrated his life to the poor people of this country, casuistry and then all the delay that can be conjured up is resorted to——"

Clark tried to interrupt, but Ashurst would not be halted. Let there be a vote on the coming Monday, he challenged. "If all are willing to vote and do vote, then I shall believe there is no filibuster."

Suddenly the Arizonan again switched off on a political tack and heaped scorn on the Republican Party for having "reached out its hands and attempted to grasp from the Supreme Court of the United States one of its members in order to mingle him in the debaucheries of politics!" Ashurst persisted in his needling of the opposite party, but eventually, under questioning by Senators Clark, Cummins, and Sutherland, he conceded: "I deny that which the *Herald* has put into my mouth, and I regret it, because the *Herald* is usually an accurate paper."

The sweetly reasonable Senator Works tried to smooth things over as he had in the subcommittee. Yes, the deliberations had been stretched out for some weeks now, but all the evidence had to be carefully sifted, case by case. A Democratic member, Senator Walsh, had taken up most of the last committee meeting reviewing one issue, said Works, and he had a perfect right to. Ashurst graciously declared his esteem and affection for his distinguished colleague from California, then again switched in midsentence to a ringing declaration of the Brandeis case as a contest between the "great inarticulate mass of people on the one hand . . . and the great, grasping corporations on the other, who want kept off the bench a man who will do all men justice!"

Senator Overman of North Carolina, one of the committee members who remained uncommitted, rose. "Some Democrats," he said, wanted to hear discussion of "three or four serious charges made against Mr. Brandeis." The Lennox case occupied most of yesterday's meeting and is still not finished. "It is a matter that necessarily takes time, but I myself have never seen any disposition to delay," the North Carolina Senator said, leaving his listeners still unsure of the way he was leaning. Then Hoke Smith of Georgia took the floor and made it clear by what a slender thread the confirmation of Brandeis was suspended:

"There has been no filibustering by anybody in that committee," said Senator Smith flatly. "Most of the time has been taken up by the Democrats, and there never has been a time when Mr. Brandeis could have obtained a favorable report from those present at a committee meeting." Then, as if offering a half-promise: "He may yet obtain it."

"Most of the time the Republicans have been in the majority. Only once or twice have we had a majority of Democrats present." Senator Reed of Missouri had been ill, Smith continued, and Shields of Tennessee was sick back in his home state.

"I say frankly for myself that there never has been a time that I have been ready to vote for a report favorable to Mr. Brandeis. I have voted to postpone the consideration of the nomination because I have not reached a conclusion, and I wanted a further investigation and more information."

With Smith's candid statement, it was out in the open that the Democrats could not yet afford to bring the nomination to a vote. Ashurst said that he would withdraw his remarks, since the Republicans had entered their disclaimer of delaying tactics. But he had succeeded in his main purpose—to bring the issues to the country by denouncing in the Senate forum, even though briefly, the evil purposes of the campaign to defeat Brandeis.

As Ashurst resumed his chair, Senator Owen of Oklahoma observed that the nomination had been pending three months to a day. Various corporations, Owen declared, had brought false charges against Brandeis, who "has been subjected to the most vicious and unjust assault ever brought against a nominee for a judgeship." Doubtless the Senator from Arizona had been led to believe the Republicans were conducting a filibuster against Brandeis because they "appear to be unanimously disposed against him and to have approved these assaults and given them such hospitable reception."

Far from the Senate chamber, people alarmed at the failure of the Judiciary Committee to act were being stirred on behalf of Wilson's nominee. From the Harvard Law School, Senator Chilton received a strong letter of endorsement of Brandeis from Professor Roscoe Pound, recently named Dean to replace the late Ezra Thayer. Pound had come to Cambridge just six years before from the College of Law of the University of Nebraska, so he observed the ingrown quality of the oldest American metropolis with the fresh view of an outsider. Precociously learned as a young man, he had become an outstanding expert in botany in his early twenties before he turned to the study of law, which he mastered with amazing celerity. Although he was now only forty-five, his teachings had gone far to stimulate the kind of reforms in American jurisprudence that Brandeis, Theodore Roosevelt, and Senator La Follette, each in his own way, had been urging through the same years. A bouncing, round-faced man with dimples in his pink cheeks, Pound in photographs had the aspect of a deadly serious, oversized kewpie, except for the little coal-black mustache, spectacles, and slicked hair parted in the center that appeared the work of a greasepencil in a mischievous hand. Pound's speech was precisely clipped in evenly accented syllables that allowed students time to absorb his thought.

It was as a teacher that Pound wrote to Chilton, stating that his purpose was to correct the mistake the nominee's friends had made in promoting Brandeis' public service work and advanced social views as his chief qualifications. It was less known, but more important, Pound informed the Senator,

> . . . that Mr. Brandeis is in very truth a very great lawyer. At the beginning of his career his article in the *Harvard Law Review* on the right of privacy did nothing less than add a chapter to our law. In spite of the reluctance of many courts to accept this, it has steadily made its way, until now it has a growing preponderance in its favor. All the cases upon this subject concur in attributing the origin of the doctrine to Mr. Brandeis' paper.

Further evidence, the Harvard law professor went on, lay in the revolutionary Brandeis brief in *Muller* v. *Oregon* and its effect on social legislation:

> The real point here is not so much his advocacy of these statutes as the breadth of perception and the remarkable legal insight which enable him to perceive the proper mode of preventing such a question.
>
> Since I came to Cambridge, not quite six years ago, I have had many opportunities of observing Mr. Brandeis, and do not hesitate to say that he is one of the great lawyers of the country. So far as sheer legal ability is concerned, he will rank with the best who have sat upon the bench of the Supreme Court.

Pound reminded Senator Chilton of the names of distinguished gentlemen who had served with Brandeis on the committee of visitors to the law school, including Justice Hughes and former Secretary of War Henry L. Stimson; and of the Harvard Board of Overseers who appointed the law school visitors, including the Honorable Henry Cabot Lodge. It was inconceivable, Pound wrote, that the Harvard board was ignorant of the charges against Brandeis, which had been common coin in Boston legal circles for some years. Nor would such eminent lawyers and gentlemen have appointed and reappointed Brandeis to the visiting committee "had they then believed him deficient in professional honor or guilty of professional misconduct."

Shortly after Chilton read Dean Pound's letter, President Lowell received a respectful, but strongly worded objection to his part in the anti-Brandeis campaign from Raymond B. Stevens, Harvard College and Law School graduate, serving as general counsel to the infant Federal Trade Commission, of which Brandeis had been one of the spiritual fathers. Surely, Stevens wrote Lowell, he must not be aware of the dishonest nature of the "brief" sent out in his name by Fox and Spence and offered for sale by C. W. Barron of *The Wall Street Journal.*

The Harvard president replied that there was nothing wrong with the mailing from 60 Wall Street. Fox was merely exercising his right "to express his opinion to his representative" and "to try to induce others who share his feelings to express their opinions." Stevens, Lowell continued, must admit that the opponents of Brandeis "are just as conscientious as you are." He completely avoided Stevens' point that the so-called brief was a slanted document that took none of the pro-Brandeis hearing testimony into account.

The Brandeis issue continued to concern Harvard men at all levels. Paul V. McNutt and his fellow members of the student committee arranging the class dinner for the third-year men at the Harvard Law School resolved to strike back at President Lowell by inviting Brandeis as their banquet speaker. But in the Yard, on the evening of May 4, the present and past editors of the Harvard *Crimson,* holding a dinner to celebrate their taking possession of the daily's new building, were startled to hear one of the speakers attack Brandeis inferentially as a muckraker. The assault was launched by Thomas W. Lamont, a former *Crimson* editor in the Class of 1892, now a banking partner of J. P. Morgan, and a Harvard overseer. ("It shows to what extent that element has gone to defeat Mr. Brandeis," one of the men present wrote to Senator Walsh. "It is perhaps the meanest of all the attacks on Mr. Brandeis I have heard.")

Lobbying for Senate votes on the Brandeis nomination continued on all sides. Austen Fox wrote again to Taft:

Although a pacifist, on occasions, I have not given orders to "cease firing," and now appeal to you to write to our friends in Augusta and elsewhere in Georgia to do what they can to stiffen Hoke Smith in his reported attitude against confirmation. . . .

We are making headway. The fight which my friends assured me was hopeless—no good fight is ever hopeless—now looks hopeful. . . . At my request the following named former Judges have written to, or made oral protests to Senator O'Gorman. . . .

Then, in afterthought:

Do not confine yourself to Georgia among the Southern States. Overman (N.C.) for instance.

Former Governor Robert Perkins Bass of New Hampshire, a strong conservationist and Roosevelt Progressive, was a dynamo of action in the Brandeis camp. He first proposed to Brandeis' informal strategy committee in Washington that he appear at the hearings as a pro-Brandeis witness. But Hapgood, Brandeis himself, Stevens of the Federal Trade Commission, and George Rublee thought this would be bad strategy. The problem was to solidify Democratic support, not antagonize potential supporters with a testimonial from a Yankee Progressive Republican. Furthermore, Rublee's own nomination as a member of the Federal Trade Commission had been held up even longer than that of Brandeis, and it was now touch and go whether the Democrats would vote against confirming Rublee out of Senatorial courtesy to the hostility of aged Senator Gallinger of New Hampshire, a conservative Republican.

For a couple of months Bass contented himself to work for Brandeis' confirmation through correspondence and personal contact with his friends. But by late April he thought the time had come for action. He wired to Brandeis' friends in Washington:

IF DESIRABLE I CAN START THE MACHINERY FOR OBTAINING A SYSTEMATIC ENDORSEMENT FOR BRANDEIS FROM EVERY IMPORTANT LABOR ORGANIZATION IN THE COUNTRY. CLOSE FRIENDS OF BRANDEIS WITH WHOM I HAVE TALKED THINK IT WOULD BE HELPFUL. THEY FEAR DELAY IS BEING SOUGHT TO ALLOW TIME FOR THE EFFECTIVE PUBLICITY MACHINERY OF THE OPPOSITION TO WORK ON THOSE SENATORS WHO ARE WAVERING. WE THINK THE ACTION I PROPOSE WOULD HAVE SALUTARY COUNTERBALANCING EFFECT. WILL YOU ASK ATTY. GEN. IF SUCH ACTION IS ADVISABLE?

Senator Henry F. Hollis, New Hampshire's first Democrat elected to the Senate since 1852, promptly approved Bass' initiative and indicated that some of his fellow Democrats in the Senate were encouraging the lobby. Senator Walsh opposed the labor-union broadside, Hollis reported, but he was not adamant about it. Senators Chilton and Ashurst both favored it very strongly, since

there is evident determination to filibuster to the end. The action outlined by you might prove very efficacious in the case of Senators whose elections are to come up this fall. I am personally satisfied that this endorsement by labor organizations would be a most excellent thing.

The Attorney General naturally dislikes to be drawn into any matter of this sort.

Bass spent much of his time the next few weeks helping direct the message campaign from New York, Boston, and Washington. Each side quickly learned what the other was doing. Norman Hapgood passed word to Senator Walsh that the opposition had added a former Senator to its staff, who was concentrating on Southern Senators. He was Joseph W. Bailey, who had retired to a Washington law practice after representing Mississippi in the United States Senate for two terms. Walsh replied that he could detect signs of "some effective work with our Southern friends."

In New York, Rabbi Stephen S. Wise, Henry Morgenthau, and Norman Hapgood put their heads together almost daily. They decided at one point that Wise should seek an appointment to try to convince Senator Borah to vote with the Democrats. Wise reported back to Morgenthau that Borah could not be counted on. Professor Felix Adler proposed to Morgenthau that the majority report of the subcommittee be sent out to the lawyers of the country, to counteract the Fox mailing. Adler gravely feared losing the votes of both O'Gorman and Hoke Smith in the Judiciary Committee. Morgenthau went again to his White House source, noting in his journal:

> *Thursday, May 4th.* I spoke to Col. House over the telephone who had just returned from Washington and he told me that the Brandeis matter looked serious; that he had talked to the President about it, who is very stubborn and even thought of sending his name in for the second time. It seems that the southern senators are fearful that Brandeis will change the attitude of the Supreme Court on the question of the Segregation Laws of Louisville. The President advised that nothing be done at present, no labor leader sent over, until he can look further into the matter. House says that Gregory also is very determined.

As day upon day passed with no official action from the Senate Judiciary Committee, Woodrow Wilson was reminded that his nomination of Brandeis had caught the popular imagination. The Reverend A. A. Berle, writing the President of a recent anti-militarism speaking crusade he had taken to eleven cities, let Wilson know that when Brandeis' name was mentioned before large crowds there had been "a wonderful outburst" of cheering in Kansas City, as well as in

St. Louis and Pittsburgh. An elderly walnut grower in Oregon wrote to Wilson that he considered the nomination of Brandeis "the most important event in the progress of our country since the emancipation proclamation of Lincoln. I was in the Union Army at the time and swung my hat for Old Abe as I now swing it for your act."

Along with the congratulations, however, came an undertone of concern that Wilson did not stand behind his nominee with sufficient vigor. From a local miners' union: "We ask you to use your good office to influence the Senate to confirm the appointment of Mr. Brandeis."

A telegram forwarded to the White House by Senator Phelan of California from a Los Angeles voter: FEELING HERE THAT BRANDEIS CONFIRMATION MAY FAIL BECAUSE OF INSUFFICIENT INTEREST OF PRESIDENT. I AM CONVINCED THAT FAILURE OF CONFIRMATION WILL LOSE WILSON MANY THOUSAND VOTES IN CALIFORNIA ALONE. PLEASE SEE THE PRESIDENT.

A letter from Chicago, expressing urgency in its underscorings: "*Stand by* Brandeis. We *need* him on the Supreme Court bench. You *can* influence his being accepted and *should* do so by *all means.*"

From Weehawken, New Jersey, the distinguished sculptor Frank Edwin Elwell wrote his former governor: "No greater political blunder could be committed at this time than to let the enemies of Brandeis triumph. The Democratic Party has done a wonderful amount of good. Your own re-election will depend on a certain kind of solid vote."

On May 5 Wilson received a plea for help from Chairman Culberson of the Judiciary Committee. If the President could write a letter explaining his reasons for nominating Louis D. Brandeis to the Supreme Court, it would strengthen the hand of the administration within the committee. None of the Democrats had been consulted in advance of the nomination, and therefore the President's precise reasons for precipitating the storm had never been made known to the administration Senators who had to steer through it.

Wilson decided that the time had come for him to act.

nine

Politics and Persuasion

When the Senate Judiciary Committee met on Monday, May 8, Senator Culberson announced that he had just received a letter from the President explaining his reasons for having sent the Brandeis nomination to the Senate. Its wording permitted no doubt that Wilson was insistent.

"I am profoundly interested in the confirmation of the appointment," Wilson wrote. He urged Culberson's committee to "accept the nomination as coming from me quick with a sense of public obligation and responsibility." The President swept aside the "many charges" against Brandeis, stating that the subcommittee report

> has already made it plain to you and to the country at large how unfounded those charges were. I myself looked into them three years ago when I desired to make Mr. Brandeis a member of my Cabinet and found that they proceeded for the most part from those who hated Mr. Brandeis because he had refused to be serviceable to them in the promotion of their own selfish interests, and from those whom they had prejudiced.

Culberson's request for his "reasons" had given Wilson an opportunity to identify his administration with everything enlightened and progressive for which Brandeis was known, and the President made the most of his chance:

> In every matter in which I have made test of his judgment and point of view I have received from him counsel singularly enlightening, singularly clear-sighted and judicial, and, above all, full of moral stimulation. He is a friend of all just men and a lover of the

right; and he knows more than how to talk about the right—he knows how to set it forward in the face of his enemies. I knew from direct personal knowledge of the man what I was doing when I named him for the highest and most responsible tribunal of the Nation.

The letter extolled Brandeis' "extraordinary ability as a lawyer," his "fairness and love of justice," his "notable services" in Massachusetts, and his "impartial, impersonal, orderly, and constructive mind." In peroration, the President declared that Brandeis "will ornament the high court of which we are all so justly proud."

Wilson's letter undoubtedly jogged the memory of some Washingtonians who knew about another letter the President had written fifteen months earlier in behalf of the same man. That had been a private note to the Admissions Committee of the Cosmos Club, an organization of men who, according to their by-laws, had achieved "distinction in the arts or sciences." Early in 1915, when Brandeis had been proposed for entrance into this select circle, a clique of sanctimonious diehards opposed his candidacy from motives similar to those exhibited in the Supreme Court seating fight: he would be an inharmonious element, who did not "belong" in a group of accomplished gentlemen. Tipped off to the trouble brewing in the Cosmos Club, of which he was a member, Wilson had written an emphatic endorsement of Brandeis as a prospective fellow member. The Boston lawyer had been duly admitted.

Wilson's letter in praise of Brandeis this time, however, was not meant to be private. It was written to demonstrate to the country that the President was standing by Brandeis as if naming him to the Supreme Court were a symbolic act by which his administration would be marked. Between the lines one could almost read the attack Wilson would launch on the predatory interests during the coming campaign, should they deny a place on the Court to Brandeis. Though it was thoughtfully composed to appeal to wavering Democratic Senators, the President had no need to employ an open letter to gain the attention of the handful who held the vital committee votes. He was seizing the opportunity to broadcast the issue beyond the Senate to the American people, as Senator Ashurst had done so effectively two weeks earlier.

The Wilson plea sparked a flareup of discussion along the old battle lines. To those on the side of confirmation, the President's message was hailed as a masterful statement; those on the opposite side found Wilson's arguments for Brandeis unconvincing. The *New Republic* cheered; the *Nation* termed the President's dismissal of the charges leveled by Brandeis' opponents "far too cavalier treatment of the eminent Boston lawyers" and the A.B.A. presidents. The charges, the *Nation* declared, "have been buttressed by sworn evidence and documents." The Fox brief, it said, had "staggered" many a

> warm friend of the nominee. . . . No wonder the Senate hesitates to confirm him. Whether it finally does so or not, the long and bitter controversy over the appointment is proof enough that it never should have been made. It is unseemly that a judge should enter the Supreme Court by the door of passion and political wrangling.

Wilson's endorsement proved a shot in the arm for the nominee's friends. "The President's letter makes us feel as if the forces of darkness haven't it all their own way," Felix Frankfurter wrote to Brandeis in a hasty note, in which he assured the recipient on the score of the Harvard law students' invitation to speak at their dinner. "If it's a relevant item, I want you to know that the desire to have you at the dinner of the graduating class comes spontaneously from the *men* [underlined, as if to make it clear that the faculty had played no part in it] and represents a deep desire." Brandeis declined the invitation with regret.

By the time Wilson's testimonial letter had been read in the Judiciary Committee, Senator O'Gorman had announced that he would not run for re-election in the fall. The President's hold on the Senator would be loosened as a consequence. But at fifty-six O'Gorman was not ready to retire altogether, and as his eye swept the benches of New York for a likely seat, he knew that the party organization expected him to bring home his share of federal patronage while he remained in office.

O'Gorman may not have known it, but the one person in Washington most responsible for his having been made a Senator in the first place had already shown considerable interest in the Brandeis case. He was a handsome, aristocratic young New Yorker named Franklin D. Roosevelt, then serving as Assistant Secretary of the Navy under Secretary Josephus Daniels. In 1911 Roosevelt had been a member of the state senate in Albany when the Tammany machine was pushing an uninspired political hack on the state legislature as its candidate for the United States Senate. Roosevelt at that time led a revolt of uncommitted legislators against the machine candidate and managed the election of the somewhat more independent Judge O'Gorman instead. Now, though the confirmation of Brandeis was not exactly in line with his Navy Department duties, Roosevelt kept a close eye on it, sending to a friend on Capitol Hill for hearing testimony of which the newspaper accounts piqued his curiosity.

Roosevelt's immediate superior, Secretary of the Navy Josephus Daniels, was one of a little group within Wilson's cabinet working most diligently for the confirmation of Brandeis. The home-state tie between Roosevelt and O'Gorman was no secret to him. And he knew, of course, how important it was to any New York Senator that the Brooklyn Navy Yard obtain its full share of the budget of Daniels' department.

A jovial, rotund newspaper editor from Raleigh, North Carolina, Daniels could teach most lifetime politicians a lesson in the way to use ties of friendship. Did O'Gorman want to return to the bench? A vote against Mr. Wilson's Justice would not open the door to a federal-court appointment. As a Senator, O'Gorman had voted against his party chief several times, and he had let it be known that he had been "treated badly" by the White House on matters of patronage. But carrying a grudge against the President in his final months as a Senator would do him no real good, and might even do him considerable harm. Brandeis, after all, had many admirers in New York; it was not a completely Irish town.

The congressional recess for the Republican National Convention was one month away. Republicans on the Judiciary Committee thanked the lucky star under which Wilson had appointed Senator Fletcher to a commission visiting South America in April; for weeks his certain vote in favor of Brandeis was missing. Senator Shields was in ill health and spent much of the spring at home in Tennessee. The Democrats were therefore immobilized until they were sure they had the votes. The Wilson letter, as Gus Karger estimated it in a note to Taft, "will further tend to solidify Republican opposition."

The former President had been disheartened in recent weeks by signs of anti-Jewish bigotry exhibited by some of his colleagues. He had let pass, without seeming to notice them, George Wickersham's expressions of antipathy to "Hebrew uplifters" of the *New Republic* —meaning Walter Lippmann, Herbert Croly, Walter Weyl, and Felix

Frankfurter. Wickersham was a Wall Streeter who scorned the liberal intellectual as he scorned the pushy little cloak-and-suiter. Taft could explain some of Wickersham's venom by his background. But to the man at Yale who clung to Gus Karger as his Washington confidant and who had appointed and kept Charles Nagel (Brandeis' brother-in-law) as his Secretary of Commerce and Labor through his entire administration, haughty expressions of anti-Semitism by those around him brought a keen distress. Some of the best-educated people, alas, had to make ill-spirited remarks to him about Brandeis as a Jew. Shortly after Taft had delivered a lecture at the Boston University Law School, for example, he received a note from Homer Albers, Dean of the school:

> *Dear Mr. President:*
> Have you heard this one?
> What is the difference between William H. Taft and Louis D. Brandeis?
> Why, the former is distinguished in Jurisprudence, and the latter in Jewish prudence!
>
> > *Sincerely yours,*
> > HOMER ALBERS, *Dean*

It was the kind of joke that William Howard Taft did not find funny.

A somewhat different form of "Jewish prudence," which Albers equated with Mephistophelian cunning, had actually impelled a number of wealthy and conservative Jews during the committee impasse to suggest to Wilson that he withdraw the Brandeis nomination. Mainly men of property and position, like Louis Marshall and Jacob Schiff, this group had boiled with rage at the way Brandeis had taken the leadership of the Zionist movement away from them in the few short years since he had taken an interest in specifically Jewish affairs. Terribly fearful that the controversy over the Brandeis nomination would give rise to new manifestations of anti-Semitism, these few conservatives counseled retreat. While Morgenthau looked forward to Brandeis on the Supreme Court as a step toward the Jews' full participation in American democracy, the timid deplored the nomination because the uproar it caused was upsetting their gradualist plans for gaining status. Wilson at first could not understand such an attitude. Josephus Daniels explained it to him in terms of an old Southern story about a Negro woman carrying a basket of live crabs on her head. ("No, suh, she wasn't afraid those crabs would crawl out and pinch her. B'cause if one of them did try to get out, the other crabs would sho' pull him back in!") These prudent, self-appointed leaders of the American Jews, Daniels assured the President, were just trying to pull Brandeis back into his proper place in the basket. Wilson laughed at Daniels' anecdote and paid no more attention to the counsel of the timid.

A more pressing question of tactics arose when Bass, Wise, Hapgood, Frankfurter, and their associates seriously considered staging mass meetings in New York and Boston to dramatize the backing Brandeis enjoyed among the people. Would the hall be "filled with Jews and labor people," as some feared, and thus give the impression of narrowness to the confirm-Brandeis campaign? Their drive to stimulate letters to Senators had already shown that many people favorably disposed to the nomination were not willing to get involved in the controversy. And though there were fine testimonials in the subcommittee report from men like Arthur D. Hill and Dean Roscoe Pound, it was obvious from a glance through its pages that the endorsements were heavily weighted with Jewish names and labor officials' titles. Rabbi Wise wrote to Hapgood on May 12:

> If you feel, as you say, that agitation is now desirable, ought not a half dozen of us get together in New York and map out the best plan? The thing should be done, as I believe it will have to be done, with great care and circumspectness.
>
> All we need do is to help the American people to see that a crime is being committed against them.

At a meeting of the Senate Judiciary Committee on May 10, Senator Sutherland, Republican of Utah, brought up an entirely new topic that he said the subcommittee should examine. Brandeis was counsel to an illegal trust! At least to a company that the Department of Justice considered in violation of the Sherman Antitrust Act.

The fresh charge involved the part Brandeis was said to have played, less than a year before, in a chain-store merger that led to the establishment of the United Drug Company chain. Sutherland declared that if it were true, as he had heard, that Brandeis was the counsel behind this giant cut-rate outfit, a trust that threatened to drive thousands of independent druggists out of business by ruthlessly underselling them, this fact would prove the nominee was a foe of trusts only when it suited his purpose. What was most promising to the opponents of the nominee in this case was that it put George W. Anderson, in his capacity as federal district attorney in Boston, in opposition to Brandeis. Hopefully, the man who had advocated the Brandeis case in February and March could be used to condemn him now. A new hearing was called for May 12.

The fresh chance for the opponents soon proved only a damp firecracker that could not be exploded. The first witness was Louis Liggett, dominant figure in the newly formed United Drug network of drug and cigar dispensers, who outlined the way in which he had brought about the merger of numerous chain retailers. Liggett's attorney, Frederick Snow, then told the Senators that District Attorney Anderson had warned him that the new combination might be in violation of the Sherman antitrust law. In order to confirm his own opinion that the merger would not be illegal, Snow said he had called on Brandeis to study the facts and give his opinion, as an expert on antitrust law. Brandeis had done so, and jointly with Snow had sent a detailed memorandum to Anderson. Its main point was that a chain of drug stores and cigar stands doing only 5 per cent of the national retail business was quite a different matter from giants like U.S. Steel, American Tobacco, or International Harvester. Anderson wound up the subcommittee hearing by explaining that he had disagreed with the judgment of Snow and Brandeis, but that no suit had been instigated. How the Department of Justice would view the United Drug merger in the future would depend on how the chain exercised its economic power, he said. Anderson gave the Republicans on the subcommittee no stones to throw at the nominee. He acknowledged that he had for a long time looked to Brandeis for advice on economic and business matters, but that in this instance they had happened to disagree. At the end of this one-day reprise, the hearings were closed for the third—and final—time.

One person who was keenly interested in the outcome of the Brandeis struggle for both personal and professional reasons expressed himself in the most restrained terms when he touched on the matter at all. The fact that he had known Brandeis for close to forty years would not excuse an old soldier like Justice Oliver Wendell Holmes for breaching the proprieties of the Supreme Court in this case. But

he could not stop others from speculating on his state of mind. Thus
Senator Walsh was assured in a letter from Thomas P. Ivy, a conservation expert who had followed the course of the hearings closely:

> A Harvard man who was unfriendly to Mr. Brandeis said to me
> that before President Wilson offered the nomination to Mr. Bran-
> deis he consulted Justice Oliver Wendell Holmes. Justice Holmes,
> so my informant said, advised that the nomination be made. Com-
> ing from the source it did, I think the statement must be true. As
> Mr. Justice Holmes is a thorough Bostonian his approval of Mr.
> Brandeis would seem to me convincing.

At that time Walsh had replied to Ivy that a somewhat different
version of the Court's thinking on the matter had spread through the
Senate cloakroom. "The impression is abroad," Walsh said, "that only
Justice Van Devanter has felt any kind of pleasure at the prospect of
Mr. Brandeis becoming an Associate Justice."

Sunday, May 14, found Justice Holmes penning a letter to Lewis
Einstein, the State Department's chargé d'affaires at the American
legation in Sofia, Bulgaria. With Einstein as with numerous others
among his correspondents, Holmes shared an interest in books and
the fine arts, and the world of ideas springing from them. Holmes'
rough hand scratched swiftly across the pages, as if at seventy-five
he could not make the wavering lines of black ink keep pace with his
crackling thought. "I saw Cabot Lodge yesterday for a moment, looking very old and tired," Holmes wrote. "You know his wife died last
summer." There had been a garden party at the White House a few
days before, an experience causing him to observe that "the average
Democratic politician is even a more odious type than his inferior of
Republican stripe. . . ."

Holmes' letters typically darted from one topic to another. He
thought Einstein might like to meet Felix Frankfurter and Harold
Laski—"two young Jews at Harvard" with whom he had been corre-
sponding. Good minds. For the life of him he could not understand
anti-Semitism, it was so illogical. Then:

> Brandeis' matter drags along, and I don't know what will hap-
> pen. You met him at our house one night and I thought didn't fancy
> him, though of course you didn't say so. He always left on me the
> impression of a good man when he called. And I have never fully

fathomed the reasons for the strong prejudice against him shown by other good men.

Whatever happens it is a misfortune for the Court, for the time being. If he is turned down the proletariat will say only tools of the plutocrats can get in. (Though the p's don't favor me, you may bet.) If he gets in many people will think that the character of the Court no longer is above question.

Well I always can hop off if I don't like it but having kept on a good time so far I should like to keep going until 80.

To Mrs. Joseph Samson Stevens, an intimate friend who had brought up the Brandeis fight in her correspondence, Holmes wrote that Brandeis "always left me when he has called feeling encouraged about the world," but added:

> There may have been things that I should criticise. I didn't like his mode of conducting the Ballinger case, and formerly he seemed to me to wish to sink the few. But we all have foibles—and the total impression that I have received, as I say, has been that of a man whom I respected and admired subject to the inquiry why it was that other good men were down on him.
>
> This of course is private as I don't think it would be proper that I should say anything on either side while the case is *sub judice*.

On the Sunday evening Holmes was writing with judicial restraint of the dispute dividing his old friends, just a block away Norman Hapgood was taking the boldest kind of direct action in Brandeis' behalf. He had invited a number of friends to his apartment on H Street for an informal Sunday evening of mixing, refreshment, and talk—among them Senators Hoke Smith and Jim Reed—to meet Louis D. Brandeis. Reed arrived at the Hapgood apartment intending to stay but a few moments. It was a chilly evening, and Mrs. Reed was left waiting for him in the car. But when he was introduced to Brandeis, Reed found something in the Supreme Court nominee that intrigued him. He lost track of the time as they sat before the open fire and talked about one subject after another for more than an hour.

This was a meeting of two men of national importance who had known about each other for some time without really becoming acquainted. Reed was a strikingly handsome Senator with a touch of silver in his hair and pure gold in his voice, who could charm crowds and juries with his mastery of oral dialectic. The color of his oratory and the praise it had won him fired in Jim Reed a burning ambition to become President of the United States. He intended this year to win re-election to his second term in the Senate, Missouri being safely Democratic, and then make a name for himself such that his party could not ignore him in 1920. In the Senate Reed sought the support of the wealthy and powerful, but he took care not to become tagged as a tool of the big interests. He cried out in behalf of the little man, but he deplored the "excesses" of the trust-busters. He consequently weighed the Brandeis nomination issue with caution, as if to see which side of the matter offered him the greater political advantage. "We were never quite sure of where Jim Reed stood on the Brandeis nomination," Senator Ashurst, an ardent admirer of the Missouri Senator, said of him later.

As he talked this evening with Brandeis, James Reed realized that the man he had come here to meet must surely have known all about the hostility he had expressed toward Brandeis on the Senate floor back in October 1914, when the Clayton antitrust bill was under debate. It was prompted by Reed's opposition to the Federal Trade Commission Act, which had been inspired by Brandeis and passed the year before over Reed's passionate objection. On that day in 1914 Senator Weeks of Massachusetts had been trying to explain the position of the United Shoe Machinery Company as defendant against charges of acting as an illegal trust. Reed intervened again and again to point out the villainy of Louis D. Brandeis in the government's prosecution of the company. Did not the Senator from Massachusetts know, Reed had asked rhetorically, that Louis D. Brandeis, "the reformer," had drawn the company's leases, which the government declared were illegal? ("I understand that the tying clause is the work of the legal ingenuity of Mr. Brandeis.") And would Weeks not state, after Massachusetts enacted a law restricting leases containing the tying clause, "who it was who devised the plan to escape the effect of that law?" It was Mr. Brandeis again, was it not? And did not Brandeis have something to do with instigating the recent litigation against the company?

Jim Reed's entire discussion in the Senate that day had been much less a debate on the merits of the antitrust law than a spiteful *ad hominem* attack on the man who sat beside him now. It was the kind of performance that would ordinarily have made Brandeis shun the company of such a person. Yet as the Senator and the nominee sat in discussion before Hapgood's fireplace, the realities of May 1916 were far more compelling than battles fought and settled two years ago.

Political creature that he was, Reed knew that even though he did not want to vote for the confirmation of Brandeis, the compulsions of politics were forcing him to it. He scorned the Boston man's concern with economic controls of business and the world of finance; he was suspicious of Brandeis' intellect and somewhat condescending about his being a Jew. But—and this was the all-important reservation to Jim Reed—Brandeis had the backing of the President, and Wilson by his widely published letter to Culberson had turned confirmation into a party matter beyond cavil. The Republicans were going to vote solidly against Brandeis; Jim Reed, aspiring to be the next party leader, would therefore have to vote for him. He might have held out if there had not been so confounded much mail pouring in on him from every little labor union in the state of Missouri and all kinds of petty storekeepers and professional "reformers," especially in St. Louis and Kansas City. And businessmen too! This man Brandeis must have a way with him, to attract this kind of following more than a thousand miles from Boston.

When Reed realized how long he had remained talking with Brandeis about everything except the Supreme Court, he suddenly rose and exclaimed: "I must go. I have left Mrs. Reed waiting outside all this time!"

As he made his departure into the chilly night, the warmth of his farewell left the impression that Senator Reed had found in Brandeis a man whose quality he had not fully visualized before. His vote, however reluctant, appeared to have been won.

If James Reed was the most ambitious among the doubtful Democratic members of the Judiciary Committee, the most firmly established and influential was Hoke Smith of Georgia. A giant of a man with a round, full face and an extroverted manner, he was the physical opposite of the lean Brandeis, whom he confronted at last in Hapgood's living room. Hoke Smith seemed to wear the lucky ring of success on his finger. He had won his right to it, however, by superior intelligence and industry. Learning law in his father's office rather than in the university lecture hall, Hoke Smith had worked his way to wealth by winning a host of compensation claims against the railroads. "The damage lawyer of Georgia *par excellence*," the

American Law Review dubbed Hoke Smith in tribute when President Grover Cleveland appointed him, at thirty-seven, his Secretary of the Interior. Twice in his middle years Smith had been elected governor of Georgia, and now in his second term in the United States Senate he was one of the experienced, forceful leaders to whom other members respectfully looked for guidance.

Woodrow Wilson and Hoke Smith had known each other slightly back in the early Eighties when they were both fledgling lawyers on Marietta Street in Atlanta. There Smith had rapidly become a success; Wilson had been a failure, closed his office, and gone north. Thirty years later Hoke Smith could not get over the ironies of fate that had brought the Marietta Street failure to the Presidency. Hoke Smith had been a strong Wilson man in 1912, and when the New Jersey governor won the election, the Georgia Senator was close to the President's ear. Wilson owed a special debt to Smith—for having found him a splendid Secretary of the Navy in Josephus Daniels. Smith had brought Daniels to Washington in the Nineties to be his chief clerk and office director in the Interior Department, and he therefore knew Daniels as an alert, honest, imaginative public servant. In 1913, when Wilson was making up his cabinet, Hoke Smith urged upon him the appointment of Daniels, who had made a fine reputation in the intervening years as editor of the Raleigh *News and Observer*.

Wilson was grateful for the Senator's help and showed it at first in the degree to which he confided in Smith. Given his seniority in the Senate and his close personal ties to the center of authority, Hoke Smith took it as his prerogative to be consulted regularly on important matters. Yet it was common gossip around Washington that Wilson had lately been trying to run the government too much as he had run Princeton University, from his own desk, and was causing himself needless trouble by not taking proud men like Hoke Smith more into his confidence.

From the very outset of the struggle over Brandeis, Hoke Smith had purposely kept everyone guessing. When the International News Service first reported that Smith would lead the fight to reject Brandeis, the Senator contradicted the dispatch, saying:

> This report is untrue. I have an open mind on the subject. I believe that every Senator will take that position. What I want to know, and what others will desire light on, is whether Mr. Brandeis

is a reformer first and a lawyer afterward, or whether the opposite is the case. If the lawyer predominates and all other things are equal there seems no reason why he should not be confirmed. I will not decide what I will do until I know all of the facts.

During the flareup on the Senate floor ignited by Ashurst, Smith had flatly acknowledged that "there never has been a time that I have been ready to vote for a report favorable to Mr. Brandeis. . . . I have not reached a conclusion."

Like Borah and Cummins, Hoke Smith was in his bones an anti-Wall Street man. He frequently bedeviled the "money power" and the trusts from the campaign platform as he sought the votes of the impoverished "wool-hat boys" of rural Georgia. This fact aligned him with Brandeis as a critic of the maldistribution of the nation's wealth. But Smith also bore in mind the residue of bitterness that powerful forces in the state harbored for those "outside agitators" who had tried to interfere with Georgia justice a year before, when the Leo Frank case had reached its crisis. At that time Brandeis had been prominent among the Jews from outside who had interceded with the governor to commute Frank's death sentence, and Hoke Smith was wary of arousing the hate pack by embracing Brandeis now. He had already been through a bitter campaign in 1914 in which his primary opponents accused him of being a Negrophile, a defender of labor-union agitators, and a friend of Samuel Gompers. Smith had no stomach for that kind of treatment again. He therefore remained officially silent during the four months of the struggle so as not to stir up the animals in the Georgia political jungle. In self-protection he dropped hints from time to time that he was leaning against the nominee, with the result that Georgia labor unions and those personal friends whom McAdoo, Morgenthau, and Daniels could reach sent him messages in the hope of winning him over.

"I am surprised to see by the public press that you are still indifferent as to whether you will support President Wilson in the Brandeis nomination," wrote one old friend, who argued at length that Smith's old foe, the "money power," lay behind the entire campaign against Brandeis.

Now the Senator was at last confronting the man whose nomination had stirred up the four-month storm. Their meeting in Hapgood's living room and their quiet conversation apart from the other guests ended in apparent cordiality on Senator Smith's part. It looked as if both Hoke Smith and Jim Reed had been won over.

Brandeis returned to Boston, having seen only these two of three Senators whom Hapgood had hoped would be willing to meet him. The third, who was now counted out as a possible favorable vote, was Senator William E. Borah of Idaho. The same force of party solidarity that was pulling, though in opposite directions, at Reed and Cummins, was also affecting Borah. Although he had always been a progressive on domestic issues, he had resisted joining the Bull Moose in 1912 and had remained neutral in the Presidential race while fighting for his own re-election to a second term to the Senate. Since January, Borah's correspondence had shown him firmly astride the fence on the Brandeis issue, though he earnestly requested his friends who opposed Brandeis to supply him with supporting data to use in denouncing the nominee, should he decide later to vote against. Early in May, when Borah was asked whether he would like to meet Brandeis quietly to talk over any matter that concerned him in the nominee's record, the Senator replied that he could see no purpose to such a conference. Then, in the one-day hearing on Friday, May 12, concerning the United Drug merger, Borah replaced Cummins on the subcommittee and revealed clearly by the slant of his questions that he was joining his Republican Party colleagues.

The events of the next week moved swiftly.

Monday, May 15

Once again the subcommittee reported favorably to the Senate Judiciary Committee, repeating the previous party line-up of three votes to two. The one-day hearing of the previous Friday had availed the opposition nothing. Press reports stated that the committee members argued for several hours without agreement, then adjourned. Two Democrats, it was asserted, were still unwilling to vote approval for the President's nominee. Perhaps the committee might report the nomination to the Senate without a recommendation. In that event, the Senate could take whatever action it might please, though a report without recommendation would openly invite the opponents to filibuster the nomination into discard. The scheduled June 3 recess of Congress for the Republican National Convention in Chicago was now only three weeks off.

At one o'clock in the afternoon the Senate galleries were cleared, the doors closed, and, as the *Congressional Record* put it by discreet custom, "the Senate thereupon proceeded to the consideration of executive business." More than four hours later when the doors were opened, newsmen learned that the Senate had rejected President Wilson's nomination of George Rublee as a member of the Federal Trade Commission by a vote of forty-two to thirty-six. There was not much comfort in the afternoon's events for those concerned with the case of Louis D. Brandeis. Although a handful of Progressive Republicans had voted with the administration Democrats to confirm Brandeis' friend as a Federal Trade Commissioner, three of the critical Democrats whose votes were needed in the Senate Judiciary Committee had sided with the Republicans to reject him. They were Senators O'Gorman of New York, Reed of Missouri, and Hoke Smith of Georgia. Senator Overman of North Carolina had stood with the losing administration forces; Senator Shields was still in Tennessee and so had not cast a vote.

The little group working on Brandeis' campaign were almost all friends of Rublee, and were spiritually with him in his months of trial. But because the attack on Rublee was a primarily one-man assault by Senator Gallinger of New Hampshire, who waved against him the flag of Senatorial courtesy, the dispute over Rublee's confirmation to the Federal Trade Commission had been obscured by the more prominent struggle over Brandeis. The moment of truth in the lesser contest, however, seemed to spell an evil omen for the greater one.

Nerves were becoming frayed and tempers on edge. George Anderson, now back in Boston after spending many days at the hearings in Washington, complained that Attorney General Gregory was hemming him in with too many restrictions on his authority as United States Attorney. But he would not quit, Anderson wrote his superior in spirited defiance, because he was too fond of Gregory:

> I would not hold this office fifteen minutes under McReynolds and submit to having the legal powers of the office cut down so as to become a non-resident clerk, for that is really what your policy comes to.

Tuesday, May 16

Gregory to Anderson:
> Go out and play a little golf, and when your liver gets in better condition consider the fact that I am dealing with a large number

of men of varying ability and character, many of them in remote
sections of the country, and that I am practically charged with all
the mistakes any of them make and with the responsibility for their
official, if not their personal, acts. I absolutely decline to get in a
row with you.

The indefatigable Norman Hapgood, alarmed at the bad turn in
Rublee's fortunes, sent a night wire to Robert Bass in New York,
urging him to try to get Theodore Roosevelt, through intermediaries,
to help win over such Progressive Senators as Cummins and Borah.
There would be a motion to reconsider the Rublee vote, and the
Brandeis matter was next.

William Hard, the free-lance writer who had been helping the
Brandeis strategists with publicity, reported to Bass that he had
managed to get an article on the issues of the Brandeis nomination
accepted by the *Outlook,* the weekly edited until recently by Colonel
Roosevelt. Furthermore, there was a good chance he could arrange
within the week for a national syndicate to take a series of ten articles
on Brandeis, one each by ten authors, to run on successive days.

In Washington, Woodrow Wilson met briefly with Henry Morgenthau to discuss a confidential and delicate mission that might settle
the Brandeis case definitely. The President had but a few minutes to
spare before his cabinet meeting, and he had many other problems to
worry about. According to the most recent dispatches, the Germans
had seized Fortress Douaumont, a key French bastion in the Verdun
sector of the Western Front. Congress had still not acted on his Army
bill; the Irish-Americans were incensed at the brutality of the British
in suppressing the Easter uprising in Dublin and were in a foul mood
against England. Theodore Roosevelt was war-shouting like a mad-
man from Oyster Bay, and the shadow of Justice Hughes was extend-
ing ever wider over the country. It was a threatening, dangerous time
for Woodrow Wilson's administration.

Wednesday, May 17

Charles W. Eliot, old friend of Louis Brandeis, at the request of
younger friends sat down at his desk in Cambridge to write a letter
to Senator Culberson. As President Emeritus of Harvard, which he
had headed for forty years, Eliot enjoyed the prestige of a Nestor in

that Athens of New England. Now in retirement, he sat close to Boston's gods. A word from such a man, the friends of the nominee hoped, would act as counterbalance to the defamation of Brandeis by President Lowell and his colleagues of the State Street counting-houses.

"I have known Mr. Louis D. Brandeis for forty years, and believe that I understand his capacities and his character," Eliot's testimonial read. As a student, Eliot continued:

> . . . he possessed by nature a keen intelligence, quick and generous sympathies, a remarkable capacity for labor, and a character in which gentleness, courage, and joy in combat were intimately blended. His professional career has exhibited all these qualities, and with them much practical altruism and public spirit.

Although he had disagreed with Brandeis on some matters, Eliot wrote that he had never questioned the nominee's honesty, sincerity, or his desire for justice.

> Under present circumstances, I believe that the rejection by the Senate of his nomination to the Supreme Court would be a grave misfortune for the whole legal profession, the court, all American business and the country.

Thursday, May 18

A few hours after the revered Eliot of Harvard had finished his plea for the acceptance of Brandeis, members of the scattered command staff in Cambridge, Boston, New York, and Washington were busily trying to insure it the widest possible publicity as soon as it should be made public on Capitol Hill. At the same time, Ambassador Morgenthau was reporting to President Wilson the result of his mission to the sulking Southern Senate leader he needed to court for the showdown vote on his Justice:

> *My dear Mr. President:*
> I was with Senator Hoke Smith for 2½ hours yesterday discussing the Brandeis matter and listening to his and his colleagues' grievances.
> Smith stated that Senators Shields, Reed of Missouri and O'Gorman would vote as he does and that "he is disposed" to vote *for*

Brandeis' confirmation. He still wants to dispel some slight doubts he has as to the Lennox case.

I feel that I made an impression upon him and that he will vote for Brandeis.

Smith feels keenly that you did not consult any of the Democratic members of the Judiciary Committee about the nomination and as it was a national position and both Massachusetts Senators are Republicans, he thinks you should have done so.

He also stated that since January he has not been at the White House for conference.

I think it would help greatly if you would send for him *after* Brandeis has been confirmed and discuss with him the English question and thereby give him back his "self-respect" about which he is so much concerned.

He and some of the other Senators have been nursing their discontent so long that it may become chronic—while a few soothing words from you will produce a prompt cure.

This reassuring report may have brought Woodrow Wilson a measure of hope that the tide was turning. That evening, Heaven itself seemed to send him an opportunity to add more strength in the Senate Judiciary Committee. Wilson had left the White House and gone to the theater, when Senator O'Gorman appeared hastily at the Executive Mansion, urgently demanding to see the President. The Senator delivered his message instead to Joseph Tumulty, Wilson's private secretary, who at once appreciated the strategic importance of assisting O'Gorman. Tumulty rushed to the theater to relay to the President O'Gorman's plea for help.

A British court-martial in Ireland had just passed a sentence of death on a man named Jeremiah C. Lynch, a resident of New York. Lynch was a naturalized American citizen who had returned to Ireland a few months before in a frenzy of patriotic zeal to fight for independence and had been caught in the suppression of the Easter uprising in Dublin. The entire Irish-American community was up in arms. America should never let the English take such vengeance on one of her citizens! Lynch was to be shot at midnight, New York time. Senator O'Gorman must get the President to intervene! The New York Senator, who outdid all others as a professional Irishman in politics, needed no prompting and was quickly on his way to get Wilson's help to stop this foul and bloody crime. Tumulty in his turn brought the facts to the President and then at his order dashed back to the State Department.

Friday, May 19

The morning newspapers told of the swift, dramatic action to save Lynch's life taken by President Wilson at the urgent request of Senator O'Gorman. The President had sent a cable to Ambassador Page in London, directing him to make every possible effort to secure a delay in the execution of the death sentence on Lynch. And although the fate of the condemned man remained uncertain during the morning hours, there was hope that the Senator and the President had stopped the execution. Later in the day it was learned that the sentence had been commuted to ten years' imprisonment. In the city to which he was soon to return, O'Gorman was the hero of the day. He had a debt now to the President who had helped him without a minute's hesitation.

Later in the day Wilson had time to send a quick note of thanks to Henry Morgenthau for his earnest efforts to win over Hoke Smith. The Georgian's difficulty, as Wilson analyzed it, came more from innate temperament than from any genuine slight he had suffered:

> I think the matter goes deep with him and is incurable, having been born with him, but, of course, I am willing to do anything that I reasonably can to accomplish the great results we have all set our hearts upon. I was heartily sorry I was tied up so as not to be able to hear about your interview in person.

Though recent developments had taken an encouraging turn, the lateness of the hour was bearing down heavily on Woodrow Wilson. Perhaps Hoke Smith had been won over by having met Brandeis socially at Hapgood's on Sunday and having poured out his vexations into Morgenthau's sympathetic ear. Perhaps, too, Jim Reed had come around, and O'Gorman had sufficiently appreciated his speedy step to boost his prestige among his Irish following in New York. But the days were running out. If he did not get Brandeis confirmed before the convention recess in two weeks, the President's chances would be far slimmer when the Republicans returned from Chicago. Stimulated by their quadrennial tribal powwow, and the selection of a new chief, they might decide to filibuster against the nomination as the opening

phase of their campaign to take over the Presidency and control of
Congress.

Gus Karger saw in the passage of each day the most encouraging
indication that Brandeis could be beaten. He reported to Taft on the
temper of the Senate as he gauged it from reconnaissance in the enemy
camp:

> I talked with Senator Jim Ham Lewis, the Democratic whip,
> about the prospects of Brandeis' confirmation. He seems quite dubi-
> ous. If it can be brought to a vote promptly, he is of the opinion that
> confirmation will be had by a majority of five.
> But the temper of the Senate is growing more and more impa-
> tient toward the administration, because of the treatment accorded
> Senators, by the President as well as by members of the cabinet. At
> first it was Mr. Wilson's practice, Mr. Lewis recalled, to visit the
> Capitol and confer with Senators of both parties with reference to
> appointments. Later, he summoned them by telephone. Now he
> doesn't know they are on earth.
> Gregory, McAdoo, Burleson and Redfield, more especially the
> two latter, have posed as the President's mouthpieces and later
> capitalized on the influence gained in behalf of their own projects.
> Now the Senators are in a state of rebellion, and the dockets of the
> committees containing contested nominations are so crowded that
> the United States Supreme Court has but little on them.
> If this condition of affairs is not relieved, opines Senator Lewis,
> Mr. Brandeis' confirmation may well be prevented.

The generally astute Karger had missed the significance of the
week-end trip that President Wilson was preparing out of special
courtesy to Senator Overman, whose vote for Brandeis was still in
doubt. Lee Slater Overman of Salisbury, North Carolina, ranking
member of the Senate Judiciary Committee after the chairman, cut an
imposing figure in his dignified Prince Albert coat, with his immense
stature and wavy hair. He had said openly at the very beginning of
the Brandeis struggle that he was "shocked" by the nomination; yet
as the weeks advanced he would not be quoted for attribution on his
views. In April Senator Chilton called on Secretary Josephus Daniels,
who was known to have influence on Overman, and told him that
Overman was muttering against Brandeis in the Senate cloakroom.
If something were not done to stiffen him, Chilton informed Daniels,

an essential committee vote might be lost. The Secretary of the Navy reassured Chilton—as well as Woodrow Wilson, to whom he relayed the information—that his fellow Carolinian was by nature a regular party man when it came to a rollcall vote. Still, it would not hurt to humor him.

The chance to do so came when Wilson was asked to attend the big patriotic celebration in Charlotte, North Carolina, on May 20, commemorating the Mecklenburg Declaration of 1775. The President accepted long before the event, then in early May indicated that his duties in Washington might prevent his making the trip after all. A flurry of communications from Charlotte descended on the offices of Secretary Daniels and of both North Carolina Senators, Overman and Simmons, appealing for them to insure the presence of the Chief Executive. Given the tense situation within the Judiciary Committee, Wilson then confirmed that he would start for Charlotte by train on Friday night, appear at the celebration on Saturday, and get back to Washington the next morning.

Saturday, May 20

As Daniels recalled the incident some years later, the Presidential train was rolling along in the early morning about a half-hour short of Overman's home town, Salisbury, when Senator Overman, considerably agitated, came to see him. The President had just told him, Overman said, that he could not deliver a rear-platform speech in Salisbury, where the Senator had already arranged for a crowd to assemble to see him arm in arm with the President of the United States. Wilson had said that he had energy and voice only for the Charlotte address. Wouldn't Daniels try, Overman pleaded, to convince the President to say just a few words in Salisbury?

Daniels needed no urging, and carried the appeal to Wilson's compartment. Overman would probably vote for Brandeis anyway, the Secretary conceded, now that Wilson was making this trip to Charlotte. But the President could please the Senator beyond measure by saying a few gracious words in his home town, where such a gesture would mean the most. In fact, this little act might transform Overman from a passive yes-voter to an active partisan of Brandeis within the committee. Wouldn't that be worth ten minutes of Wilson's time and a little effort with his voice?

When the train slowed to a stop in the Salisbury railroad yard, a crowd of several thousand people gathered around the rear car and broke into cheers when their own Senator and the President appeared together on the observation platform. Beaming with pride, Overman introduced the President to his neighbors. Wilson, turning on all his charm, declared "how glad I am to find myself in Senator Overman's home town. You have reason to be proud of your Senator, and I am very glad to give him the tribute of my praises, and if he will permit me to add it, of my friendship."

Then addressing himself indirectly to Senator Overman as he ostensibly spoke to the throng before them, Wilson turned his fire against those whom he termed "the men who are trying to hold us back." Such men, he declared, now control the Republican Party:

> They have their heads over their shoulders. They are looking backward, not forward. They do not know the problems of the new day. Whenever I try to show my sympathies for the forward-looking men of their own party by nominating men of that sort, they at once try to block progress; they have no sympathy for the forward-looking men of their own party. I am for forward-looking men, not backward-looking men.

The reference to blocking men "of their own party" was an obvious reference to the nomination of George Rublee, a Progressive Republican, to the Federal Trade Commission. But Wilson's remarks applied allegorically, and just as aptly, to the nomination of Brandeis. The listening Overman had voted to approve Commissioner Rublee in the Senate; his vote in committee on the prospective Justice was still to come.

The rest of the day, though a big one for Charlotte and a tiring one for the President and Mrs. Wilson, provoked less comment than the early-morning stop in Salisbury. Bands blared, patriotic societies paraded, and the mayor of Charlotte delivered a twenty-minute oration in introducing the President's fifteen-minute address. Charlotte had seldom seen such crowds or heard such cheering, amid the flags, feasting, and fireworks. That evening as his train headed back toward Washington, Wilson took with him Secretary Daniels' comforting assurance that Overman was now his man to the end of the Brandeis affair. It had been a good day's work.

On the same Saturday, May 20, Senator Walsh could notify a constituent that the date for voting on the Brandeis nomination had at last been appointed:

> It affords me much pleasure to say to you that after the tedious delay before the Committee a unanimous agreement has been arrived at for a final disposition by the Committee on Wednesday next.
>
> Even at this late day it is impossible to predict what the report will be, although it looks now as if it could be no worse than a return of the matter to the Senate without recommendation. The result in the Senate is not open to much doubt. The votes are there to confirm regardless of the action which may be taken by the Judiciary Committee, as those who have made a careful canvass assert.

Monday, May 22

Writing again to Karger, Taft confessed his feeling of apprehension over events to come:

> The nightmare of Brandeis constantly rises before me. I fear he is likely to be confirmed.
>
> I see that President Eliot is going to write in his favor. Eliot usually says something very severe about somebody. He will probably attack the Presidents of the American Bar Association. Eliot has reached a time where it would be well for him to retire from the position of General Censor, but as he grows older, he grows more voluble. It would not surprise me if he were to attack me. In dealing with me twice he has made such egregious mistakes of fact that one never knows what he will do when he sets his blunderbuss going.
>
> Wilson seems to have him completely in leash and to make him do what he chooses.

Rumored to be on its way to Washington for the past day or two, the Eliot letter was made public by Culberson even as Taft was contemplating the senility of its author. The generous space given it in the press brought cheer to the Brandeis group. This authoritative voice, sounding from the stronghold of reaction against the calling of Brandeis to the Supreme Court, was just what was needed to buoy their spirits. By nightfall another piece of good news was on the wires: Hoke Smith had announced that he would vote for confirmation on May 24. He had reached his decision, Senator Smith told reporters, on Saturday night after conducting what he termed his own "diligent

and exhaustive investigation" both of the hearing record and of facts
that lay beyond it:

> My investigation has convinced me that Mr. Brandeis is an hon-
> est, conscientious, able lawyer, and that his great purpose in public
> service has been to do good.
> The opposition to Mr. Brandeis' confirmation has gone over his
> entire professional career, hunting acts for criticism. There are some
> things in his record that I do not approve of, but none of them in-
> volves conduct that fairly can justify doubt as to his integrity, when
> fully and thoroughly considered.
> What lawyer with thirty-five years of experience at the bar can go
> over what he has done during that period without feeling that it
> would have been better not to have done some of the things that
> he has done?

Tuesday, May 23

In commenting on the Georgia Senator's determination to vote the
next day for the confirmation of Brandeis, the Atlanta *Constitution*
pointed out a surprising ambivalence in Hoke Smith's posture. He
was going to vote in favor of Brandeis, characterized in the newspaper
as "one of the most zealous and persistent advocates" of the Stevens
price-fixing bill when it was before the previous Congress. Yet Senator Smith had voted against confirming George Rublee as a member
of the Federal Trade Commission solely on the ground that Rublee
had been in favor of the Stevens bill. Evidently a view of economics
sufficient to bar one man from a government regulatory agency did
not, in Hoke Smith's view, make another man unfit for the Supreme
Court of the United States.

Smith stuck to his position when the administration Democrats that
afternoon made one final effort to confirm Rublee as a Federal Trade
Commissioner. On a motion to reconsider its rejection of the previous
week, the Senate produced a tie vote, 38 to 38, with the effect that
the motion to reconsider was lost. Hoke Smith and O'Gorman of New
York were among the ten Democratic Senators who joined the Republicans to defeat Wilson's nominee to the commission. Reed of
Missouri, while not voting, was announced as paired against the
motion to reconsider. Senator Overman of North Carolina voted with
the administration as he had done eight days previously. Senator

Shields was still absent from the Senate. Despite all the appeals that had reached these five Democratic members of the Judiciary Committee on behalf of the President, only one had voted in favor of Mr. Wilson's nominee. The augury for the morrow again seemed cloudy.

Taft's collaborator, George Wickersham, was still trying to bring pressure to bear on the Senate, apparently unaware that the committee vote had been set for Wednesday. He penned a hasty word to his old chief from his Wall Street office, sadly taking note of "Eliot's pronouncement" and "Hoke Smith's conversion." No newspaper, Wickersham complained, had published a summary of the testimony indicting Brandeis. So much effort and expense without publicity! Did Taft think that "Professor-Governor Baldwin would be willing to write and publish a summary statement of just what *was* established by the evidence? It would help immensely. What is wanted is something to give moral support to weak-backed Senators."

By this time Taft had left New Haven for Melrose, Massachusetts, a Boston suburb where he was scheduled that evening to address a meeting of the Federation of Church Schools on "A Complete Education." After his talk, Taft went into Boston to spend the night at the Commonwealth Avenue home of his cousins, Mr. and Mrs. Samuel Carr. Neither he nor Wickersham, anyone on Capitol Hill, nor even President Wilson or Louis D. Brandeis, was aware that a train from Knoxville, Tennessee, was carrying Senator Shields back to Washington.

ten

Ten to Eight

John Knight Shields was a throwback to the time of Andrew Jackson. In appearance and manner, the Senator from Tennessee gave the impression that he would have fitted comfortably into the period of rugged frontier Democracy, with its symbolism of log cabin, hard cider, and coonskin cap. In Washington he wore a cutaway, as befitted a former chief justice of the supreme court of his home state, but tobacco-chewing went with it as a counterbalance, as did his protestations whenever he was offered champagne: "I'm from Tennessee, and I drink nothing but red whiskey."

The dark hair, dark eyes, and black mustache against a pale skin, and the thin, wiry frame added to the total effect of tough independence that the first-term Senator from Knoxville consciously cultivated. "Senator Shields reminded me more of a pirate than any man I ever saw," was the recollection of one veteran observer in the Senate press gallery.

From the beginning of the Brandeis struggle, the administration had never been certain of Shields' vote. The opposition had almost counted on winning him over. In March, George Wickersham had received an encouraging word on Shields from John J. Vertrees, a Tennessee lawyer whom Taft's Attorney General hoped to exploit as his go-between with the Senator. Vertrees, at Wickersham's suggestion, had been brought into the 1910 Ballinger investigation as special counsel to present the Wickersham-Ballinger side of the matter. After weeks of bitter combat with Brandeis at that time, Vertrees had technically won his battle, but his distaste for the Boston lawyer who had so neatly and publicly dissected his clients still burned in his mouth after six years.

"I am sure that Senator Shields will vote against confirmation," Vertrees had written confidentially to Wickersham. Vertrees said that he had explained to Shields his special competence to judge the man, and had declared Brandeis "wanting in the courage and moral qualities required . . . his elevation to the Supreme Bench would be a calamity." Wickersham had dutifully passed Vertrees' good word on his lobbying on to Taft.

It was fortunate for Woodrow Wilson that his son-in-law, Secretary of the Treasury McAdoo, had spent his formative years in Tennessee before seeking his fortune in New York. As the vote Shields held close to his chest took on ever more crucial importance, McAdoo set about stirring up every old friend and loyal Democrat he knew in the state to press the need for Brandeis' confirmation on their Senator. One of his agents was Robert B. Cooke of Chattanooga, who had expressed dismay in January at the readiness of his local bar-association colleagues to urge the President to appoint Taft. Now, McAdoo wrote, Cooke could strike a blow for democracy by stiffening Shields. Confirmation of Brandeis was a major political issue, the Secretary explained:

> I hope you will understand the real motives back of the implacable opposition of the selfish and reactionary interests of this country who are moving heaven and earth to defeat his confirmation as a Justice of the United States Supreme Court. I earnestly hope that Senator Shields will not be misled by the character of this campaign against Mr. Brandeis. . . .
>
> I feel so earnestly that Mr. Brandeis' defeat would be an injury to the country, to say nothing of an injury to the Democratic Party if any Democrats contributed to that defeat, that I am most anxious that such a result shall not come about. I do not know just where Senator Shields stands on this matter, but I understand that he is in doubt. . . . I wish you would drop him a line and ask him if he won't stand by a Democratic President and the Democratic Party in its efforts to put on the Supreme Bench an unusually high-minded and able man.

In the final days before the committee was scheduled to vote, the recalcitrant Shields was reached in numerous ways with the President's message. At least once when he was in Washington, the Senator was called away from a dinner party by telephone and asked to come to the White House for a talk with the President. He not only

had his difficulties with Wilson over patronage, like those of O'Gorman and Hoke Smith; he was also in sharp disagreement with the
President over his own pending bill concerning federal water-power
policy. These points of irritation had taken on a somewhat changed
aspect for Shields since the Tennessee primary in early spring had
resulted in the defeat of the senior Senator, Luke Lea, by Representative Kenneth McKellar. In 1917 Shields would automatically become
senior man in the Senate from his state and therefore be in a position
to control far more patronage through his office than before. Shields
realized, however, that Senators who displease the President lose the
juiciest patronage plums to those from other states who play the party
game. By his very promotion, therefore, his freedom of maneuver had
become more circumscribed.

On the morning of May 24, fifteen full weeks after the hearings
in the Brandeis case had been opened in the Senate Judiciary Committee room, the committee members gathered in the same place to
render their decision. The excitement generated by the crowd of
spectators in February was missing now, but the atmosphere of
tension among this group of irreconcilable men seemed to pervade
every corner of the room as they took their seats at the long conference table. On the Republican side sat aged Clarence Clark of
Wyoming, who had served on the subcommittee for a few days; Knute
Nelson of Minnesota, still smarting from the pain of his Pyrrhic victory in exonerating Ballinger long ago; Dillingham of Vermont; and
Brandegee of Connecticut, who had been relatively quiet throughout
the drawn-out struggle; aristocratic-looking George Sutherland of
Utah, with his trim, gray beard and pince-nez, who has bristled with
indignation in April when Ashurst had accused his side of stalling
and filibustering in committee; Borah of Idaho, his firm mouth set
with determination, who had permitted his party loyalty to drown
out the nagging voice within him, and had made up his mind to vote
as he had on the final subcommittee report; and the tepid Progressive from California, Senator Works. Cummins of Iowa, his proxy
vote against confirmation arranged with the chairman, was out of
town busily directing his campaign for the Presidential nomination.
Culberson of Texas was in the chair at the head of the committee
table, the votes of eight other Democrats as good as in his pocket.

Chilton, Fletcher, Walsh, and Ashurst had long since shown where they stood. In recent days the chairman had learned that, one by one, the votes of Senators O'Gorman, Overman, Reed, and Smith had been secured by the manipulation of forces outside the committee room. Now it was only a question of Shields. There had been no certain word from him. Would he fail to arrive on time for the vote? If so, the motion to approve the Brandeis nomination would be passed by a narrow nine-to-eight margin. But if he should arrive, there would be a doubt. He might possibly vote to confirm. But should Shields vote *No,* the nomination would be returned to the Senate without recommendation. In that event, the opponents of Brandeis might easily stage a filibuster against him on the Senate floor that would tie the body up until the convention recess.

Arriving early by train at Union Station, Shields that morning had gone to Hoke Smith's office for a conference, then returned to his own suite. Just as Culberson was preparing to call the roll, Shields walked into the committee room. Except for a few terse greetings, hardly a word was spoken as the Senators quietly faced the climax of the Brandeis affair. The poll moved down the table by seniority. When the names were called, *Aye* or *No* sounded from each Senator as expected.

"Senator Shields?"

"Aye!"

A gasp escaped from several members who had pinned their hopes on Shields to deadlock the committee. The Brandeis nomination was approved for Senate action by a vote of ten to eight. Every Senator had voted the policy of his political party.

Woodrow Wilson received the news in New York City, where he had gone by train to attend the wedding that afternoon of his close friend and personal physician, Dr. Cary Grayson. As he rode back to Washington in the evening, his sense of jubilation over the victory was indeed sweet. There would be no stopping the confirmation now, because the Democrats had the votes in the Senate to force it through. The Republicans had made the nomination a party matter, and in so doing had helped Wilson gather up all his partisan forces to oppose them. The imminence of the Republican National Convention had brought out the true Democratic spirit in every man. He had insisted on Brandeis and he had won, when only yesterday he had failed when the Senate rejected his nomination of George Rublee as a Federal Trade Commissioner.

Former President Taft was also on a train when the committee acted, en route from Boston to Saratoga Springs. He wrote a longhand letter in pencil to his Aunt Delia as clearly as the swaying of the train would permit, oblivious of the outcome of the committee vote in Washington. The dark fears Taft had expressed for weeks, though always tinged with the silver of hope, were finally confirmed at the end of his journey. He made no comment to reporters, but went before his audience as scheduled that evening and earnestly told an assemblage of Methodists that the United States should build its Navy to a strength equal to that of Germany. Three days later, on Saturday, Taft was in Washington to say a few appropriate words at a meeting of the Supreme Court bar, held to honor the memory of Taft's old Georgia friend and appointee to the Court, the late Justice Lamar. Presiding over the solemn occasion was the senior Senator from Georgia, Hoke Smith. Brandeis spared Taft's feelings by remaining in Boston.

The New York Times could not concede Lamar's seat on the Supreme Court to Brandeis without going on record to deplore the change. "We remain of the opinion," *The Times* declared in a lengthy editorial after the committee vote, "that if Mr. Brandeis is to enter public life, the legislative hall, not the Bench of the Supreme Court, is the proper theatre for the exercise of his abilities." The editorial conceded that Brandeis had not been proved corrupt, but regretted that the case against him on the grounds of deficient professional ethics had failed to convince a partisan majority of the committee. It then pointed sadly to the dismal future of the Supreme Court that the confirmation of Brandeis implied:

> The Supreme Court, by its very nature, must be a conservative body; it is the conservator of our institutions, it protects the people against the errors of their legislative servants, it is the defender of the Constitution itself. To place on the Supreme Bench judges who hold a different view of the function of the court, to supplant conservatism by radicalism, would be to undo the work of John Marshall and strip the Constitution of its defenses. It would introduce endless confusion where order has reigned, it would tend to give force and effect to any whim or passion of the hour, to crown with

success any transitory agitation engaged in by a part of the people, overriding the mature judgment of all the people as expressed in their fundamental law.

The Republican Senators saw no point in continuing the struggle, and agreed to vote without debate on the nomination two days before the recess for their Chicago convention. Secretary McAdoo wrote exultantly to Brandeis that with this concession, the last shadow of obstruction had been overcome: "The opposition has entirely collapsed and you will be confirmed by a very large majority. I believe I am as much gratified as you must be by the splendid way in which you have been vindicated by the hearings before the Committee."

McAdoo dismissed too casually the depth of conviction of Brandeis' opponents in the Senate. All eight Republican members of the Judiciary Committee signed a report roundly condemning the man whose "vindication" had been voted by the ten Democrats. Adopting in full the previously printed views of Senators Cummins and Works, the Republican report went on to summarize the opposition case against Brandeis in far stronger language than the two subcommittee members had seen fit to employ. Declaring that each of the charges against Brandeis had been "proved," it appealed to the Senate to vote *No,* with these words of righteous certitude:

> The facts upon which our conclusions are based are undisputed. They present a condition that should make the confirmation of this man by the United States Senate impossible. Never before in the history of the country has a man been appointed a Justice of the Supreme Court of the United States whose honesty and integrity were seriously brought in question. It must be evident to any thinking and unbiased mind that this appointment has resulted from something other than the qualifications and fitness of the appointee for the office.
>
> We regard it as a great misfortune and a distinct lowering of the standard heretofore maintained in making appointments to this high office that one should be selected for the place whose reputation for honesty and integrity amongst his associates at the bar has been proved to be bad, which reputation has been justified by his own course of conduct. We cannot conscientiously give our consent to such an appointment.

But these were only words for the record. A few minutes before 5 P.M. on June 1, the Senate galleries were cleared and the Senators went into executive session to vote on the Brandeis nomination. Everything had been said or written; there was not a word of debate. The vote was an anticlimactic formality. When the doors were opened a half-hour later, Vice-President Marshall announced that the nomination of Louis D. Brandeis had been confirmed by a vote of forty-seven to twenty-two.

Of the Democrats present and voting, only Senator Newlands of Nevada had deserted to the Republicans. After the vote had been announced, Newlands rose to explain his solitary gesture as if he anticipated criticism by his colleagues and constituents: "Regarding my vote, I should like to say that I have great admiration for Mr. Brandeis as a propagandist and publicist, but I do not regard him as a man of judicial temperament, and for that reason I voted against his confirmation."

Seven of the eight Republicans who had voted against confirmation in committee were present to cast their ballots against the nominee on the rollcall. Only Borah, who had been in the chamber earlier in the afternoon, did not vote. In his absence he was paired with another absentee of his own party, a Progressive Republican who saw the Brandeis issue the other way.

Preconvention activity in Chicago had already lured a number of Republican Senators from Washington, and this was the case with Weeks, favorite-son candidate of Massachusetts. Henry Cabot Lodge, the convention keynote speaker, remained in Washington to vote against Brandeis, as did Senator Harding of Ohio, Taft's choice for convention chairman, and Senator Albert B. Fall of New Mexico, who was scheduled to nominate Theodore Roosevelt at Chicago.

Although Senator La Follette's influence as Progressive Republican leader was insufficient to win for Brandeis the support of Senators Cummins, Works, and Borah, he was not altogether wrong in the estimate he had ventured to the President in January. Joining La Follette in the Senate vote to confirm Brandeis were George Norris, a Progressive Republican from Nebraska with the temperament of an unfettered free agent, and Miles Poindexter, junior Senator from Washington, who would face the voters in a few months to seek vindication of his principles. In addition to these three, there were two other Progressive Republicans close to La Follette whose votes for Brandeis would have been cast had they been needed. They were Senators Clapp of Minnesota and Gronna of North Dakota, who were paired on the *Aye* side of the vote against absent Republicans who would have voted *Nay*. To this degree, then, was the Senate "La Follettized," as Taft had complained four months earlier when the Brandeis issue first came before it.

A conference of campaigners for woman suffrage was in progress in New York City when the newspapers announced BRANDEIS CONFIRMED TO SUPREME COURT. One woman at the meeting looked at the headline, then turned to a young lady just a year out of Bryn Mawr College who happened to be sitting next to her.

"I see they confirmed that Jew Brandeis as a Justice of the Supreme Court!" she remarked with distaste in her voice.

Susan Brandeis stiffened, then replied in a cutting tone: "You certainly are speaking to the right person, madam. Mr. Brandeis happens to be my father!"

While the Senate was voting, Louis Brandeis was returning from his downtown office to his summer home in Dedham on the late afternoon train. He read the confirmation news on his wife's face as he entered the house, and heard it in her greeting, "Good evening, Mr. Justice Brandeis."

That day Alice Brandeis had received a cordial invitation from Belle La Follette, to whom she had been drawn in intimate friendship since the joint legislative fights of their husbands had developed into a close working comradeship. Mrs. La Follette had written that after the Senate vote

> . . . there will be an end to all this wicked business. As soon as Louis is a member of the Court his enemies will take to cover. I suppose some of them will be claiming they made him Judge. The fight has been a bitter, desperate one but it will end with the oath of office. . . . We will have a quiet dinner. Quiet to the outside world but we will draw the shades and dance on the table and do whatever we feel like doing in the way of jubilation.

Throughout the Brandeis struggle, La Follette had been disgusted by the way his Progressive colleague Cummins had run with the reactionary pack baying after Brandeis, on the false scent of his supposedly "deficient professional ethics." In his own Wisconsin paper, *La Follette's Weekly*, the Progressive leader had declared that the furor over the nominee's ethics was a completely false issue. The true one was the anger of the privileged over his pursuit of social

justice for the common man, his advocacy of economic reforms that
had shrunk their purse and curbed their power. The morning after
Senate confirmation, precisely this approach to the Brandeis case
was taken by *The Christian Science Monitor,* the Boston daily renowned from coast to coast for its thoughtful editorial page:

> The antagonism to Mr. Brandeis has profited the nation in that
> it has laid bare the grounds upon which one great element in politics
> bases its opposition to the policies of another. It has served to show,
> for the millionth time, that when one undertakes to champion any
> great reform he must be prepared to encounter the allied and bitter
> opposition of all those engaged in practices and enterprises in need
> of reformation.
>
> The antagonism to Mr. Brandeis extended far beyond any inter-
> ests he attacked, or could have attacked in the course of his career.
> He had touched points of moral conduct in business in which all
> were concerned, and there was a correspondingly wide range for the
> feeling that was stirred against him.

The *Monitor* turned its back on the long list of allegations against
Brandeis and scrutinized instead what motives had driven his opponents to their attack on him:

> It has been difficult, and in some cases seemingly impossible,
> for certain of the opponents of Mr. Brandeis to credit him with
> worthy motives in his warfare against social and industrial injus-
> tice. These opponents apparently could not understand how a man
> of his great natural ability, his exceptional talents, his marvelous
> energy, could freely give thought and time to the advancement of
> the public good. They have questioned his every act, thrown sus-
> picion upon his every move. They could not, seemingly, bring them-
> selves to the point of believing that a great and successful lawyer
> should, out of regard for the rightness of things, become an al-
> truist. . . .

To *The Christian Science Monitor,* the fact that Brandeis was a Jew
had played no part at all in the events of the preceding four months.
But Woodrow Wilson was receiving a stream of letters of gratitude
from those who saw his recognition of Brandeis as a hopeful pillar of
fire for every Jew in America.

From Syracuse, New York: "Though character and fitness was the
motive of this nomination, I think the 'world of Judaism' next No-

vember will return in full this fine compliment you have conferred upon their race in placing this high honor upon Mr. Brandeis."

From the United Hebrew Citizens of Luzerne County, Pennsylvania, came word that a special meeting had been held on June 2 to adopt resolutions honoring the new Justice, and declaring to the President that "this honor conferred on a Jew is highly appreciated by all the Jews of this country, and we as an association thank you for conferring this honor on one of our kind. . . ."

From a pharmacist in Brooklyn: "You have done as much for the Jews as Cyrus did so many centuries ago."

The victory over anti-Semitism was merely one element of the affair that District Attorney George Anderson mentioned when sending congratulations to Wilson from Boston:

> It is fitting that one who had played his small part in the fight for genuine democracy in this old New England community should pay his tribute of respect and admiration to the President who had the courage, insight and persistency to make Louis D. Brandeis a member of the Supreme Court.
>
> You, the Attorney General and others who have never lived in New England do not, I think, even now appreciate what this appointment, fought to a successful finish in the confirmation of yesterday, means to us of New England.
>
> This victory is a new victory for freedom; freedom from the trammels of race prejudice; freedom from subservience to money power; freedom to think and to speak as men ought to think and act and speak in a real democracy.

From New York the President received a note of felicitation from Henry Morgenthau, who reminded Wilson of a political fence needing his hand for its repair: "I hope that in the midst of your many other duties you will *not forget* to ask Hoke Smith to call on you for a conference."

On Monday, June 5, the President replied to Morgenthau that he was

> . . . indeed relieved and delighted at the confirmation of Brandeis. I never signed any commission with such satisfaction as I signed his. I understand that he is to be sworn in today.
>
> Next time I see you I want to say a word to you about consulting with the senior Senator from Georgia. . . .

That same morning a few hundred yards north from the White House on 16th Street, Brandeis left the Lafayette Hotel for the ride to the Capitol with Chief Justice White. On the way the two men chatted about the proprieties of the Supreme Court, the disposition of securities held by the new Justice, the procedure of the swearing-in ceremony. In the presence of the other Associate Justices in their private courtroom in the Capitol, White administered the oath of allegiance to the federal Constitution. Then, dressed for the first time in the black silk robe of a judge, Brandeis took his place at the end of the line of Justices. They proceeded across the corridor through a buzzing throng of friends and curious onlookers who had been unable to squeeze into the crowded Court chamber.

It was a historic moment, as Chief Justice White entered the pillared chamber and led the nine black-robed figures down the aisle to the bench. An awesome dignity pervaded the hushed hemicycle, this classical room in which the Senate had met for fifty years while thunder rolled from Webster, Benton, and Sumner, from Calhoun and Henry Clay. Since that time, this meeting place of the Supreme Court had witnessed a vast unfolding of federal power announced to the country under a Supreme Court headed in turn by Chief Justices Taney, Chase, Waite, and Fuller. Their busts in graven marble looked down now on this new moment of transition in the history of their continuing Court.

The nine men moving toward their places on the bench bore on their shoulders the weight of a Constitution regulating the affairs of a nation that had expanded from a newly liberated colonial past to a present of mighty industrial power and world influence. Two of the nine, the Chief Justice and Holmes, had fought against one another in the Civil War. One among them, Justice Hughes, might within the week be called upon to leave this Court to become a candidate for the Presidency. Another among them, the lean, robed figure, now the center of attention, who filed in last and stopped at the clerk's desk while the others mounted the bench, had only yesterday been the focal point of a Supreme Court struggle without precedent. Everyone in the room sensed that the advent to the Supreme Court of Louis D. Brandeis, the man more hated and at the same time more beloved than any other at the American bar, marked the beginning of a new era.

The slightly graying man with the sensitive aspect of a beardless

Lincoln of slightly Semitic cast raised his hand and repeated the oath of office:

> I, Louis Dembitz Brandeis, do solemnly swear that I will administer justice without respect to persons, and do equal right to the poor and to the rich, and that I will faithfully and impartially discharge and perform all the duties incumbent upon me as Associate Justice of the Supreme Court of the United States, according to the best of my abilities and understanding, agreeable to the Constitution and the laws of the United States, so help me God.

With Congress in recess while the Republican National Convention displaced most other news from the front pages, Senator Walsh received his just share of compliments from friends who recognized how doggedly he had worked to bring the new Supreme Court Justice through his trial to the bench. From Boston, Anderson sent Walsh a hearty "well done," with the wry comment that plenty of others would now rush in to claim credit for the successful outcome of the affair. From Helena, Montana, the secretary of a miners' lodge hailed the Catholic Senator's fight to overcome "bigotry, prejudice and hatred against a race that has been persecuted for centuries. Your magnanimity and fairness to do justice entitled you to greatest praise and laudation, and all lovers of justice owe you a debt of gratitude."

Walsh, in response, sought gently to assess the struggle in a somewhat different light:

> No doubt much of the hostility toward Mr. Brandeis had its origin in the senseless racial prejudice, but I am altogether convinced that the more formidable part of the opposition sprang from the ardent sympathy he has displayed with the efforts in which some of us have been engaged to secure better conditions of life for the toiling masses. . . .
> The brunt of the battle fell upon me, and it is comforting indeed to know that it is recognized generally by those who have followed the contest that it was not unworthily borne.

To another correspondent in Massachusetts, Walsh sent a breakdown of the communications reaching the Judiciary Committee that gave a vastly different picture from that painted by the opponents of Brandeis. They had claimed a "wave of protest" had greeted the Brandeis nomination, coming from the men in his own city and state who knew him best. Walsh observed that the opponents of Brandeis in Massachusetts had been tightly concentrated in Boston. Letters from Boston lawyers had totaled 190 against Brandeis and 175 in his favor. Yet, Walsh declared, the committee "received 620 letters from lawyers in Massachusetts endorsing the nomination, and only eight in the state at large, or outside the city of Boston, were opposed to him."

Watching the reports of the Republican convention early in the week, McAdoo advised Wilson that the Brandeis affair might become a useful campaign issue:

> If the Republicans, as the newspapers intimate, should adopt a platform declaring strongly for social justice, so-called, would it not be an admirable thing if the Democratic platform, in treating of this subject, should point out that when you nominated for the Supreme Bench a man who, in a most conspicuous way, was the very embodiment of the highest principles of social justice and had, for years, waged a fight against social abuses and privileges, the Republican party in the Senate unanimously voted against him? I am enclosing a very significant editorial from the *Christian Science Monitor* of June 2nd bearing upon this point.

With the nomination of Charles Evans Hughes by the Republican convention on Saturday, June 10, and his immediate resignation from the Supreme Court in order to accept, President Wilson found himself facing the same problem as in January—selection of a new Associate Justice. He did not want to invite another struggle like the one just completed. Should he surmount his difficulties the easy way, by naming a Southern man who would be accepted at once by such potential troublemakers as Hoke Smith, Jim Reed, and Shields? The President considered nominating Attorney General Gregory, a Texan, the man who above all others around him had encouraged him to name Brandeis. But word came back to Wilson through Norman Hapgood that the new member of the Supreme Court considered Gregory, as a thoroughgoing progressive, most valuable right where he was:

> Mr. Brandeis elaborated . . . his belief that the Attorney General is a good lawyer and that it is extremely difficult to get a sufficiently good lawyer who is as genuine a progressive as he is. After all, it is the progressive spirit that we have to consider at this moment, as well as from the more permanent point of view.

To Wilson's considerable relief, a month later the Senate quickly approved his selection of Judge John H. Clarke from the federal Circuit Court of Appeals in Cincinnati, the court in which Taft had spent the most comfortable and rewarding years of his life. Clarke was a forward-looking judge of the new school of thought on broad social questions, but his nomination stirred none of the animosities that had been aroused by Brandeis.

With summer in 1916, the country quickly turned its attention to other battles—the Wilson-Hughes election campaign, the great naval engagement off Jutland between the German and British fleets, the heartbreaking failure, at tragic and bloody cost, of the Allied summer offensive in France. Woman suffrage and Prohibition came forward as issues to arouse excitement; behind them the American people could hear the war drums rolling closer. It was a time of too great preoccupation elsewhere for a retrospective analysis of the struggle over the Brandeis nomination. Yet one magazine article, written while the issue was still in the balance and not in print until it was resolved, with a clearer perspective than all others summed up the ironic duality of Brandeis' character that had invited the invidious assault upon him. It was written for *The Outlook* by William Hard, one of the few journalists with whom Brandeis had felt completely at ease and in whom he was willing to confide during his nomination fight.

I am moved once more [Hard wrote] . . . to admire and to execrate the skill with which life sometimes seizes upon a man's best quality as the very instrument with which to endeavor to compass his ruin.

Here is a man who, almost as if his mother had taken him as a child to the Temple of Justice and had dedicated him to its singular service, has spent his life trying, above all things else, to cultivate in himself the power and the habit of thinking impartially—so much so that an amazingly large part of his practice as a contentious advocate at the bar has not been contentious at all, but has consisted either of giving impartial business advice to business clients about their own business affairs or else of actually serving as a sort of arbitrator between conflicting business interests—as a sort, that is, of private judge.

Yet he now finds that certain things which he never could have done if he had not been impelled to them by the excessive judicialness of his temperament are the very things which in the mouths of

his adversaries are the chief charges brought against him to prove
his "unfitness" for a United States Supreme Court judgeship.

If Mr. Brandeis should ever wish to compose the world's best
essay on irony, all he would need to do would be to call in his
stenographer and dictate his autobiography.

Hard dissected in his article the three cases which he termed the
most important among the anti-Brandeis charges: the railroad rate
case, the United Shoe Machinery Company matter, and the Lennox affair. In each, he declared, Brandeis made the mistake of pre-
suming that other people would see clearly his position and his
motives. He was too much the idealist to protect himself against the ill-
will of others. His fault lay in not appreciating the discontent and
suspicion of those whom he would not blindly serve for a lawyer's
fee. Here, Hard concluded, lay the great irony of the long weeks of
attack upon the reputation of Louis Brandeis, candidate for the bench:

> For the matter immediately in hand, this fault, this excess of
> independence, this forgetfulness of personal issues in the midst of
> issues of truth and of right—what is it, this fault, but the very
> qualifying virtue of a judge?

Author's Postscript

(*Informally combining bibliography, acknowledgments, footnote material, personal comment, and guideposts for others who may follow me down the same path.*)

The inspiration to write *Justice on Trial* came a few years ago while I was reading a lengthy fictional best-seller. That book concerned a battle that erupted in the United States Senate when the President appointed a highly controversial figure to an important office. The story line of the novel held my interest, but the characters seemed cut from cardboard and much of their actions and speech seemed unrealistically contrived.

"But there was a *real* one!" I suddenly thought—an actual case where the Senate and the country were bitterly divided over just such a controversial nomination. I had known vaguely of the storm that had greeted Woodrow Wilson's naming Louis D. Brandeis as an Associate Justice of the Supreme Court, so I turned from the novel to look up the record, to see whether the event merited retelling. I concluded that it did.

Because the congressional investigation of persons, as opposed to subjects, has become a fixture of our national politics, an account of the Brandeis nomination struggle, now that many private papers bearing on it are open to research, may give us a helpful perspective from which to evaluate other confirmation fights that surely lie ahead. Men have become excited about the Supreme Court once again. Many people care about its membership as passionately as when Wilson's nomination of Brandeis divided the country nearly two generations ago. Parallels, similarities, and differences are left for each reader to determine for himself.

In the research for this book I used the obviously relevant periodicals, histories, biographies, and books of social analysis. Three printed sources were of special value: First, the hearings and reports of the Senate Judiciary Committee, 64th Congress, 1st session, "Nomination of Louis D. Brandeis." Second, *Brandeis: the Personal History of an American Ideal* by Alfred Lief, a short biography published in 1936 during the lifetime of Justice Brandeis and of many people whose names dot this book. Third, *Brandeis: a Free Man's Life,* by Professor Alpheus T. Mason of Princeton University, published in 1946. This is a detailed, scholarly biography, based on Professor Mason's years of study of Justice Brandeis' life and work and on his close personal contact with the Justice. Both the Lief and Mason biographies include two chapters on the nomination struggle to which *Justice on Trial* is devoted. Insofar as possible, I have tried to add to their accounts rather than to duplicate.

Another source meriting special mention is the undergraduate thesis of John Pryor Furman, Princeton '42, written under the direction of Professor Mason and devoted entirely to the Brandeis nomination fight. Mr. Furman did the basic sifting through the Brandeis papers concerning the nomination struggle at the University of Louisville Law School library. He lent his remarkably thorough unpublished thesis to me for my research.

Most of my documentary research was carried out in the Manuscript Division of the Library of Congress in Washington, where the papers of many of the actors in this drama are deposited. The most fruitful collections were those of Presidents Theodore Roosevelt, William Howard Taft, and Woodrow Wilson; of Senators William E. Borah and Thomas J. Walsh; and of Josephus Daniels, Thomas W. Gregory, Oliver Wendell Holmes, Charles Evans Hughes, William G. McAdoo, Henry Morgenthau, Sr., the National Consumers League, Amos Pinchot, and Elihu Root.

For Chapters One and Three, the National Consumers League papers in the Library of Congress were especially valuable in documenting the social scene in 1915–1916, the role of the Supreme Court at the time, and the part played by Brandeis in the League's activities.

In Chapter Two (p. 31), the Solicitor General John W. Davis mentioned to President Wilson as a possible Supreme Court nominee was the same John W. Davis who was the Democratic candidate for the Presidency in 1924. Davis' long legal career reached its climax with the 1954 school-segregation cases, in which he was the principal advocate on the losing side before the Supreme Court.

Governor Bilbo of Mississippi (p. 30) was later United States Senator Bilbo. Robert F. Wagner (p. 36), a state senator in New York, was later United States Senator Wagner, father of Mayor Robert Wagner of New York.

The full record of the part played in the Brandeis nomination affair by Senator Robert M. La Follette (p. 37) is unfortunately not yet open to research workers, nearly forty years after La Follette's death. It is easily possible that this part of the story may be enriched when the voluminous La Follette papers now in the Library of Congress are ready for general use by historians.

When I visited the National Archives in 1962 to look at the official Brandeis nomination paper (p. 39) signed by President Wilson, the document was missing from its assigned place. I called the attention of the staff to its disappearance. The paper was still missing in November 1963, when I checked again.

The present-day Boston law firm of Nutter, McClennen & Fish at 75 Federal Street is the successor to the original firm of Warren & Brandeis (p. 41). I found that its files still contain a number of Brandeis' folders antedating his taking his seat on the Supreme Court, although his pre-Court papers were supposedly all deposited at the University of Louisville Law School and were thoroughly examined by Professor Mason and his colleagues. The Boston files include letters, memoranda, and clippings on the Leo Frank trial and miscellaneous personal correspondence, including several notes from Felix Frankfurter.

The fight waged by Brandeis and others (p. 46) at the turn of the century for public control of the Boston transit system doubtless played a part in Boston's being one of the first major cities in the country to turn to municipal transit. The Metropolitan Transit Authority of Boston is, in that sense, a Brandeis legacy.

The resemblance between Brandeis and Abraham Lincoln (p. 56) was impressed on me recently upon entering Ford's Theatre in Washington, now a Lincoln Museum. There the plaster busts of Lincoln before he grew his beard, viewed from the right profile, look startlingly like pictures of Brandeis at about the same age. My own grandfather, Francis E. Leupp, called public attention to this resemblance in February 1916, in an article he wrote for the *Nation* under the pseudonym "Tattler." Leupp as a schoolboy had seen the beardless Lincoln shortly before the 1860 election, and observed Brandeis in Washington fifty years later.

Federal Judge Landis (p. 64) who complimented Brandeis was already nationally famous for having fined Standard Oil $29,000,000 in antitrust cases. A few years later he was appointed the first Commissioner of Baseball, in the wake of the 1919 Black Sox scandal, and held that post until his death in 1944.

A detailed account of Wilson's desire to name Brandeis his Attorney General in 1913 (p. 67), and his decision against the appointment, is found in *Wilson: the New Freedom*, by Arthur S. Link. Although John F. ("Honey Fitz") Fitzgerald, grandfather of the late President John F.

Kennedy and then Democratic leader in Boston, had frequently clashed with Brandeis before 1913, members of the Kennedy family assured me that there are no Fitzgerald papers extant by which the role of "Honey Fitz" in this affair can be documented.

Justice Felix Frankfurter told me that it was a talk by Brandeis on the opportunities for public service in the law, probably that delivered on May 4, 1905, in Phillips Brooks House (p. 68), that inspired his own career in juridical scholarship, which later led to the Supreme Court.

It has been asserted in various published works that Judah P. Benjamin was offered a Supreme Court justiceship (p. 70) by President Fillmore but that he declined the offer before it was sent to the Senate. My own research, however, has led me to believe there is no primary evidence to document this story. The point is of importance only in terms of the "first" to be credited to Brandeis—whether he was the first Jew "picked" for the Supreme Court, as the New York *Sun* put it, or the first actually nominated. To answer the question as to how much of a role anti-Semitism played in the Brandeis nomination struggle is for each reader to determine after reading the evidence. Because this is a point in which there is intense interest today, I sought all the material I could on this aspect of the story.

The *Sun* proved wrong (p. 71) in predicting that Wilson could not be re-elected without carrying New York state. In 1916 Hughes carried New York, with its large Jewish vote, yet Wilson won the election.

Senator James J. Wadsworth (p. 72), not reelected in 1920, later spent many years in the United States House of Representatives. His son, James J. Wadsworth, Jr., has served as United States Representative to the United Nations.

James M. Curley (p. 74) was later governor of Massachusetts and a congressman. John F. Fitzgerald (p. 74), formerly major of Boston and member of Congress, was the unsuccessful Democratic candidate in 1916 for the Senate seat held by Henry Cabot Lodge. David I. Walsh (p. 75) later held the same Senate seat from 1926 to 1946, when he was defeated by Lodge's grandson, Henry Cabot Lodge II. In turn the younger Lodge lost his "family seat" in 1952 to Fitzgerald's grandson, John Fitzgerald Kennedy. Ten years later, in a special election, Edward M. Kennedy won his older brother's seat in a contest with George Lodge, great-grandson of the 1916 Senator.

The original letters from William Howard Taft to Gus Karger (p. 77 et seq.) are in the possession of Colonel Alfred Gus Karger of Cincinnati, the son of Taft's confidant. It was urged upon me both by Colonel

Karger and by Mrs. Helen Taft Manning, daughter of William Howard Taft, that Taft was free of the anti-Semitic bigotry that marked some of the men around him (pp. 78, 179, 217). I am convinced from my research that this is quite true. While serving as Chief Justice from 1921 to 1930, Taft developed a genuine affection and respect for Brandeis as a person, despite their differences on matters of law.

It was from Faneuil Hall (pp. 83–84) that John F. Kennedy made his televised wind-up campaign speech for the Presidency on the eve of his election in November 1960.

Arthur D. Hill (p. 85) was again at odds with some of his conservative Boston friends a few years later when he took an active part in the campaign for a new trial for Sacco and Vanzetti.

Much of the correspondence of Senator Henry Cabot Lodge (p. 85 and following) is taken from his papers in the Massachusetts Historical Society which his grandson, Ambassador Henry Cabot Lodge, granted me permission to examine, with the understanding that passages to be quoted be shown to him. When the book manuscript was finished I discussed the selected quotations with George Cabot Lodge, who represented the Lodge family. The point at issue was whether today's reader might misconstrue Senator Lodge's reason for opposing the appointment of Brandeis to the Supreme Court. The Lodge family firmly believes that Senator Lodge was primarily concerned with what he considered Woodrow Wilson's misusing a Supreme Court appointment to attract the Jewish vote. But in his denunciation of the appointment, they believe, he used words which today might misrepresent him as anti-Semitic. I leave the record to the judgment of the reader.

Despite a careful search, I was unable to find any confirmation of Senator Lodge's statement (p. 88) that Theodore Roosevelt was "pretty thoroughly against" Brandeis. My research included calling on the memories of three Roosevelt children: Archibald Roosevelt, Mrs. Nicholas Longworth, and Mrs. Richard Derby.

Higginson's letter to Lodge (p. 89) gives what I consider a likely, though unproved, clue to the financing of the long campaign against Brandeis. Fox told the Senate Judiciary Committee (p. 119) that he was employed by five members of the protesting Boston group, acting on behalf of all. According to Higginson, these men were organized at the initiative of the United States Steel general solicitor, Bolling, and a director, James H. Reed, who traveled to Boston for that purpose. Mr. John H. Osmers of Blue Ridge, New Jersey, private secretary to Chairman Elbert H. Gary of the United States Steel board, assured me that Judge Gary would never have taken part in such an affair. Mr. Osmers told me: "I personally saw to the dispersal of Judge Gary's files after his death." Bolling, who lived in Greenwich, Connecticut, was killed in action in France in 1918. Reed died in 1927. I could not locate any papers of either man.

The papers of President Lowell of Harvard (p. 92 and thereafter) were consulted at Widener Library, under permission from the Harvard Board of Overseers.

Senator John W. Weeks (pp. 92–94) considered the United Shoe Machinery case the principal black mark against Brandeis, according to the recollection of his son, Sinclair Weeks.

Details of the personal appearance, characteristics, and background of a number of 1916 Senators (p. 96 and elsewhere, especially Chapters Eight, Nine, and Ten) are based in part on my interviews with the late Senator Henry F. Ashurst. Several times I checked on his feats of memory and found them remarkably accurate on the most obscure details, of which he could not have been reminded before I questioned him. Ashurst, who died May 31, 1962, was the last survivor of the 1916 Senate.

Clarence W. Barron (p. 103) for whom *Barron's Weekly* is named, kept a detailed diary in shorthand at this time, of which excerpts were printed in the book *They Told Barron* and others. Yet my hunt for Barron's original diaries, despite the help of staff members of *The Wall Street Journal* and of Mr. Arthur Lissner, Barron's secretary, was fruitless. Another researcher will, I hope, find them.

Professors Pound, Scott, and Frankfurter (pp. 107–108) of the Harvard Law School of 1916 recalled their memories of the Brandeis nomination for me in interviews in 1961 and 1962. All were in accord that they had no fear of retaliation from President Lowell for standing in favor of Brandeis when Lowell was opposed. Pound at the time was under consideration for appointment as Dean of the Harvard Law School, and received the appointment from Lowell while the Brandeis case was still hanging in the balance. Justice Frankfurter told me that the spirit of the group of men who were actively working to promote Brandeis' confirmation was a confident one, like that of a fighter in the ring: "We went into that fight planning to win, not to lose," Justice Frankfurter said.

Dr. Henry I. Dorr (p. 116) came through handsomely on this promise, and in fact was one of the most generous donors to medical and dental education of his day. A physician, dentist, and expert on anesthesiology, Dorr gave heavily both to Harvard and to Temple University for many years. My research did not discover either the source of his wealth, unusual for a medical man, or the reason for his caring so passionately about the Brandeis nomination.

In the Taft papers I found that Robert A. Taft (p. 108), later a United States Senator from Ohio, was dissuaded by his father from accepting the offer of a year's clerkship with Justice Oliver Wendell Holmes after graduation. In view of Holmes' distinguished record as scholar and judge, leading students at the Harvard Law School vied eagerly for the position. But the elder Taft advised his son that he would do better to go back to Cincinnati and get into the practical work of property law, because a year with Holmes would be pretty much a loss of his time. One can only wonder how the mind of Robert A. Taft would have been influenced had he rejected this advice of "Papa."

Memories of Austin G. Fox (p. 112 et seq.) were given me by Dr. John C. A. Gerster of New York, Fox's son-in-law, and by Mr. Clifton P. Williamson, a close friend. Justice Frankfurter in his book *Felix Frankfurter Reminisces* wrote that he once told a colleague who was looking at a portrait of Fox in the Harvard Club of New York: "That's a study in unbeaten brass."

The papers of Kenneth Spence (p. 115), like those of Fox, appear to have been lost, according to the information I gathered from members of both families.

Nowhere in the public or private records could I find the terms on which Fox was retained (p. 119, also p. 89), or exactly who paid him, if indeed he was paid.

The fact that Samuel Gompers (p. 120) was quietly consulted by Woodrow Wilson on the Brandeis nomination was recalled for me by John L. Lewis, President Emeritus of the United Mine Workers of America. In 1916 Lewis was a personal assistant to Gompers.

The papers of Governor Robert Perkins Bass (p. 121) were presented to Baker Library, Dartmouth College, in 1961, by former Representative Perkins Bass, who guided me to this rich collection of Progressive Era documents.

For students of this period, the partial collection of unsorted personal papers of Norman Hapgood (p. 126) may prove a fruitful source of documentation. Mrs. Norman Hapgood, of New York and Petersham, Massachusetts, furnished me at her summer home a number of items bearing on her husband's close relationship with Brandeis, Wilson, and others.

A memo I found in the Woodrow Wilson papers breaks down the religious composition (p. 137) of the Supreme Court at the time of Brandeis' appointment.

Shortly after his appearance (p. 152) to testify in favor of Brandeis, Newton D. Baker was named Secretary of War by President Wilson.

The Frances Perkins (p. 152) who sought signatures in Brandeis' behalf was later Secretary of Labor in the cabinet of Franklin D. Roosevelt.

Background of the refusal of Jacob M. Dickinson (p. 161) to join in the A.B.A. presidents' protest is explained in his papers in the Tennessee State Library and Archives in Nashville. Likewise, the Henry St. George Tucker papers, University of North Carolina Library, explain why this A.B.A. president (1904–1905) would not sign the Root-Taft-Baldwin letter. Tucker had proposed a softer wording that was unacceptable to the others.

Shortly before his death in 1962, Mr. Henry Hurwitz (p. 182) expressed to me a feeling that Brandeis had let him down in 1916, in not having made a fight of the Harvard Club matter. The Richard Whitney (p. 182) who wrote this letter to Brandeis was dropped from the Harvard Club in the 1930s after his conviction and prison sentence for fraud as President of the New York Stock Exchange.

The oracular interpretation of Charles Evans Hughes' message (p. 184) per Henry L. Stoddard is based on my reading of Stoddard's handwritten report to George Perkins, in the Perkins papers, Butler Library, Columbia University.

Henry Morgenthau, Sr. (p. 184), was the father of Secretary of the Treasury Henry Morgenthau, Jr., in the Franklin D. Roosevelt administration. His published version of the New London incident some years later differs in minor detail from my version, which is based on his diaries in the Library of Congress.

According to his children, Senator O'Gorman (p. 194) left no papers. But Senator Reed of Missouri (p. 194) did leave numerous files which are at the home of his widow, Mrs. Nell Quinlan Reed, in Kansas City. They were in the process of being arranged for the use of scholars as this book was written.

Senator Borah (p. 195) was quoted in later years as deeply regretting his mistake in having voted to reject the nomination of Brandeis.

On Theodore Roosevelt's attitude (pp. 197–199), see earlier note on Lodge letter, p. 88.

Senator George Sutherland (p. 204) later served on the Supreme Court with Brandeis.

It was from Senator Hollis (p. 210), good friend and golfing companion of Franklin D. Roosevelt (p. 215), then Assistant Secretary of the Navy, that the future President obtained his copy of the Brandeis hearing record. In his White House years F.D.R. leaned heavily on Brandeis for advice, and dubbed him "Isaiah" for what he considered Brandeis' prophetic ability. In 1937, Brandeis played a vital behind-the-scenes role in defeating Roosevelt's attempt to "pack" the Supreme Court and so counterbalance the "nine old men," Brandeis among them.

The same Cosmos Club (p. 214) in Washington attracted national attention in the early 1960s because of a dispute over admission of the first Negro proposed for membership.

My reading of Holmes' hand in the Holmes-to-Einstein letters (pp. 220–221), Library of Congress, is not perfectly certain on a few words. When I consulted Mr. Lewis Einstein, he told me that reading Holmes' handwriting at age seventy-five "requires a new Rosetta Stone."

Holmes (p. 221) actually remained on the Supreme Court until he was close to ninety-one.

Professor Mark DeWolfe Howe of the Harvard Law School, biographer of Holmes, supplied me with the letter (p. 221) to Mrs. Stevens.

For much information on the personality of Hoke Smith (p. 223) I am indebted to his biographer, Professor Dewey Grantham of Vanderbilt University, as well as to Senator Ashurst. The memory of the Leo Frank case (p. 225, also p. 12) and the lynch cries against "Northern Jews" incited in that affair in Georgia by demagogues like Tom Watson, were still vivid in the spring of 1916.

Because of the sensitive position of Senator Smith (p. 225) Brandeis' friends were relieved to find, after a search, that nowhere in the entire record had there been an act that could be interpreted as a challenge to white supremacy in the South.

The New York Times (p. 242) spoke in quite a different voice in 1939 when Brandeis retired from the Supreme Court. *The Times'* editorial tribute read in part:

The retirement of Justice Brandeis takes from the bench of the Supreme Court one of the great judges of our time. Nearly a quarter of a century has passed since Woodrow Wilson sent his nomination to the Senate. The storm against him at that time seems almost incredible now. From the first he vindicated the wisdom and the confidence of the far-sighted President who appointed him to office. Year by year his stature as a judge has increased. His learning, his extraordinary ability to get at facts, the clarity of his reasoning, the crisp precision of his language, his intellectual energy and his great integrity have long destined him to occupy a seat among the foremost judges of the court. In the respect and affection of the American people he has come to occupy a place like that reserved for

Justice Holmes, his intimate friend, his frequent colleague in dissent, his boon companion on new frontiers. . . .

A few years after voting against the confirmation of Brandeis, Senator Harding (p. 244) as President ran one of the most corrupt administrations in American history. His Secretary of the Interior, Albert Fall (p. 244), went to the federal penitentiary for his complicity in the Teapot Dome oil scandal.

The incident on page 245 was recalled for me by Mrs. Susan Brandeis Gilbert, daughter of Justice Brandeis. She and her husband, Mr. Jacob Gilbert, helped me with reminiscences of her father.

Exactly how many votes the Brandeis nomination won for Woodrow Wilson in the 1916 election campaign (pp. 250–251) can, of course, never be told. But the evidence is overwhelming that large numbers of people saw the appointment as an important symbolic act that marked Wilson as a true progressive and the Republican opponents of Brandeis as reactionaries. Wilson's margin of victory was so thin that the Brandeis issue, or each of a number of others, could alone be credited for it. For example, a shift of only 1983 votes from Wilson to Hughes in California, where one million votes were cast, would have elected Hughes to the Presidency.

Brandeis spent the summer of 1916 studying in preparation for his first term on the Court. In October, however, the diabolically clever schemer that his opponents had pictured showed that he could be as forgetful as any normal freshman. On October fifth he said good-bye to his Boston associates at his old law firm on Devonshire Street, then boarded the train for Washington. A little later his secretary received a telegram from the Providence station:

LEFT MY GREEN BAG IN STATION RESTAURANT. PLEASE BRING IT TO
WASHINGTON.

L. D. BRANDEIS

Alice Grady knew that even the brilliant new member of the Supreme Court could make a human mistake. Her wire to Brandeis in reply:

TELEGRAM RECEIVED. BAG FOUND IN OFFICE. WILL BRING IT ALONG.

ALICE H. GRADY

A. L. Todd
Chevy Chase, Maryland
February, 1964

Bibliography

BOOKS

Amory, Cleveland: *The Proper Bostonians* (New York, E. P. Dutton, 1947)

Bacon, Edwin M.: *Book of Boston: Fifty Years' Reminiscences* (Boston, The Book of Boston Co., 1916)

Baker, Ray Stannard: *Woodrow Wilson, Life and Letters* (7 volumes, New York, Charles Scribner's Sons, 1931, 1935, 1937)

Bates, Ernest Sutherland: *The Story of the Supreme Court* (Indianapolis, Bobbs-Merrill Co., 1936)

Bowen, Catherine Drinker: *Yankee from Olympus* (Boston, Little, Brown and Co., 1944)

Brandeis, Louis D.: *Business: A Profession* (Boston, Small, Maynard and Co., 1914)

Brandeis, Louis D.: *Other People's Money* (New York, Frederick A. Stokes Co., 1914)

Brandeis, Louis D.: *Women in Industry* (New York, National Consumers' League, 1908)

Bray, Thomas J.: *The Rebirth of Freedom* (Indianola, Iowa, Record and Tribune Press, 1957)

Cotter, Arundel: *The Authentic History of the U. S. Steel Corporation* (New York, The Moody Magazine and Book Co., 1916)

Cotter, Arundel: *United States Steel—A Corporation with a Soul* (Garden City, N. Y., and Toronto, Doubleday, Page and Co., 1921)

Cramer, Clarence H.: *Newton D. Baker* (Cleveland, World Publishing Co., 1961)

Daniels, Josephus: *The Wilson Era: Years of Peace, 1910–1917* (Chapel Hill, The University of North Carolina Press, 1944)

De Haas, Jacob: *Louis D. Brandeis* (New York, Bloch Publishing Co., 1929)

Diamond, William: *The Economic Thought of Woodrow Wilson* (Baltimore, The Johns Hopkins Press, 1943)

263

Dunnington, Miles William: *Senator Thomas J. Walsh and the Vindication of Louis D. Brandeis* (Lithoprinted, part of Ph.D. thesis, University of Chicago, 1943)

Forcey, Charles: *The Crossroads of Liberalism* (New York, Oxford University Press, 1961)

Frankfurter, Felix: *Felix Frankfurter Reminisces* (New York, Reynal, 1960)

Frankfurter, Felix: *Law and Politics* (New York, Harcourt, Brace and Co., 1939)

Garraty, John A.: *Henry Cabot Lodge* (New York, Knopf, 1953)

Garraty, John A.: *Right-hand Man* (New York, Harper, 1960)

Goldman, Eric: *Rendezvous with Destiny* (New York, Knopf, 1952)

Goldmark, Josephine C.: *Impatient Crusader* (Urbana, University of Illinois Press, 1953)

Grantham, Dewey W.: *Hoke Smith and the Politics of the New South* (Baton Rouge, Louisiana State University Press, 1958)

Haines, Lynn: *The Searchlight on Congress* (Washington, 1916–1927)

Haines, Lynn: *The Senate from 1907 to 1912* (Washington, the National Capitol Press, 1912)

Handlin, Oscar: *Adventure in Freedom* (New York, McGraw-Hill, 1954)

Handlin, Oscar: *American Jews: Their Story* (New York, Anti-Defamation League of B'nai B'rith, 1958)

Hatch, Alden: *Edith Bolling Wilson* (New York, Dodd, Mead, 1961)

Herlihy, Elisabeth M., Ed.: *Fifty Years of Boston* (Boston, 1932)

Huthmacher, J. J.: *Massachusetts People and Politics* (Cambridge, Belknap Press of Harvard University Press, 1959)

Jessup, Philip C.: *Elihu Root* (New York, Dodd, Mead, 1938)

Johnson, Claudius O.: *Borah of Idaho* (New York, Toronto, Longmans, Green, 1936)

Karger, Alfred Gus: *Thinking American* (New York, D. Ryerson, Inc., 1941)

LaFollette, Belle and Fola: *Robert M. LaFollette* (2 volumes, New York, Macmillan, 1953)

LaFollette, Robert M.: *LaFollette's Autobiography* (Madison, University of Wisconsin Press, 1960)

Lamar, Clarinda P.: *Life of Joseph R. Lamar* (New York, G. P. Putnam's Sons, 1926)

Leopold, Richard W.: *Elihu Root and the Conservative Tradition* (Boston, Little, Brown, 1954)

Leupp, Francis E. ("Tattler"): *National Miniatures* (New York, A. A. Knopf, 1918)

Lief, Alfred: *Brandeis: The Personal History of an American Ideal* (Harrisburg, Stackpole Sons, 1936)

Link, Arthur S.: *Wilson: the New Freedom* (Princeton, Princeton University Press, 1956)

Link, Arthur S.: *Wilson: the Road to the White House* (Princeton, Princeton University Press, 1947)

McKenna, Marian C.: *Borah* (Ann Arbor, University of Michigan Press, 1961)

Madden, James William: *Charles A. Culberson* (Austin, Texas, Gammel's Book Store, 1929)

Madison, Charles Allan: *Critics and Crusaders* (New York, H. Holt and Co., 1947)

Madison, Charles Allan: *Leaders and Liberals in 20th Century America* (New York, F. Ungar Publishing Co., 1961)

Mason, Alpheus T.: *Brandeis: A Free Man's Life* (New York, The Viking Press, 1946)

Mason, Alpheus T.: *Brandeis and the Modern State* (Princeton, Princeton University Press, 1933)

Mason, Alpheus T.: *Bureaucracy Convicts Itself* (New York, The Viking Press, 1941)

Mason, Alpheus T., and Staples, H. L.: *The Fall of a Railroad Empire* (Syracuse, N. Y., Syracuse University Press, 1947)

Meade, Robert D.: *Judah P. Benjamin* (New York, London, etc., Oxford University Press, 1943)

Meriwether, Lee: *Jim Reed, Senatorial Immortal* (Webster Groves, Mo., International Mark Twain Society, 1948)

Morgenthau, Henry: *All in a Lifetime* (Garden City, N. Y., Doubleday, Page and Co., 1922)

Mowry, George E.: *Theodore Roosevelt and the Progressive Movement* (Madison, The University of Wisconsin Press, 1946)

O'Keane, Josephine: *Thomas J. Walsh* (Francestown, N. H., M. Jones and Co., 1955)

Pennington, Mary V., and Bolling, John R.: *Chronology of Woodrow Wilson* (New York, Frederick A. Stokes and Co., 1927)

Perkins, Dexter: *Charles Evans Hughes and American Democratic Statesmanship* (Boston, Little, Brown, 1956)

Pollack, Ervin H., Ed.: *The Brandeis Reader* (New York, Oceana Publications, 1956)

Pound, Arthur, Ed.: *They Told Barron* (New York, London, Harper and Brothers, 1930)

Pringle, Henry F.: *The Life and Times of William Howard Taft* (2 volumes, New York, Toronto, Farrar and Rinehart, Inc., 1939)

Pusey, Merlo J.: *Charles Evans Hughes* (2 volumes, New York, etc., Macmillan, 1951)

Samuels, Charles and Louise: *Night Fell on Georgia* (New York, Dell Publishing Co., 1956)

Schriftgiesser, Karl: *The Gentleman from Massachusetts: Henry Cabot Lodge* (Boston, Little, Brown and Co., 1944)

Solomon, Barbara Miller: *Ancestors and Immigrants* (Cambridge, Harvard University Press, 1956)

Tarbell, Ida M.: *The Life of Elbert H. Gary* (New York, D. Appleton and Co., 1925)

Thomas, Helen Shirley: *Felix Frankfurter: Scholar on the Bench* (Baltimore, Johns Hopkins Press, 1960)

U. S. Congress, Senate Committee on the Judiciary, 64th Congress, 1st Session: *Nomination of Louis D. Brandeis* (Washington, U. S. Government Printing Office, 1916)

U. S. Congress: *Albert B. Cummins—Memorial Addresses* (Washington, U. S. Government Printing Office, 1927)

U. S. Congress: *Memorial Services for Duncan U. Fletcher* (Washington, U. S. Government Printing Office, 1938)

U. S. Congress: *Lee S. Overman—Memorial Addresses* (Washington, U. S. Government Printing Office, 1931)

U. S. Congress: *Memorial Services for Thomas J. Walsh* (Washington, U. S. Government Printing Office, 1934)

U. S. Government: *Statistical Abstract of the United States—1916*

U. S. Steel Corporation: *Elbert Henry Gary* (New York, U. S. Steel Corporation, 1927)

Villard, Oswald G.: *Fighting Years* (New York, Harcourt, Brace and Co., 1939)

Vorspan, Albert: *Giants of Justice* (New York, Union of American Hebrew Congregations, 1960)

Warren, Charles: *The Supreme Court in U. S. History* (3 volumes, Boston, Little, Brown and Co., 1922)

Wehle, Louis B.: *Hidden Threads of History* (New York, Macmillan, 1953)

Who's Who in America, 1916–1917

Who's Who in New England, 1916

Wilson, Edith Bolling: *My Memoir* (Indianapolis, New York, The Bobbs-Merrill Co., 1939)

PERIODICALS (in addition to newspapers mentioned in the text and index)

Arena	*Leslie's Weekly*
Collier's Weekly	*Literary Digest*
Congressional Record	*The Nation*
Harper's Weekly	*New Republic*
Harvard Alumni Bulletin	*The Outlook*
Harvard Graduates' Magazine	*Review of Reviews*
The Independent	*The Survey*
LaFollette's Magazine	*World's Work*

Index

Adair v. *U.S.*, 11
Adams, Charles Francis, 106, 119, 181
Adler, Dr. Felix, 203, 211
Albers, Homer, 217
Allen, William Reynolds, 30
American Bar Association, 31, 90, 115, 129, 132, 158–163, 235, 260
American Federation of Labor, 36, 38
American Law Review, 224
American Tobacco Company, 50
Anaconda Copper Mining Company, 142
Anderson, George W., 113, 151, 162, 168, 219, 227, 247, 249
Armstrong, William W., 51–53
Ashurst, Henry Fountain, 194, 204–207, 210, 222, 241, 258, 261
Atlanta *Constitution,* 236
Atlantic Monthly, 44

Bacon, Robert, 184
Bailey, Hollis Russell, 108–109, 116
Bailey, Joseph W., 211
Baker Library, Dartmouth College, 259
Baker, Newton D., 152, 260
Baldwin, Simeon, 132, 159, 161, 162
Ballinger, Richard A., 75–77, 122, 125, 126, 128–129, 131, 146–147, 152, 170, 188, 191, 192, 195
Barron, Clarence W., 103–106, 109, 115, 145, 188, 209, 258
Barron's Weekly, 258
Bass, Representative Perkins, 259
Bass, Robert Perkins, 121, 168, 210, 211, 218, 228, 259

Batts, Robert Lynn, 157
Beagle, Ralph, 30
Benjamin, Judah P., 256
Bennet, William S., 28–29
Benton, James M., 30
Berle, Reverend A. A., 211
Bigelow, A. S., 189
Bilbo, Theodore G., 30, 254
Blatchford, Justice Samuel, 193
Bolling, Raynal C., 89–90, 257, 258
Borah, William Edgar, 195, 199, 211, 226, 228, 244, 254, 260
Boston & Maine Railroad, 60–62, 105
Boston Elevated Railway Company, 46
Boston News Bureau, 103
Boston *Post,* 73, 107, 120, 158
Boston University Law School, 217
Brandegee, Frank B., 204, 240
Brandeis, Alice, 245
    (*see also* Goldmark, Alice)
Brandeis brief, 56, 58–59
Brandeis, Dunbar and Nutter, 51, 55, 124, 255
Brandeis, Elizabeth, 55
Brandeis, Louis Dembitz, background, 40–68
    see Ballinger, Richard A.
    and Boston gas system, 48–49
    and Boston transit, 45–47, 255
    Chicago Bar Association address, 168–169
    confirmed, 243–245
    economic theories of, 62–64
    see Equitable Life Assurance Society

Brandeis, Louis Dembitz, Faneuil Hall
    address, 84
  see Gillette Safety Razor Company
    and Harvard, 40–41, 42, 43, 117
  see Illinois Central Railroad
  see Interstate Commerce Commis-
    sion
    and labor movement, 44–45, 84,
    136–137, 153
  see Lennox bankruptcy
    and liquor laws, 43–44
    and Morgenthau, 184–185
    and *Muller* v. *Oregon,* 56–59,
    208
  see New York & New England Rail-
    road
  see New York, New Haven & Hart-
    ford Railroad
    nominated, 37–39
  see Old Dominion Copper & Smelt-
    ing Company
    personality, 47, 53–56
    and politics, 65
    resemblance to Lincoln, 56, 248–
    249, 255
    and "right to privacy," 43
    and savings bank life insurance, 53
    and Senator Reed, 221–223
    and Senator Smith, 223–226
    sworn in, 248–249
    and Theodore Roosevelt, 65, 197–
    199
  see United Drug Company
  see United Shoe Machinery Com-
    pany
    views on Constitution, 202
  see Warren will case
    and Woodrow Wilson, 66–67
    and Zionism, 137, 181
Brandeis, Susan, 245
  (*see also* Gilbert, Susan Brandeis)
Brewer, Justice David J., 59
Brown, Justice Henry B., 25
Brushaber v. *Union Pacific Railroad,*
    37
Business—a Profession, 67
Butler Library, Columbia University,
    260
Butler, Nicholas Murray, 196

Cannon, James, 155–156
Carleton & Moffat, 94

Carr, Samuel, 237
Catchings, Waddill, 123–124
Charleston *Gazette,* 96
Chattanooga Bar Association, 34
Chicago Bar Association, 168
Chilton, Horace, 30
Chilton, Senator William Edwin, 94,
    96, 103, 105, 125, 185–188, 210,
    232, 241
Choate, Charles, 146
Choate, Joseph H., 57, 159, 161, 162
Christian Science Monitor, 246, 250
Cincinnati Law School, 23
Cincinnati *Times-Star,* 77
Clapp, Senator Moses E., 244
Clark, Champ, 30
Clark, Senator Clarence, 97, 102, 105,
    109, 114, 204, 205, 206, 240
Clarke, John H., 251
Clayton Antitrust Act, 67, 111, 114,
    222
Cleveland, Grover, 18, 23, 72, 193,
    224
Coburn, Frederick, 140
Collier's Weekly, 66, 76–77, 115, 120–
    121, 125, 126
    (*see also* Ballinger, Richard A.)
Colt, James D., 119
Commercial Club of Boston, 51–52,
    149
Committee to Visit the Law School,
    107
The Common Law, 19
Consolidated Gas Company, 148
Cooke, Robert B., 239
Cooke, Thomas H., 34
Coolidge, Louis A., 89, 95, 158, 163
Coppage v. *Kansas,* 10–11, 169
Cosmos Club, 214, 261
Crane, Charles R., 152
Cree, Reverend Howard, 17
Croly, Herbert, 216
Culberson, Senator Charles Allen, 72,
    94, 193–194, 195, 212–213, 240
Cummins, Senator Albert Baird, 97,
    100–103, 125, 151, 165, 185, 190–
    191, 201, 206, 226, 228, 240, 245
Curley, James Michael, 74, 84, 256

Danbury Hatters, 10, 36, 37, 38
Daniels, Josephus, 215, 216, 217–218,
    232–234, 254

Davis, John W., 31, 170, 254
Day, William A., 203
Day, Justice William Rufus, 11, 19, 36, 137, 183
Dedham Polo Club, 130, 152
Dembitz, Lewis, 40
Derby, Mrs. Richard, 257
Detroit *Free Press,* 73
Dickinson, Jacob M., 31, 161, 260
Dillingham, William P., 240
Dorr, Dr. Henry Isaiah, 108
Dow-Jones Company, 104

Earl, E. T., 175
Einstein, Lewis, 220, 261
Eliot, Charles W., 41, 183, 229, 235
Elwell, Frank Edwin, 212
Equitable Life Assurance Society, 51–52, 149, 150, 170, 177, 187
Eshleman, John M., 99–100
Ewing, Presley K., 30

Fall, Senator Albert B., 244, 262
Faneuil Hall, 83–84, 257
Federal Trade Commission, 62, 67, 208, 210, 222, 227, 234, 236
Filene, Edward, 47
Fillmore, President Millard, 256
Fish, Stuyvesant, 123
Fisk, Charles J., 30
Fitzgerald, John F. ("Honey Fitz"), 65, 74, 255, 256
Fitzgerald, William F., 142, 163–165
Fletcher, Senator Duncan U., 96, 102, 103, 112, 185, 188, 216, 241
Foraker, Joseph B., 23
Ford's Theatre, 255
Fox, Austen George, 112, 113, 115, 119, 122–126, 159, 164, 165, 170, 173, 174, 196, 201, 209, 257, 259
Frank, Leo M., 12, 13, 225, 255, 261
Frankfurter, Felix, 107, 116, 132, 162, 168, 177–178, 197, 215, 217, 218, 220, 255, 256, 258, 259
French, Asa P., 153, 154, 168
Frick, Henry C., 38
Fuller, Chief Justice Melville W., 18, 25
Furman, John Pryor, 254

Gallinger, Senator Jacob H., 210, 227
Garrison, Lindley M., 121

Gary, Elbert H., 38, 63, 89, 257, 258
Gerster, Dr. John C. A., 259
Gilbert, Jacob, 262
Gilbert, Susan Brandeis, 262
  (*see also* Brandeis, Susan)
Gillette Safety Razor Company, 124, 170, 187
Glavis, Louis P., 75–77, 122, 126, 188
  (*see also* Ballinger, Richard A.)
Goldmark, Alice, 47
  (*see also* Mrs. Louis D. Brandeis)
Goldmark, Josephine, 57, 58
Goldsmith, N. F., 150
Gompers, Samuel, 36, 38, 79, 120, 225, 259
Gotcher, Mrs. Elmer, 57
Grady, Alice H., 262
Grantham, Dewey, 261
Graves, W. W., 30
Gray, Justice Horace, 24, 42
Grayson, Dr. Cary, 241
Green, William, 136
Gregory, Stephen S., 161
Gregory, Thomas W., 30, 37, 74, 113, 157, 161, 201, 202, 211, 227, 250, 254
Gronna, Asle J., 244

Hale, Shelton, 107
Hand, Learned, 197
Hapgood, Norman, 66, 76, 113, 121–122, 126, 152, 162, 210–211, 218, 221, 228, 250, 259
Hapgood, Mrs. Norman, 259
Hard, William, 228, 251–252
Harding, Warren G., 195–196, 244, 262
Harlan, Justice John Marshall, 11
Harper's Weekly, 63, 121
Harriman, Edward H., 61, 123–124, 187
Harrison, Benjamin, 23
Hart, John C., 30
Harvard Alumni Bulletin, 140, 173
Harvard Board of Overseers, 258
Harvard Club of New York, 182–183, 259
Harvard *Crimson,* 209
Harvard Ethical Society, 68
Harvard Law Review, 43, 208
Harvard Law School, 41–42, 107, 207, 258, 259

Harvard Law School Association, 42
Herrick, Myron T., 28
Hester, Andrew, 136
Higginson, Henry Lee, 89–90, 95, 257
Hill, Arthur D., 85–89, 107, 144–146, 154, 218, 257
Hilles, Charles D., 195
Hollis, Henry F., 210, 260
Holmes, Joseph D., 201
Holmes, Justice Oliver Wendell, 11, 13, 18–19, 24, 28–29, 42, 55, 87, 137, 202, 219–221, 248, 254, 261
The Homestead, 14, 16–17
Hornblower & Weeks, 93
House, Colonel Edward M., 203, 211
Howard, Clarence, 138
Howe, Mark A. DeWolfe, 140
Howe, Professor Mark DeWolfe, 261
Hughes, Justice Charles Evans, 11, 13, 19–20, 51, 53, 137, 183–184, 196–197, 208, 248, 250, 254, 256, 262
Hull, Cordell, 37
Hurwitz, Henry, 182–183, 260
Hutchins, Edward, 144

Illinois Central Railroad, 61, 123–124, 152, 170, 177, 187
Illinois Law Review, 168
International Harvester Corporation, 12, 74, 81
Interstate Commerce Commission, 61–63, 98–101, 103, 170, 187, 191, 192
Ivy, Thomas P., 220

Jackson, Justice Howell Edmunds, 23
James, Ellerton, 130–131
James, Senator Ollie M., 30
Jaretzki, Alfred, 124
Johnson, Joseph, 36
Jones, Charles H., 90–91
Jones, Stiles, 141

Kahn, Otto H., 80
Karger, Colonel Alfred Gus, 256
Karger, Gus J. (*see* Taft, William H., Karger-Taft correspondence)
Kelley, Mrs. Florence, 57, 152
Kellogg, Frank B., 161
Kellogg, Paul U., 152, 153
Kelly, Judge William J., 125
Kelsey, Clarence, 27

Kennedy, Edward, 256
Kennedy, John F., 255, 256, 257
Kent, William, 134
Kerby, Frederick, 146–147, 188
Kidder, Peabody and Company, 48
King, Alexander Campbell, 30

LaFollette, Belle (Mrs. Robert M.), 245
LaFollette, Robert Marion, 37, 63, 64, 65, 71, 79, 245, 254–255
Lamar, Justice Joseph Rucker, 13–14, 17, 26–27
Lamar, Lucius Quintus Cincinnatus, 13
Lamont, Thomas W., 209
Landis, Kenesaw Mountain, 64, 255
Lansing, Robert, 3, 16
Laski, Harold, 220
Lawler v. *Loewe* (*see* Danbury Hatters)
Lea, Luke, 240
Lee, Higginson & Company, 89
Lehmann, Frederick W., 161
Lennox bankruptcy, 105, 117–118, 170, 187, 191, 192
Lennox, James, 117–118
Lennox, Patrick, 117
Lennox, Dr. Patrick, 119
Leslie's Weekly, 170, 172
Leupp, Francis E., 176–177, 255
Lewis, Senator James Hamilton, 232
Lewis, John L., 259
Lewis, William Draper, 197
Library of Congress, 254, 260, 261
Lief, Alfred, 254
Liggett, Louis, 219
Lincoln, Abraham (*see* Brandeis, Louis D., resemblance to)
Lippmann, Walter, 152, 162, 216
Lissner, Arthur, 258
Lloyd, Henry Demarest, 44
Lochner v. *New York,* 9, 57, 169
Lodge, George Cabot, 256, 257
Lodge, Senator Henry Cabot, 24, 36, 71, 74, 79, 82–92, 106, 128–131, 176, 181–182, 184, 198, 199, 208, 220, 244, 257
Lodge, Henry Cabot II, 256, 257
Loewe, Dietrich E., 10, 36
(*see also* Danbury Hatters)
Long, B. F., 30
Longworth, Mrs. Nicholas, 257

Los Angeles *Evening Express,* 175
Los Angeles *Morning Tribune,* 175
Los Angeles *Times,* 201
Lourie, David, 138
Lowell, A. Lawrence, 89, 92–94, 106–108, 140–141, 159, 173–174, 178, 208–209, 258
Lurton, Justice Horace H., 22, 29
Lusitania, 3
Lynch, Jeremiah C., 230–231

McAdoo, William Gibbs, 30, 34, 70, 239, 243, 250, 254
McClellan, Thomas Cowan, 30
McClennan, Edward, 114–115, 118, 149, 153, 164
McCulloch, Edgar Allen, 30
McElwain, William H., 44
McKellar, Kenneth, 240
McKenna, Justice Joseph, 18, 19, 23, 137
McKinley, William, 18, 19, 20, 21, 23, 24
McLean, W. C., 30
McNair, M. P., 140
McNamara brothers, 201–202
McNeely, Robert N., 16
McNutt, Paul V., 209
McReynolds, Justice James Clark, 17, 20, 21, 27, 31, 36, 61, 67, 137, 183
Manning, Mrs. Helen Taft, 256
Marbury v. *Madison,* 8
Marshall, John, 8
Marshall, Louis, 80, 217
Mason, Alpheus T., 254, 255
Massachusetts Historical Society, 257
Massachusetts Institute of Technology, 45
Mayflower, 35
Meldrim, Peter W., 159, 161, 162
Mellen, Charles S., 59–61, 109
Menorah Journal, 183
Menorah Society, 183
Metropolitan Club of Washington, 140
Metropolitan Transit Authority of Boston, 255
Montague, Andrew Jackson, 30
Morgan, J. Pierpont, Sr., 52, 60, 63, 209
Morgenthau, Henry, 184–185, 203, 211, 217, 228, 229–231, 247, 254, 260

Morse, John Torrey, 129–130
Moskowitz, Henry, 153
Muller, Curt, 57
Muller v. *Oregon,* 56–59, 169, 208

Nagel, Charles, 217
The Nation, 176, 177, 215
National Archives, 255
National Consumers League, 57, 152, 254
National Progressive Republican League, 65
Nelson, Knute, 195, 240
New Republic, 177–180
New York & New England Railroad, 125, 146, 150, 170, 187
New York, New Haven & Hartford Railroad, 59–62, 105, 150, 188
New York *Evening Mail,* 183
New York *Sun,* 69–71, 256
The New York Times, 3, 74, 242–243, 261–262
New York *World,* 73, 203
Newlands, Francis G., 244
Noble, John, 119
Norris, George, 244
Nutter, McClennen & Fish, 255

Ochs, Adolph S., 74
O'Gorman, James A., 194, 209, 211, 215, 216, 227, 230–231, 236, 241, 260
Old Dominion Copper & Smelting Company, 144, 163–165, 170, 189
Order of Railway Conductors, 136
Osmers, John H., 257, 258
Other People's Money, 67
The Outlook, 251
Overman, Lee Slater, 72, 94, 194, 206, 209, 227, 232–234, 236, 241
Owen, Robert L., 31–32, 207

Page, Walter Hines, 231
Parker, Alton B., 132, 161
Peabody, Francis, 147, 148, 151–152
Peck, George, 162
Pelletier, Joseph, 108–109
Perkins, Frances, 152, 260
Perkins, George W., 35, 38, 63, 66, 80, 183, 184, 260
Persia, 16, 17, 36
Phagan, Mary, 12
Phelan, James D., 212

Phelps-Dodge Corporation, 164
Philadelphia News Bureau, 103
Phillips Brooks House, 68, 256
Pillsbury, Albert, 147–149
Pinchot, Amos, 134, 139–140, 254
Pitney, Justice Mahlon, 11, 13, 17, 20, 137
Plant, Thomas G., 50
Poindexter, Miles, 244
Pound, Roscoe, 107, 108, 116, 207–208, 218, 258
Protective Liquor Dealers' Association, 43, 155
Public Franchise League, 46, 48, 130, 166–167
Pulitzer, Joseph, 73

Rackemann, Charles, 119
Railway Business Association, 38, 73
Raleigh *News and Observer,* 224
Rawle, Francis, 159, 160, 162
Reed, Senator James A., 194, 221–223, 227, 236, 241, 260
Reed, James Hay, 89–90, 257, 258
Reed, Nell Quinlan (Mrs. James A.), 260
Review of Reviews, 49
Richards, James L., 48–49
Roosevelt, Archibald, 257
Roosevelt, Franklin D., 215, 216, 260, 261
Roosevelt, Theodore, 19, 20, 21, 26, 32–33, 36, 88, 184, 196, 197–199, 254, 257
Root, Elihu, 24, 25, 36, 128–129, 132, 158–159, 178, 184, 254
Rublee, George, 210, 227, 234, 236–237

St. Louis Businessmen's League, 138
St. Louis *Globe-Democrat,* 160
Schiff, Jacob, 80, 181, 217
Scott, Austin, 107, 258
Seabury, Samuel, 197
Seibert, Albert, 143
Seibert, Paddock & Cochran, 95
Sherman Antitrust Act, 10, 50, 62
Shields, John Knight, 195, 216, 227, 237–241
Shiras, Justice George, Jr., 24
Simmons, Senator F. M., 233
Smith, Charles Sumner, 165
Smith, Senator Hoke, 195, 200, 203,

206–207, 209, 211, 221, 227, 229–231, 235–236, 241, 242, 261
Snow, Frederick, 219
Spelling, Thomas C., 103, 170–172
Spence, Kenneth, 115, 146, 170, 201, 259
Speyer, James, 80
Standard Oil Company, 12, 50, 161, 255
Stevens, Mrs. Joseph Samson, 221, 261
Stevens, Raymond B., 208–209, 210
Stimson, Henry L., 208
Stockton *Record,* 175–176
Stoddard, Henry L., 183–184, 260
Storey, Moorfield, 115–117, 125, 159, 162
Straus, Oscar S., 152
Stuart, Henry C., 30
Sullivan & Cromwell, 123–124
Sullivan, Mark, 121–123, 125
Sumner, Senator Charles, 115, 159, 248
The Survey, 152
Sutherland, George, 204–206, 218, 240, 260

Taft, Charles P., 23, 196
Taft, Henry W., 80, 81
Taft, Robert Alphonso, 108, 132, 196
Taft, William Howard, 14, 18, 20, 75, 178, 195, 209, 242, 254, 256
  and A.B.A. petition, 157–159, 162
  background, 21–29
  and Ballinger, 75–77, 131
  and bigotry, 216–217, 256–257
  and Hughes, 196–197
  and Karger, 77–80, 81, 101, 132–133, 158–159, 162–163, 180–181, 200, 216, 232, 235
  and Lodge, 181–182
  and *New Republic,* 179–180
  and 1912 campaign, 32–33, 76–77
  and Supreme Court vacancy, 33–34
Taft, Mrs. William H. (Nellie), 23
"Tattler," 176–177, 255
  (*see also* Leupp, Francis E.)
Teal, Joseph, 101
Tennessee State Library and Archives, 260
Thayer, Ezra, 108, 117
Thayer, James Bradley, 42
Thorne, Clifford, 97–102

Tillman, "Pitchfork Ben," 72
Tucker, Henry St. George, 260
Tumulty, Joseph, 135, 139, 230

Ullman, Isaac, 79
United Drug Company, 218–219
United Hatters of North America, 10
United Mine Workers of America, 136, 259
United Shoe Machinery Company, 49–51, 95, 105, 111–112, 113–114, 151, 170, 177, 187, 191, 222
United States Chamber of Commerce, 138
United States Steel Corporation, 2, 4, 38, 63, 74, 89–90, 95, 257
University of Louisville Law School, 254, 255
University of North Carolina Library, 260

Van Devanter, Justice Willis, 17, 20, 137, 220
Vanderlip, Frank A., 203
Vertrees, John J., 238, 239
Villa, Pancho, 36

Wadsworth, Senator James J., 72, 256
Wadsworth, James J., Jr., 256
Wagner, Robert F., 36, 254
Walker, Joseph, 153, 154
Wall Street Journal, 1, 2, 38, 73, 103–104, 188, 258
Wallerstein, David, 135
Walsh, David Ignatius, 75, 256
Walsh, Thomas J., 97, 102, 103, 104, 109, 119, 122–123, 125, 141–144, 164, 165, 185, 188–190, 201, 202, 210, 211, 241, 249–250, 254
Warner, Roger, 119
Warren and Brandeis, 41–42, 53, 55, 255
Warren, Edward (Ned), 126–127
Warren, Professor Edward H., 107
Warren, Edward R., 166–167
Warren, Samuel D., 41–43, 109–110, 126–127
Warren will case, 105, 109–111, 116–117, 126–127, 170, 177, 186, 191, 192
Washington *Evening Star,* 36, 73
Washington *Herald,* 27, 204, 206
Washington *Post,* 72
Washington *Times,* 28, 37, 174

Watson, Tom, 261
Weeks, John Wingate, 71, 79, 92–94, 222, 258
Weeks, Sinclair, 258
Wehle, Louis Brandeis, 121
Wendell, Barrett, 91
West End Railway, 45
Wetmore, Edmund, 162
Weyl, Walter, 216
Whipple, Sherman, 117–119, 133, 177
White, Chief Justice Edward Douglas, 17–18, 25, 27, 31, 36, 81, 137, 193, 248
White, Henry, 31
Whitney, Richard 182–183, 260
Wickersham, George, 61, 75–76, 81, 95, 131–132, 179–180, 196, 217, 237
 (*see also* Ballinger, Richard A.)
Widener Library, Harvard University, 258
Williamson, Clifton P., 259
Wilson, Woodrow, 3, 20, 121, 254, 262
 and Brandeis appointment, 37–39, 133–139
 and cabinet, 66–67
 and Lamar death, 14–17, 30–34
 and 1912 campaign, 26, 32–33, 65–66
 Presidential duties, 35–36
 and Senator Culberson letter, 212–214
 and Senator O'Gorman, 230–231
 and Senator Overman, 232–234
 and Senator Shields, 239–240
 and Senator Smith, 224, 229–231, 247
Wilson, Mrs. Woodrow, 14, 35
Wing, Henry, 132
Winslow, Sidney, 50, 111–112, 113–114
Wise, Rabbi Stephen S., 152, 181, 211, 218
Wood, General Leonard, 184
Works, John Downey, 114, 151, 165, 185, 191–192, 201, 240
Wyman, Bruce, 60

Yale University, 23, 26
Young, George M., 30
Youngman, William, 124–127, 165–166

About the Author

A. L. Todd is a freelance writer whose articles have appeared in numerous national magazines. His previous book, the widely praised *Abandoned,* published by McGraw-Hill in 1961, was an account of the tragic and heroic Greely Arctic Expedition of 1881–1884. A graduate of the Phillips Exeter Academy and Swarthmore College, Mr. Todd was a teacher, shipyard machinist, parachute infantryman and news reporter before turning to magazine and book writing. Born in Washington, D.C., and now living in Chevy Chase, Maryland, he haunts the Library of Congress, where it is both his vocation and his avocation to dig out stories of the past and bring them to life, combining the best elements of research and journalism with superb storytelling.